D1155123

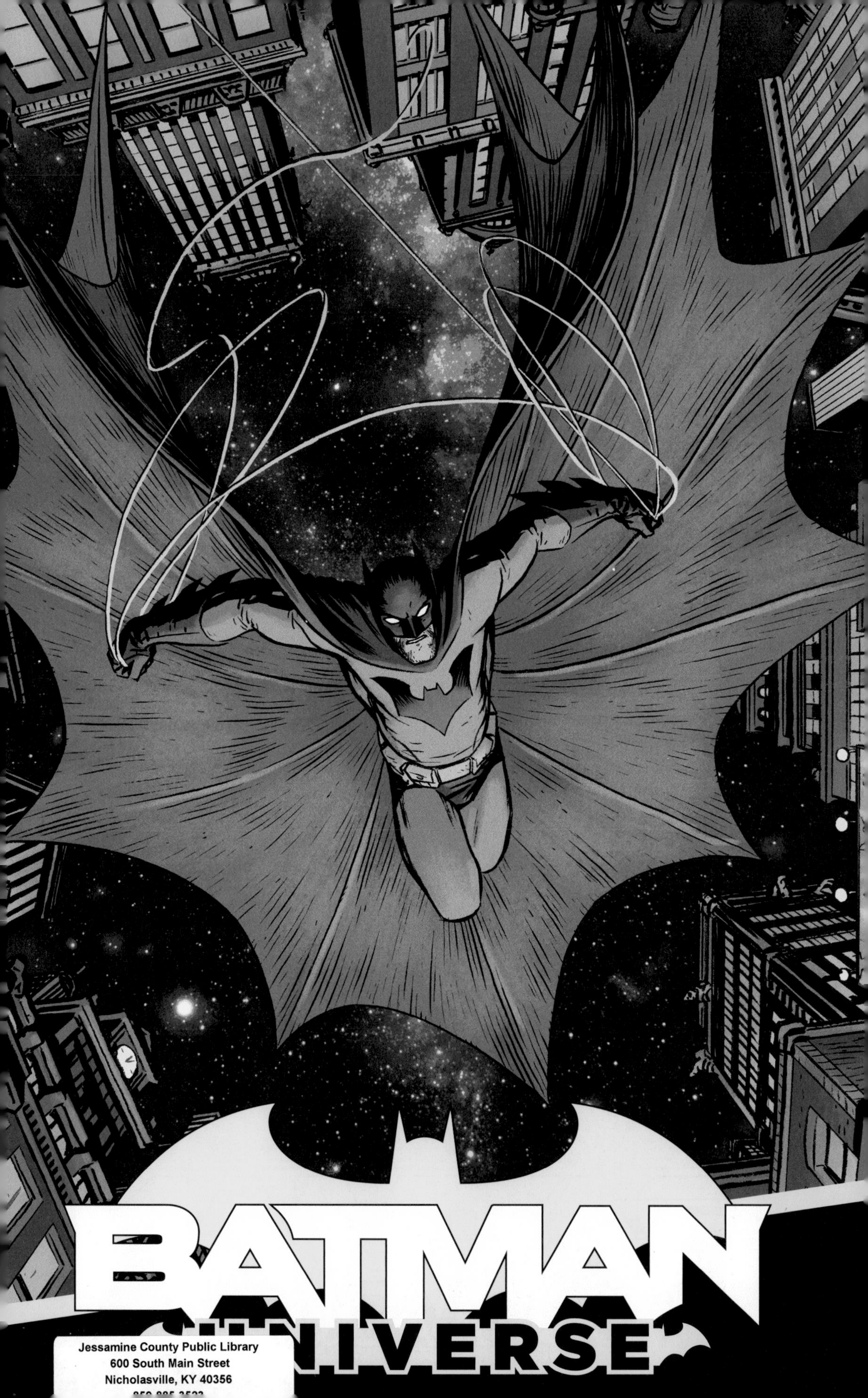
BATMAN
NIVERSE

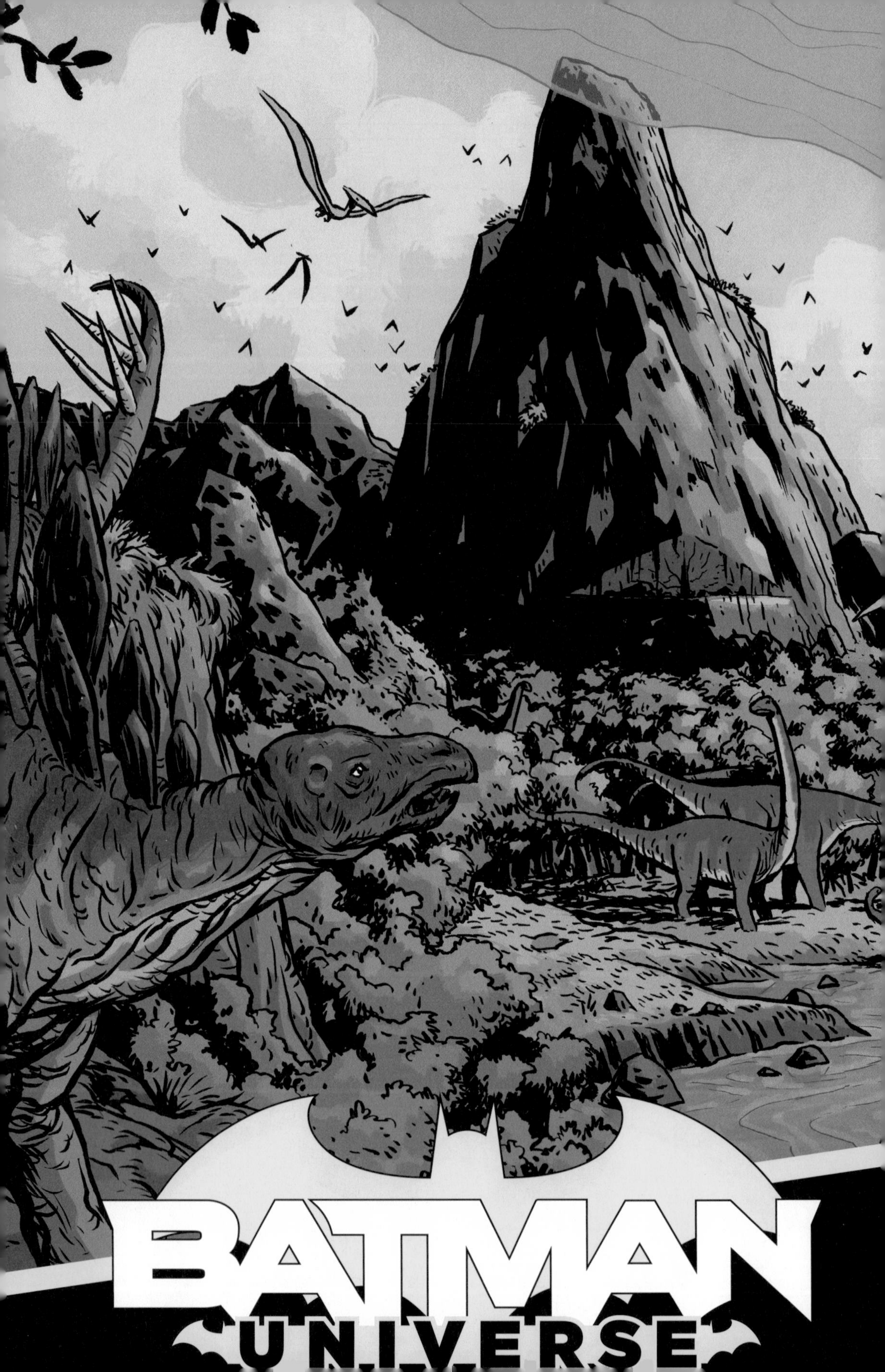
BATMAN
UNIVERSE

BRIAN MICHAEL BENDIS
writer

NICK DERINGTON
artist

DAVE STEWART
colorist

JOSH REED
CARLOS M. MANGUAL
TOM NAPOLITANO
ALW's TROY PETERI
letterers

NICK DERINGTON
series and collection cover artist

BATMAN created by BOB KANE with BILL FINGER   SUPERMAN created by JERRY SIEGEL and JOE SHUSTER

BATMAN: UNIVERSE

Published by DC Comics. Compilation and all new material Copyright © 2020 DC Comics. All Rights Reserved. Originally published in single magazine form in *Batman: Universe* 1-6 and *Batman Giant* 3-14. Copyright © 2018, 2019 DC Comics. All Rights Reserved. All characters, their distinctive likenesses, and related elements featured in this publication are trademarks of DC Comics. The stories, characters, and incidents featured in this publication are entirely fictional. DC Comics does not read or accept unsolicited submissions of ideas, stories, or artwork. DC – a WarnerMedia Company.

DC Comics
2900 West Alameda Ave., Burbank, CA 91505
Printed by LSC Communications,
Kendallville, IN, USA. 2/14/20.
First Printing. ISBN: 978-1-4012-9484-7

Library of Congress
Cataloging-in-Publication Data is available

PEFC Certified
This product is from sustainably managed forests and controlled sources
PEFC/29-31-337
www.pefc.org

AND OF THE SEVENTEEN DINNER GUESTS YOU HAVE WAITING FOR YOU HERE IN STATELY WAYNE MANOR...

...THERE IS ONE LOVELY WOMAN NAMED LORELAI WHO IS BOTH AGE AND INTELLECTUALLY APPROPRIATE FOR YOU.

THERE'S NOTHING I CAN DO ABOUT THAT NOW, ALFRED.

SERVE THE APPETIZER.

AND I WILL ALSO RECOMMEND YOUR GUESTS CHEW SLOWLY.

WHAT WAS THE RIDDLER'S MOST RECENT RIDDLE?

REAL NAME-
EDWARD NYGMA

HEIGHT-
6'1"

WEIGHT-
183 LBS (83.0 KG)

ALIASES-
THE PRINCE OF PUZZLES, QUIZMASTER E. NIGMA, EDWARD NASHTON

POWERS-
CHAMELEON, ESCAPE ARTIST, GADGETRY, SWORDSMANSHIP

PLEASE DON'T MAKE ME READ IT AGAIN.

I CAN'T READ THE ENCRYPTION FROM HERE.

WORD FOR WORD.

POSTED TO YOU ON THE DARK WEB: "WHEN IS THE RIDDLER NOT THE RIDDLER?"

SO DISAPPOINTING.

IT DOES SEEM A LITTLE PEDESTRIAN FOR HIM.

IS EVERYTHING CAPITALIZED AND--?

SPELLED CORRECTLY.

YES, SIR.

I MAY NOT HAVE EXPRESSED THIS TO YOU IN THE PAST, BUT I ALWAYS REGARDED THE RIDDLER AMONG YOUR MOST CLEVER ADVERSARIES.

I ALWAYS APPRECIATED THE AMOUNT OF EFFORT HE PUT FORTH.

THIS RIDDLE... IT'S QUITE BENEATH HIM.

I'LL MAKE SURE TO TELL HIM HE LOST A FAN.

FSSHHOOO

I'M DOING THIS MANUALLY.

OH GOOD LORD, SIR. WHY?

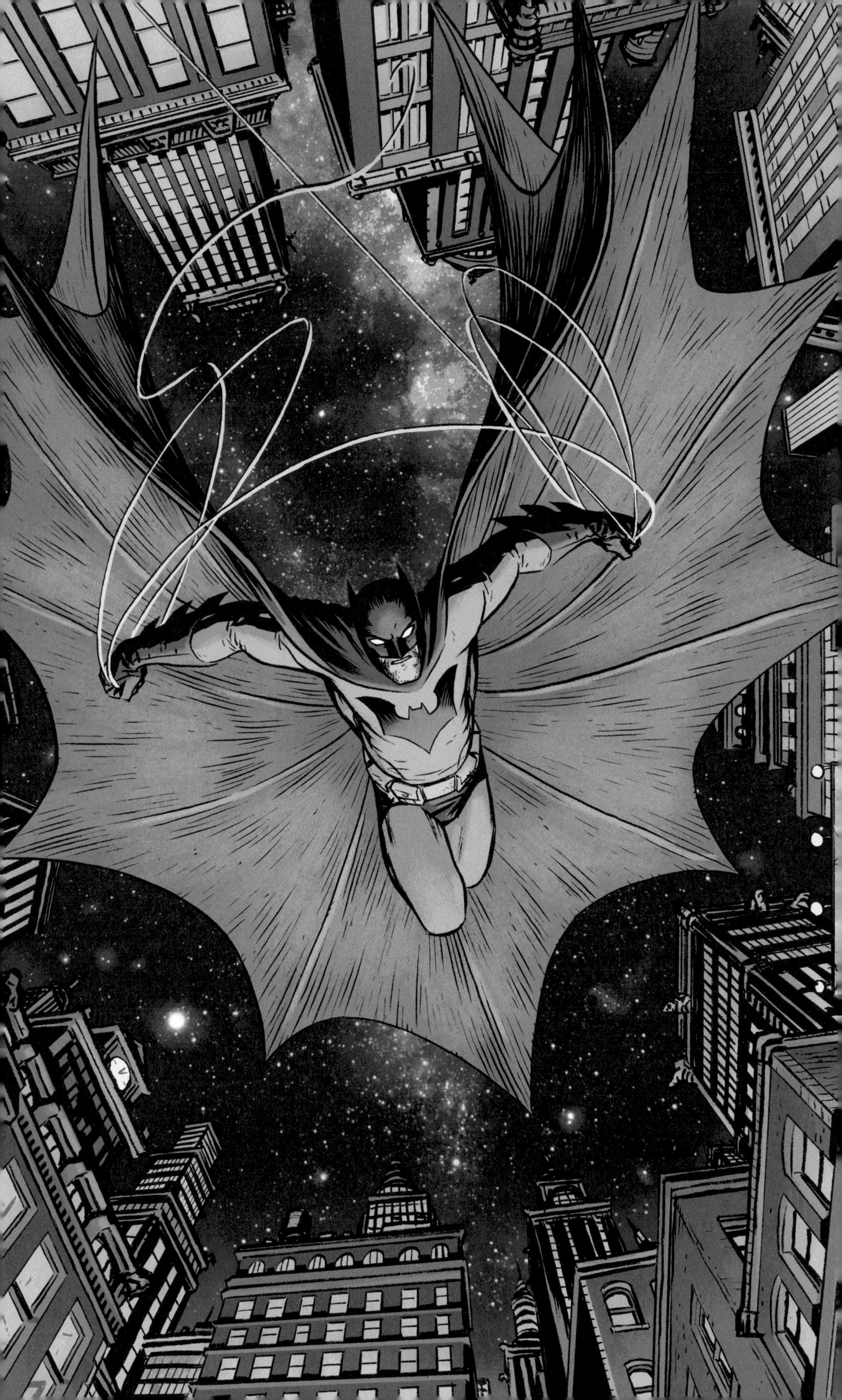

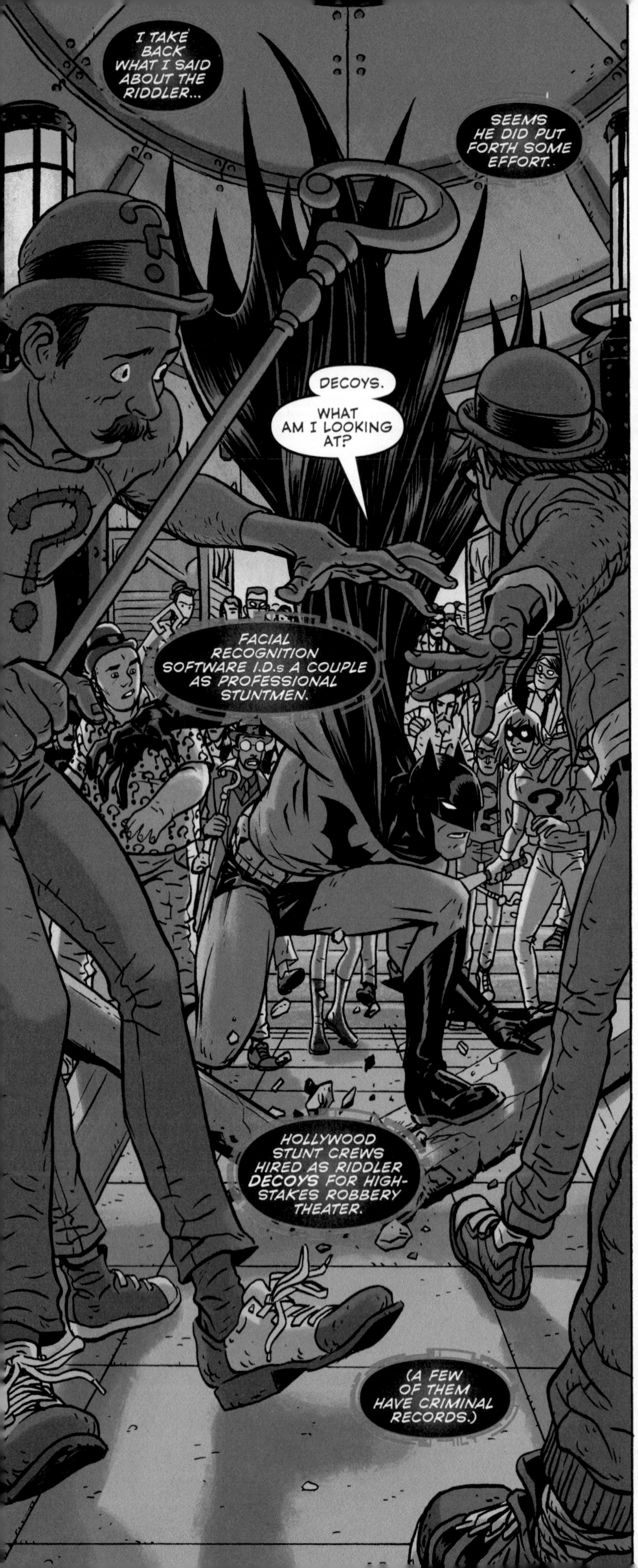
I TAKE BACK WHAT I SAID ABOUT THE RIDDLER...
SEEMS HE DID PUT FORTH SOME EFFORT..
DECOYS.
WHAT AM I LOOKING AT?
FACIAL RECOGNITION SOFTWARE I.D.s A COUPLE AS PROFESSIONAL STUNTMEN.
HOLLYWOOD STUNT CREWS HIRED AS RIDDLER DECOYS FOR HIGH-STAKES ROBBERY THEATER.
(A FEW OF THEM HAVE CRIMINAL RECORDS.)
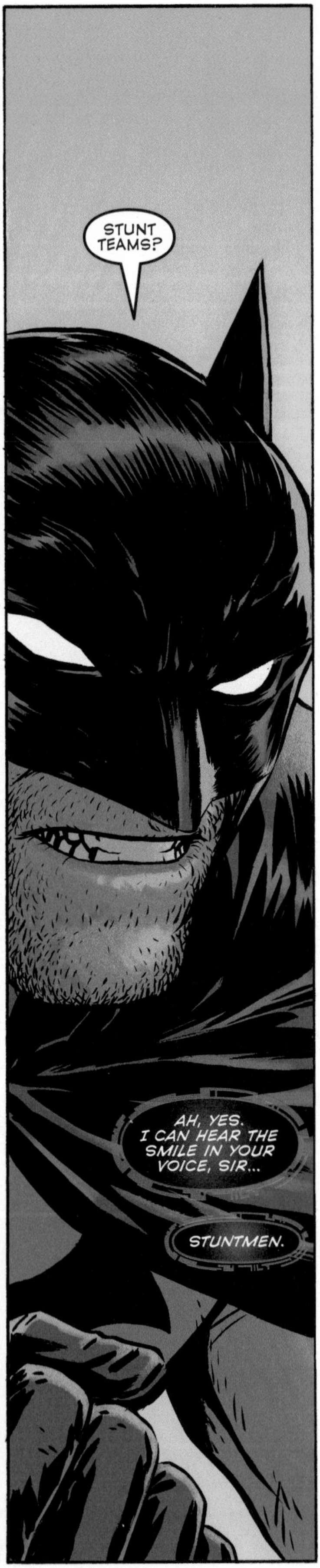
STUNT TEAMS?
AH, YES. I CAN HEAR THE SMILE IN YOUR VOICE, SIR...
STUNTMEN.

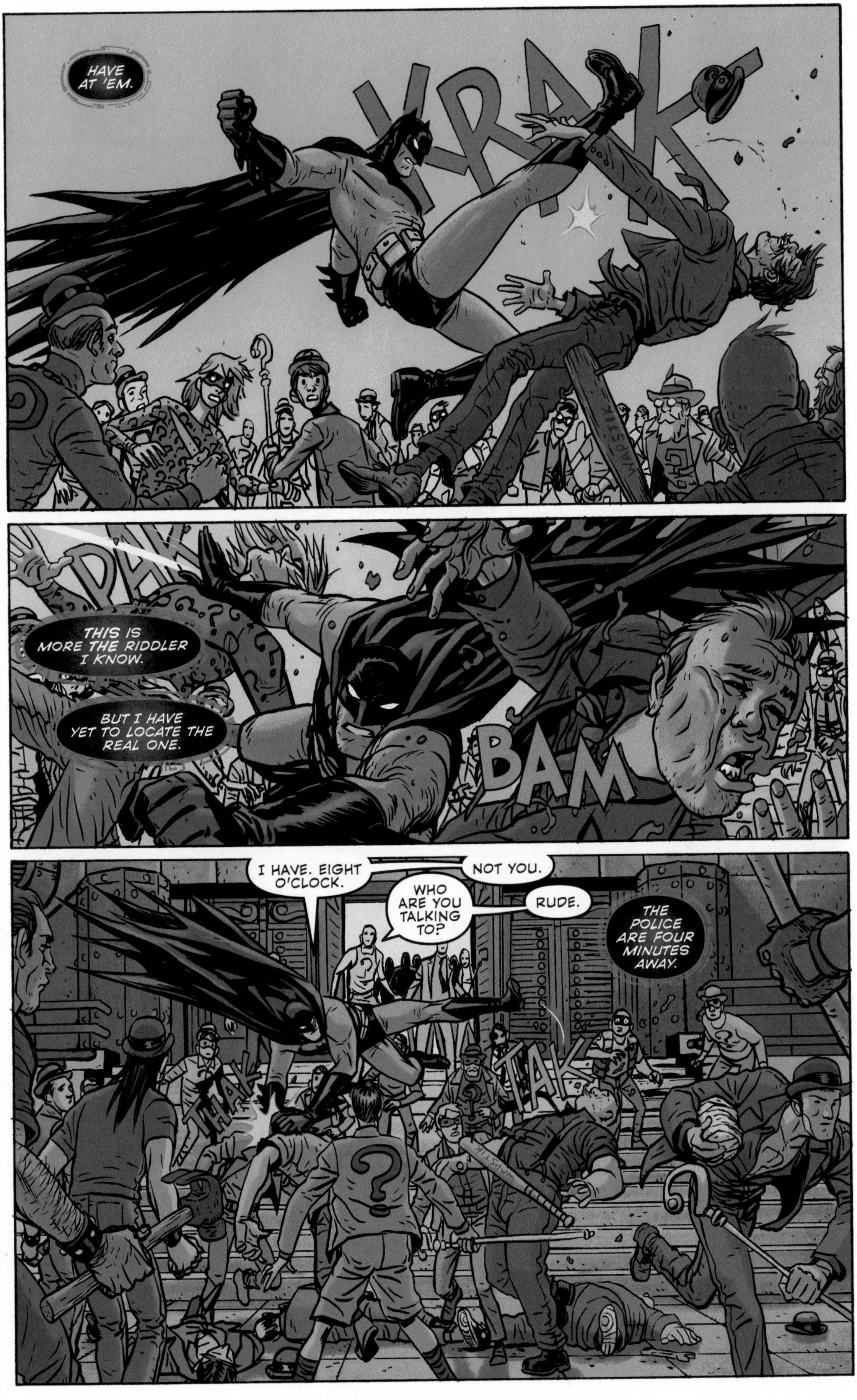
HAVE AT 'EM.
VRAK
THIS IS MORE THE RIDDLER I KNOW.
BUT I HAVE YET TO LOCATE THE REAL ONE.
BAM
I HAVE. EIGHT O'CLOCK.
NOT YOU.
WHO ARE YOU TALKING TO?
RUDE.
THE POLICE ARE FOUR MINUTES AWAY.
TAK

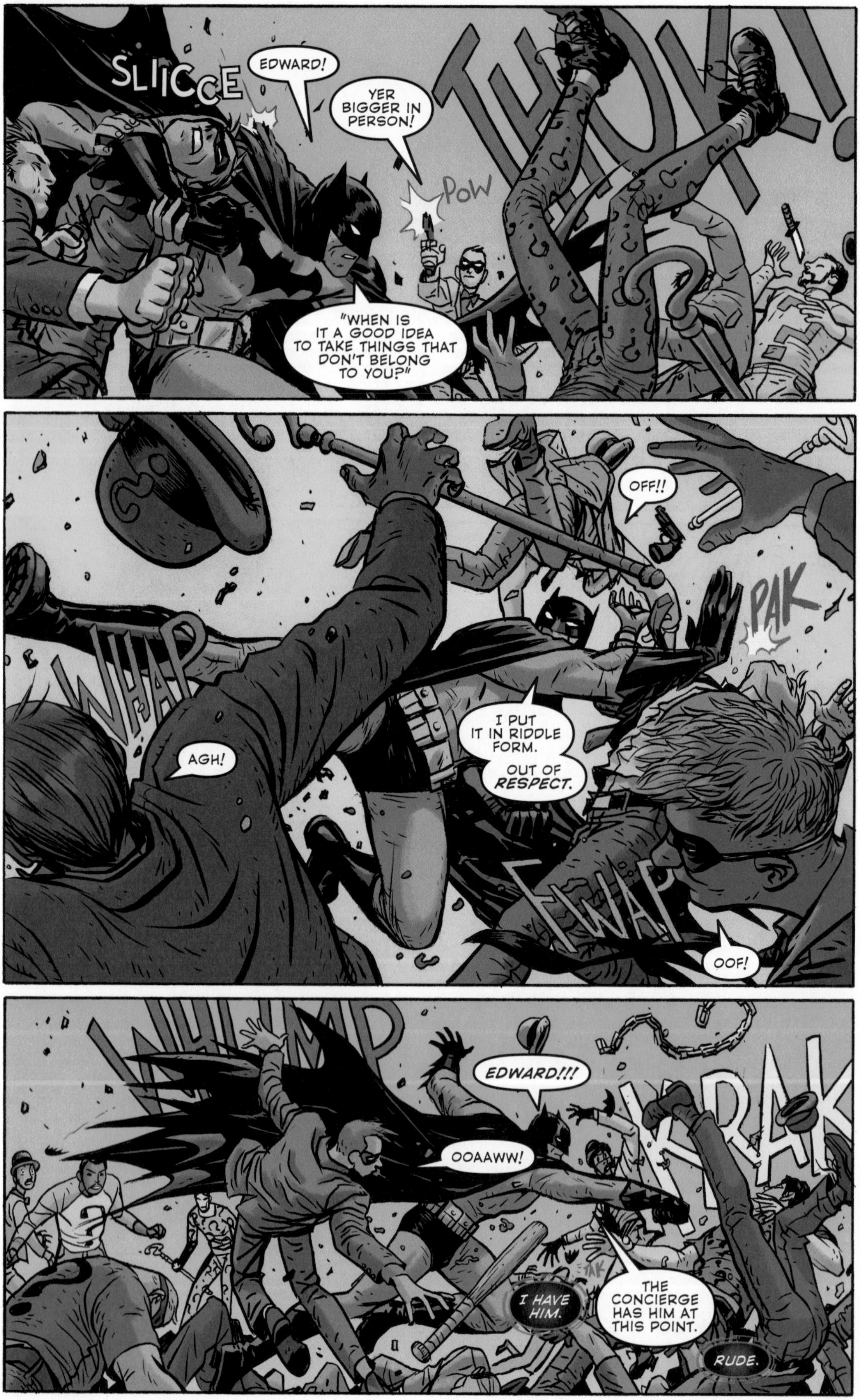
SLIICCE
EDWARD!
YER BIGGER IN PERSON!
THOCK!
POW
"WHEN IS IT A GOOD IDEA TO TAKE THINGS THAT DON'T BELONG TO YOU?"
OFF!!
PAK
WHAP
AGH!
I PUT IT IN RIDDLE FORM.
OUT OF *RESPECT*.
FWAP
OOF!
WHUMP
EDWARD!!!
KRAK
OOAAWW!
I HAVE HIM.
THE CONCIERGE HAS HIM AT THIS POINT.
RUDE.

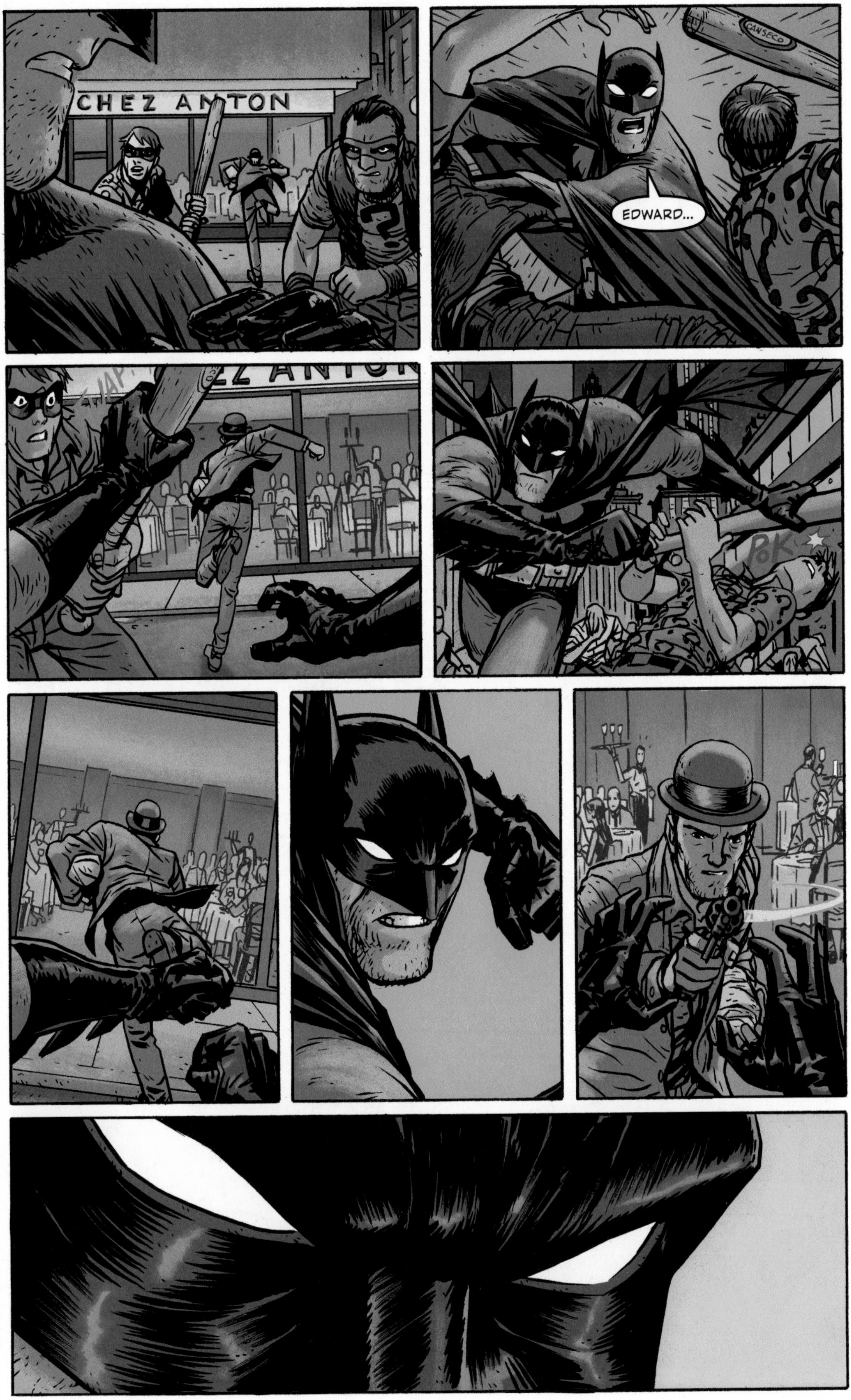
CHEZ ANTON
CANSECO
EDWARD...
POK

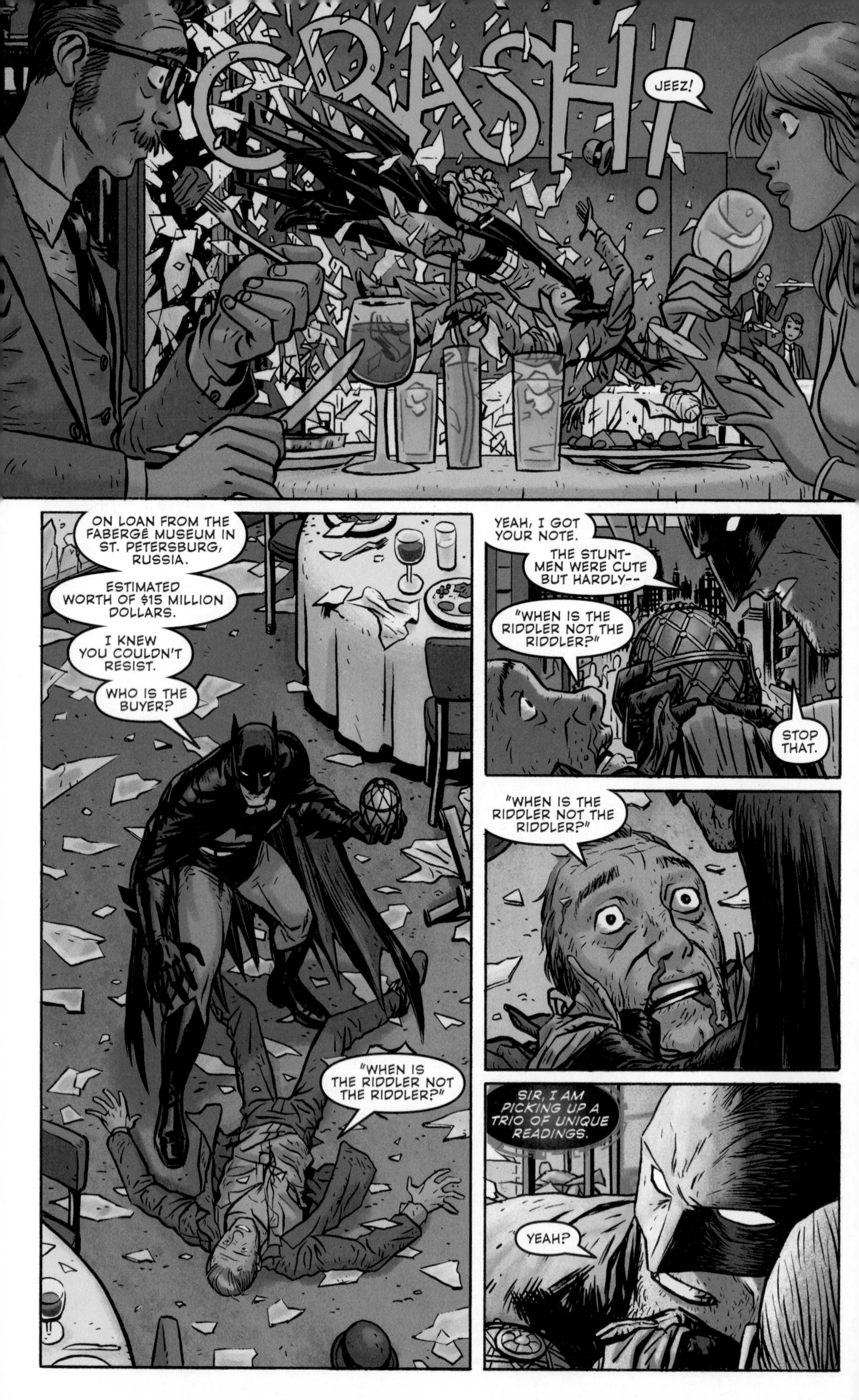
CRASH!
JEEZ!
ON LOAN FROM THE FABERGÉ MUSEUM IN ST. PETERSBURG, RUSSIA.
ESTIMATED WORTH OF $15 MILLION DOLLARS.
I KNEW YOU COULDN'T RESIST.
WHO IS THE BUYER?
"WHEN IS THE RIDDLER NOT THE RIDDLER?"
YEAH, I GOT YOUR NOTE.
THE STUNT-MEN WERE CUTE BUT HARDLY--
"WHEN IS THE RIDDLER NOT THE RIDDLER?"
STOP THAT.
"WHEN IS THE RIDDLER NOT THE RIDDLER?"
SIR, I AM PICKING UP A TRIO OF UNIQUE READINGS.
YEAH?

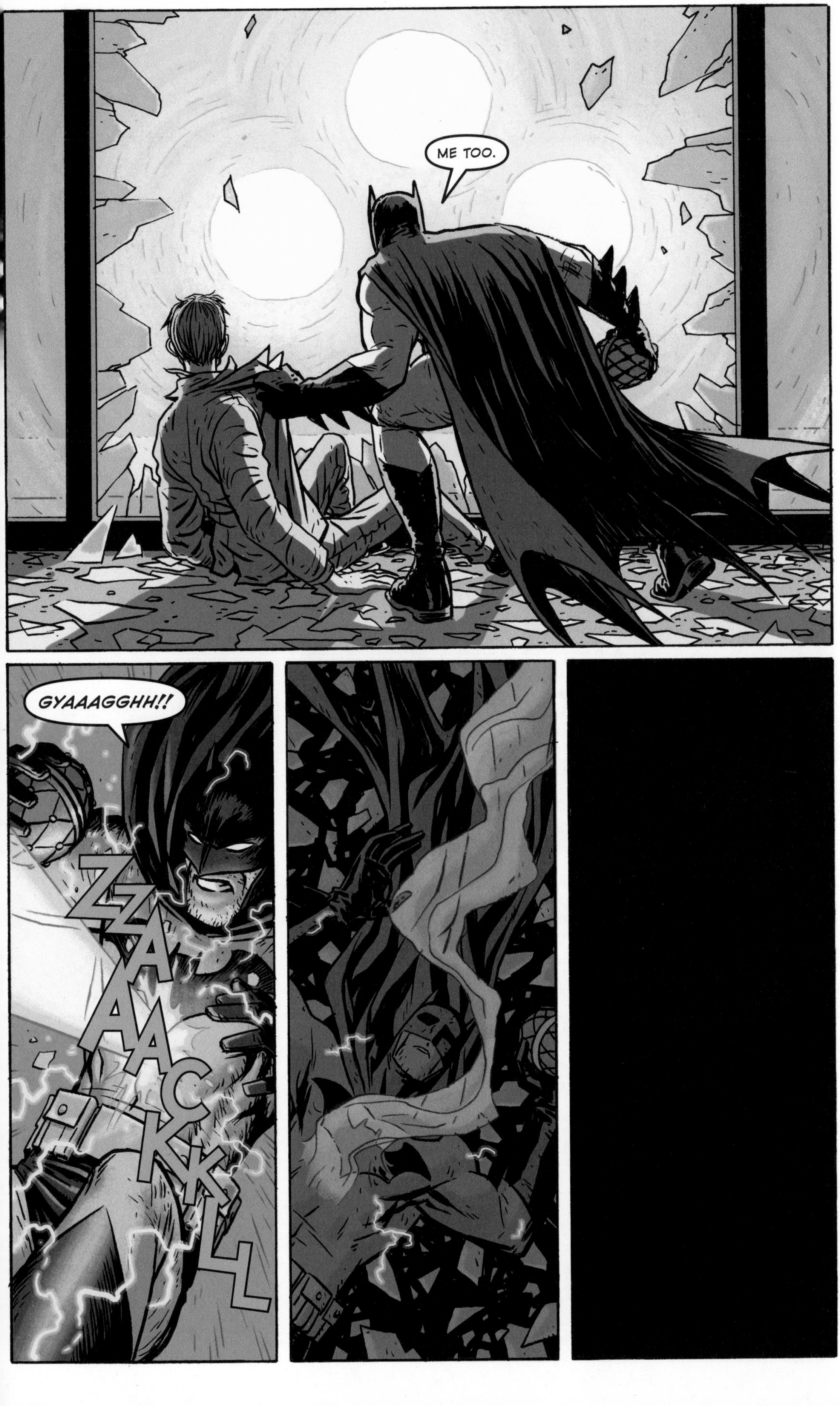
ME TOO.
GYAAAGGHH!!
ZZAAACKKLL

GO AHEAD.

BE MY GUEST.

MAYBE HE CAN'T BREATHE.

SURE, KID.

TAKE OFF HIS MASK.

HE WON'T MIND.

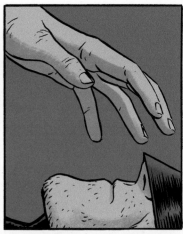

PLEASE DON'T.

WHERE'S THE EGG?

YOU ORDERED EGGS?

WHERE'S *THE* RIDDLER?

ALL THE RIDDLERS ARE BEING LOADED INTO THE PADDY WAGON.

NO.

THE REAL ONE.

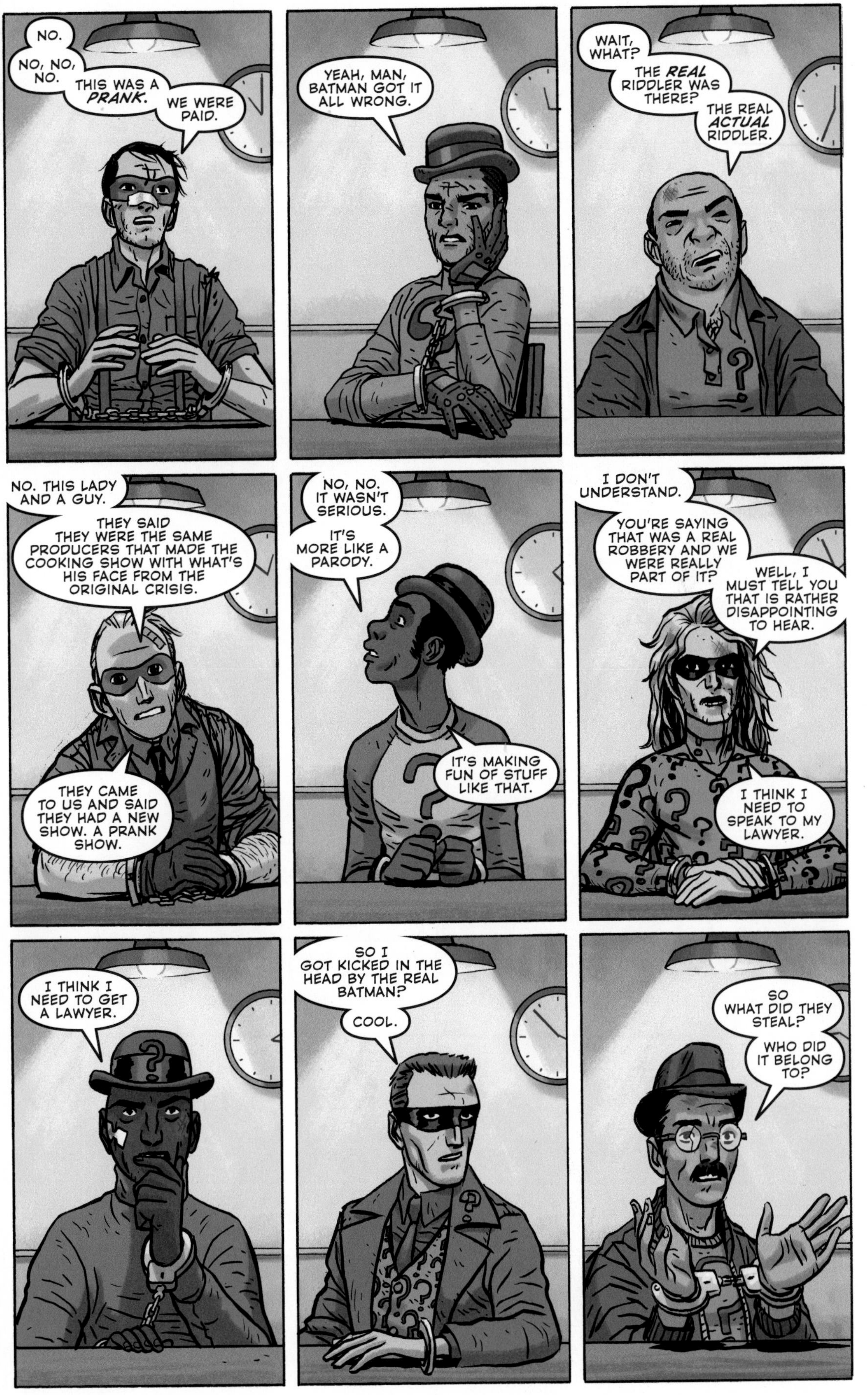
NO.
NO, NO, NO.
THIS WAS A *PRANK.*
WE WERE PAID.
YEAH, MAN, BATMAN GOT IT ALL WRONG.
WAIT, WHAT?
THE *REAL* RIDDLER WAS THERE?
THE REAL *ACTUAL* RIDDLER.
NO. THIS LADY AND A GUY.
THEY SAID THEY WERE THE SAME PRODUCERS THAT MADE THE COOKING SHOW WITH WHAT'S HIS FACE FROM THE ORIGINAL CRISIS.
THEY CAME TO US AND SAID THEY HAD A NEW SHOW. A PRANK SHOW.
NO, NO. IT WASN'T SERIOUS.
IT'S MORE LIKE A PARODY.
IT'S MAKING FUN OF STUFF LIKE THAT.
I DON'T UNDERSTAND.
YOU'RE SAYING THAT WAS A REAL ROBBERY AND WE WERE REALLY PART OF IT?
WELL, I MUST TELL YOU THAT IS RATHER DISAPPOINTING TO HEAR.
I THINK I NEED TO SPEAK TO MY LAWYER.
I THINK I NEED TO GET A LAWYER.
SO I GOT KICKED IN THE HEAD BY THE REAL BATMAN?
COOL.
SO WHAT DID THEY STEAL?
WHO DID IT BELONG TO?

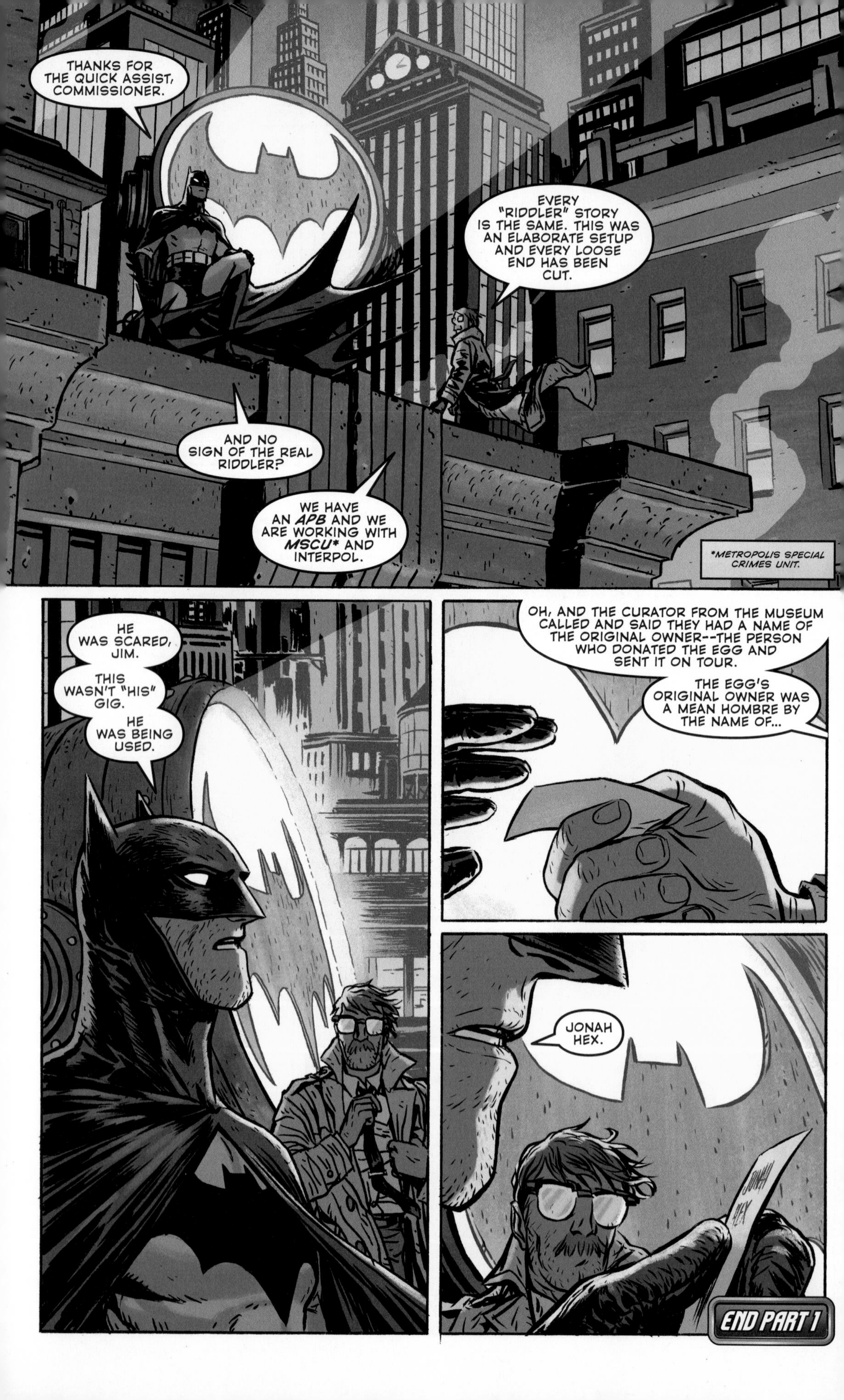
THANKS FOR THE QUICK ASSIST, COMMISSIONER.
EVERY "RIDDLER" STORY IS THE SAME. THIS WAS AN ELABORATE SETUP AND EVERY LOOSE END HAS BEEN CUT.
AND NO SIGN OF THE REAL RIDDLER?
WE HAVE AN *APB* AND WE ARE WORKING WITH *MSCU** AND INTERPOL.
*METROPOLIS SPECIAL CRIMES UNIT.
HE WAS SCARED, JIM.
THIS WASN'T "HIS" GIG.
HE WAS BEING USED.
OH, AND THE CURATOR FROM THE MUSEUM CALLED AND SAID THEY HAD A NAME OF THE ORIGINAL OWNER--THE PERSON WHO DONATED THE EGG AND SENT IT ON TOUR.
THE EGG'S ORIGINAL OWNER WAS A MEAN HOMBRE BY THE NAME OF...
JONAH HEX.
JONAH HEX
END PART 1

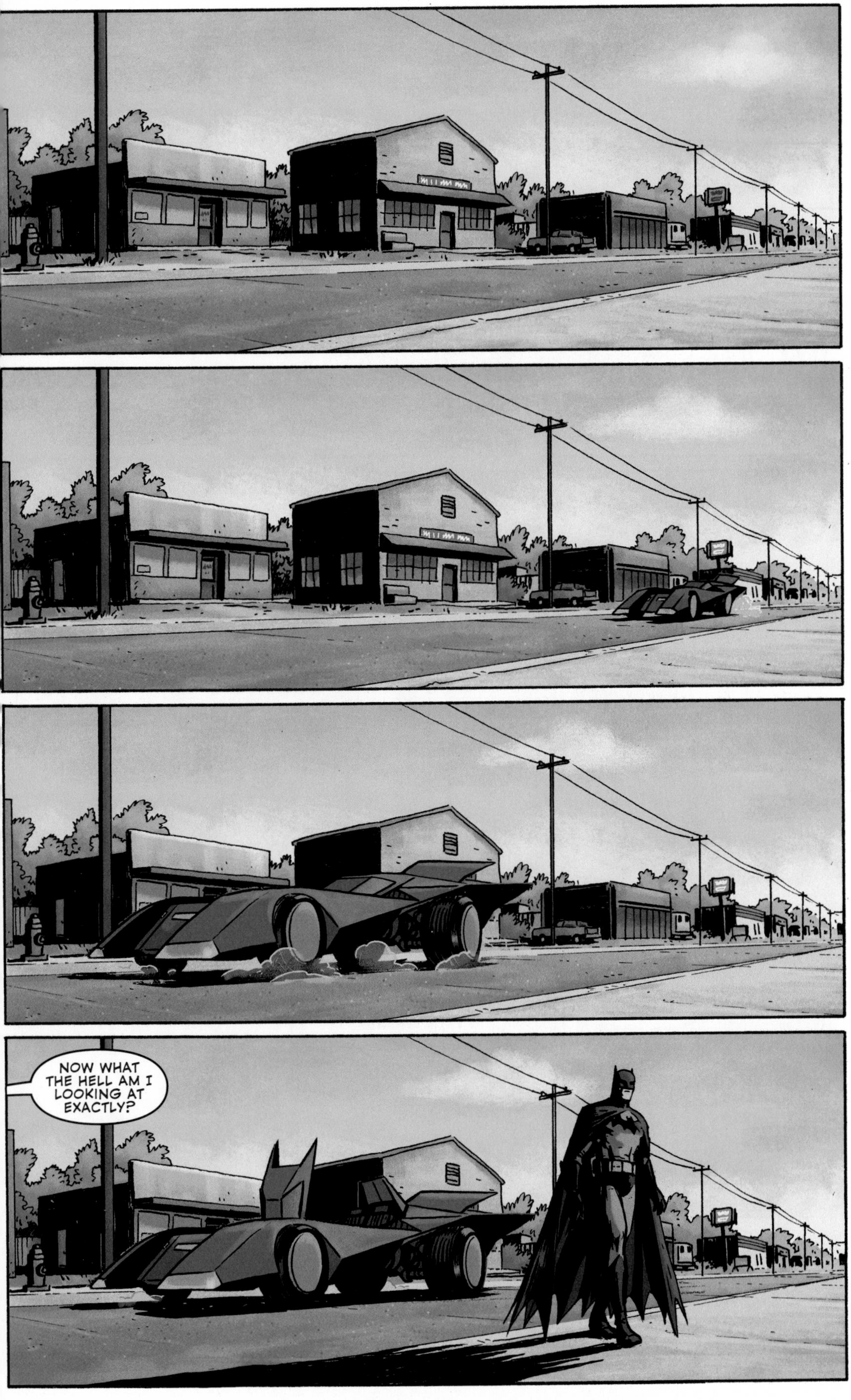
NOW WHAT THE HELL AM I LOOKING AT EXACTLY?

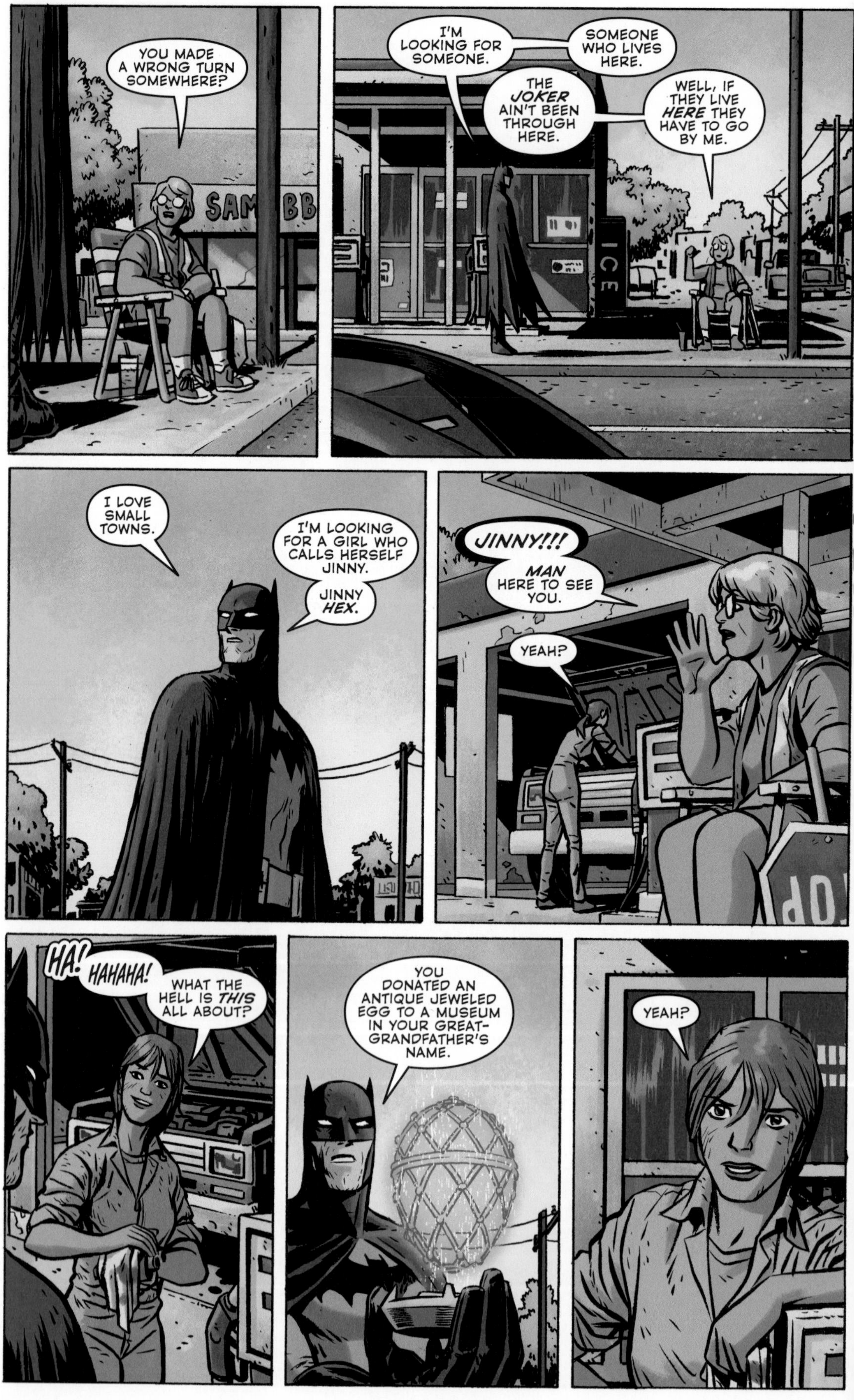
YOU MADE A WRONG TURN SOMEWHERE?
SAM BB
I'M LOOKING FOR SOMEONE.
SOMEONE WHO LIVES HERE.
THE *JOKER* AIN'T BEEN THROUGH HERE.
WELL, IF THEY LIVE *HERE* THEY HAVE TO GO BY ME.
ICE
I LOVE SMALL TOWNS.
I'M LOOKING FOR A GIRL WHO CALLS HERSELF JINNY.
JINNY *HEX.*
JINNY!!!
MAN HERE TO SEE YOU.
YEAH?
HA! HAHAHA!
WHAT THE HELL IS *THIS* ALL ABOUT?
YOU DONATED AN ANTIQUE JEWELED EGG TO A MUSEUM IN YOUR GREAT-GRANDFATHER'S NAME.
YEAH?

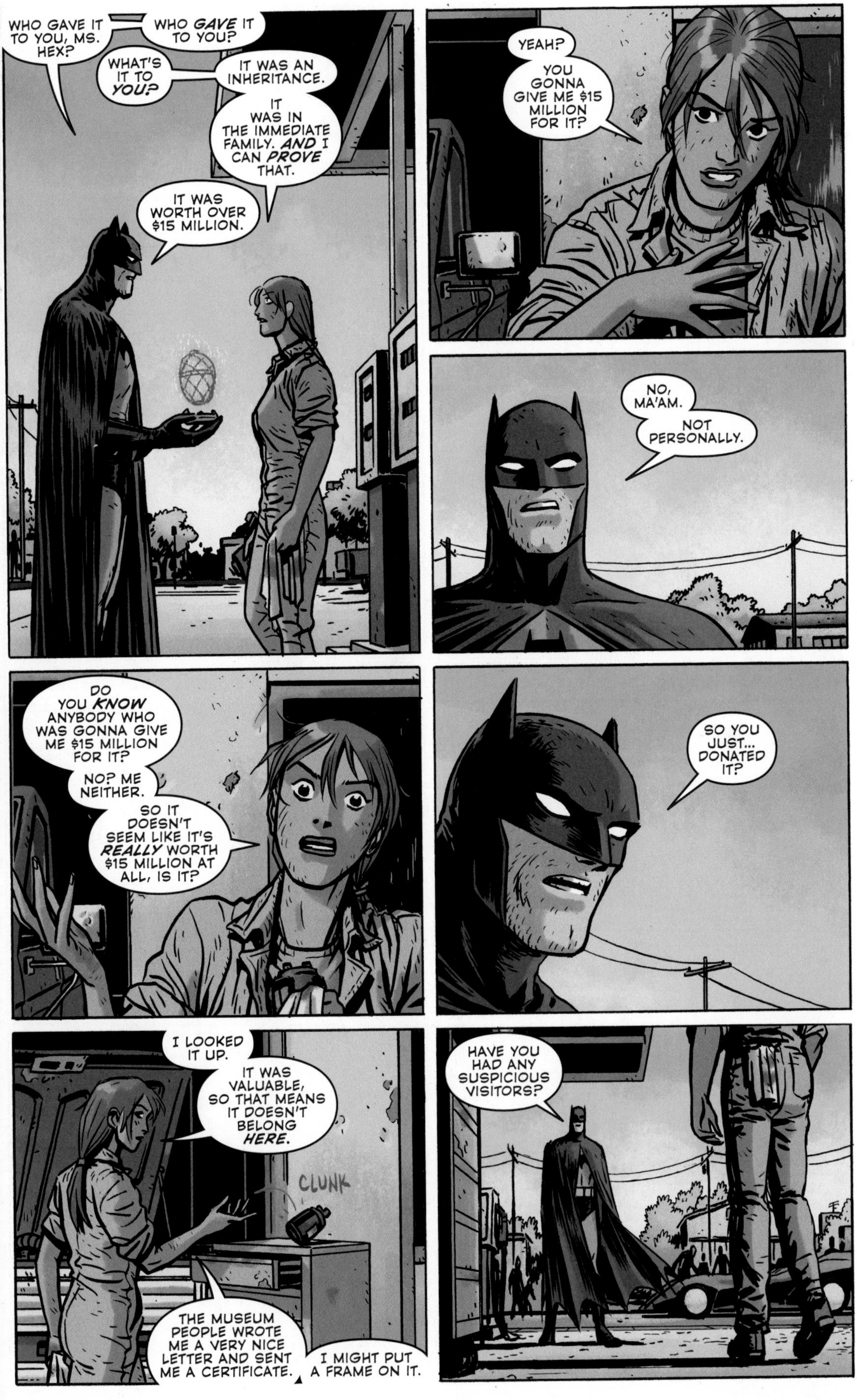
WHO GAVE IT TO YOU, MS. HEX?
WHO GAVE IT TO YOU?
WHAT'S IT TO YOU?
IT WAS AN INHERITANCE.
IT WAS IN THE IMMEDIATE FAMILY. AND I CAN PROVE THAT.
IT WAS WORTH OVER $15 MILLION.
YEAH?
YOU GONNA GIVE ME $15 MILLION FOR IT?
NO, MA'AM.
NOT PERSONALLY.
DO YOU KNOW ANYBODY WHO WAS GONNA GIVE ME $15 MILLION FOR IT?
NO? ME NEITHER.
SO IT DOESN'T SEEM LIKE IT'S REALLY WORTH $15 MILLION AT ALL, IS IT?
SO YOU JUST... DONATED IT?
I LOOKED IT UP.
IT WAS VALUABLE, SO THAT MEANS IT DOESN'T BELONG HERE.
CLUNK
THE MUSEUM PEOPLE WROTE ME A VERY NICE LETTER AND SENT ME A CERTIFICATE.
I MIGHT PUT A FRAME ON IT.
HAVE YOU HAD ANY SUSPICIOUS VISITORS?

YOU KNOW I HAVE.

A GUY DRESSED UP LIKE BATMAN SHOWED UP...

AND STARTED GETTING IN MY FACE ABOUT SOMETHING THAT WAS TOTALLY NORMAL.

YOU INHERITED AN EGG AND IT'S BEEN--

I NEVER SAW IT BEFORE IN MY LIFE UNTIL MY MAMA KEELED OVER.

SEEMS LIKE SHE HAD A BIG PILE OF SECRETS THAT SHE KEPT FROM ME.

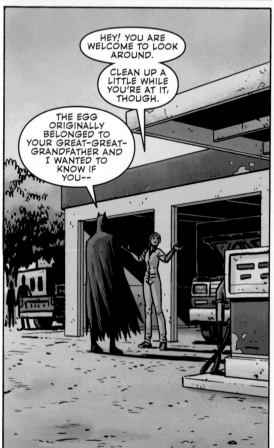

HEY! YOU ARE WELCOME TO LOOK AROUND.

CLEAN UP A LITTLE WHILE YOU'RE AT IT, THOUGH.

THE EGG ORIGINALLY BELONGED TO YOUR GREAT-GREAT-GRANDFATHER AND I WANTED TO KNOW IF YOU--

I KNOW. HIS NAME IS JONAH.

HE WAS ONE BAD HOMBRE.

WAS THE EGG STOLEN? IS *THAT* THE THING?

BECAUSE I DIDN'T DO IT.

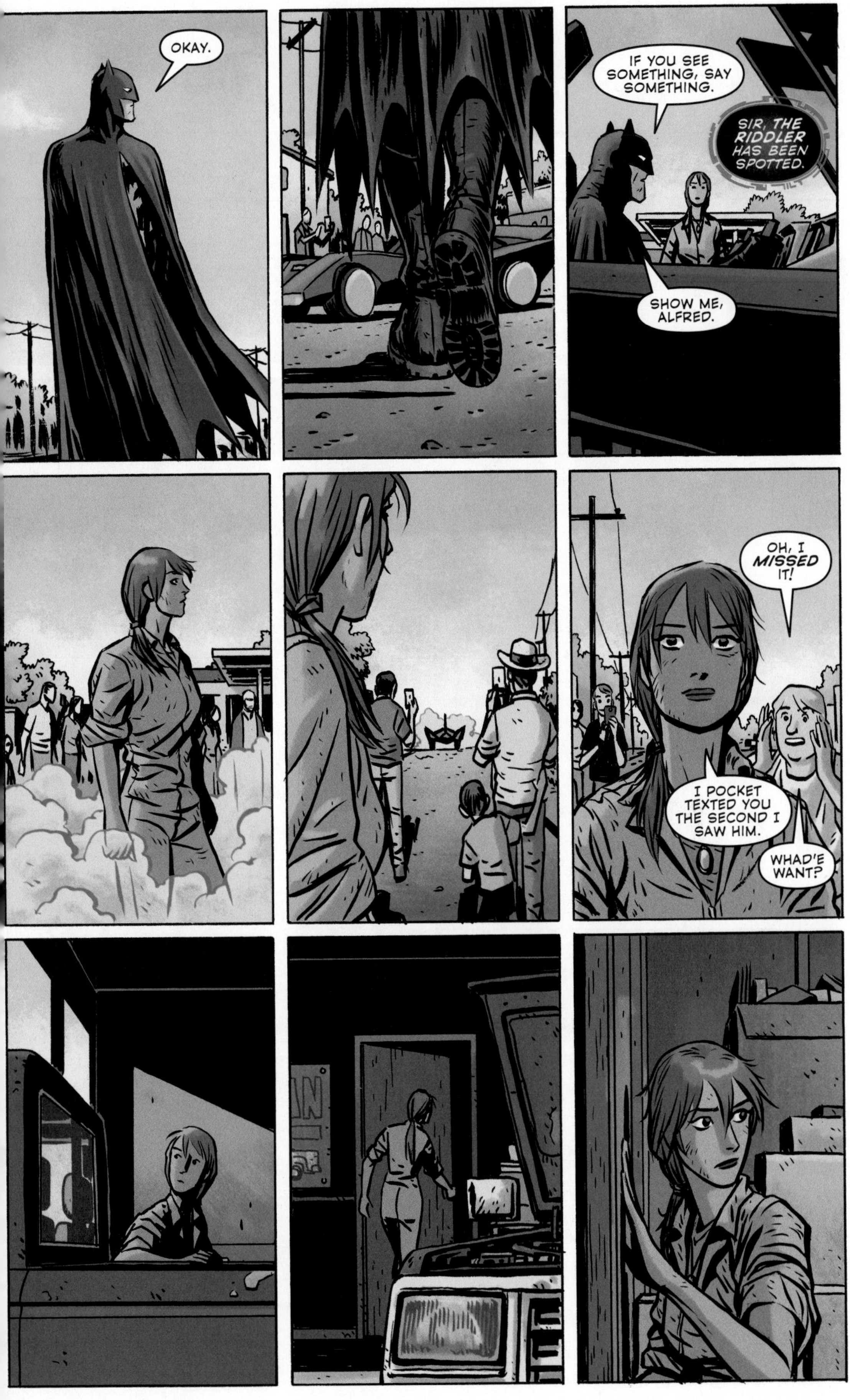
OKAY.
IF YOU SEE SOMETHING, SAY SOMETHING.
SIR, THE RIDDLER HAS BEEN SPOTTED.
SHOW ME, ALFRED.
OH, I MISSED IT!
I POCKET TEXTED YOU THE SECOND I SAW HIM.
WHAD'E WANT?

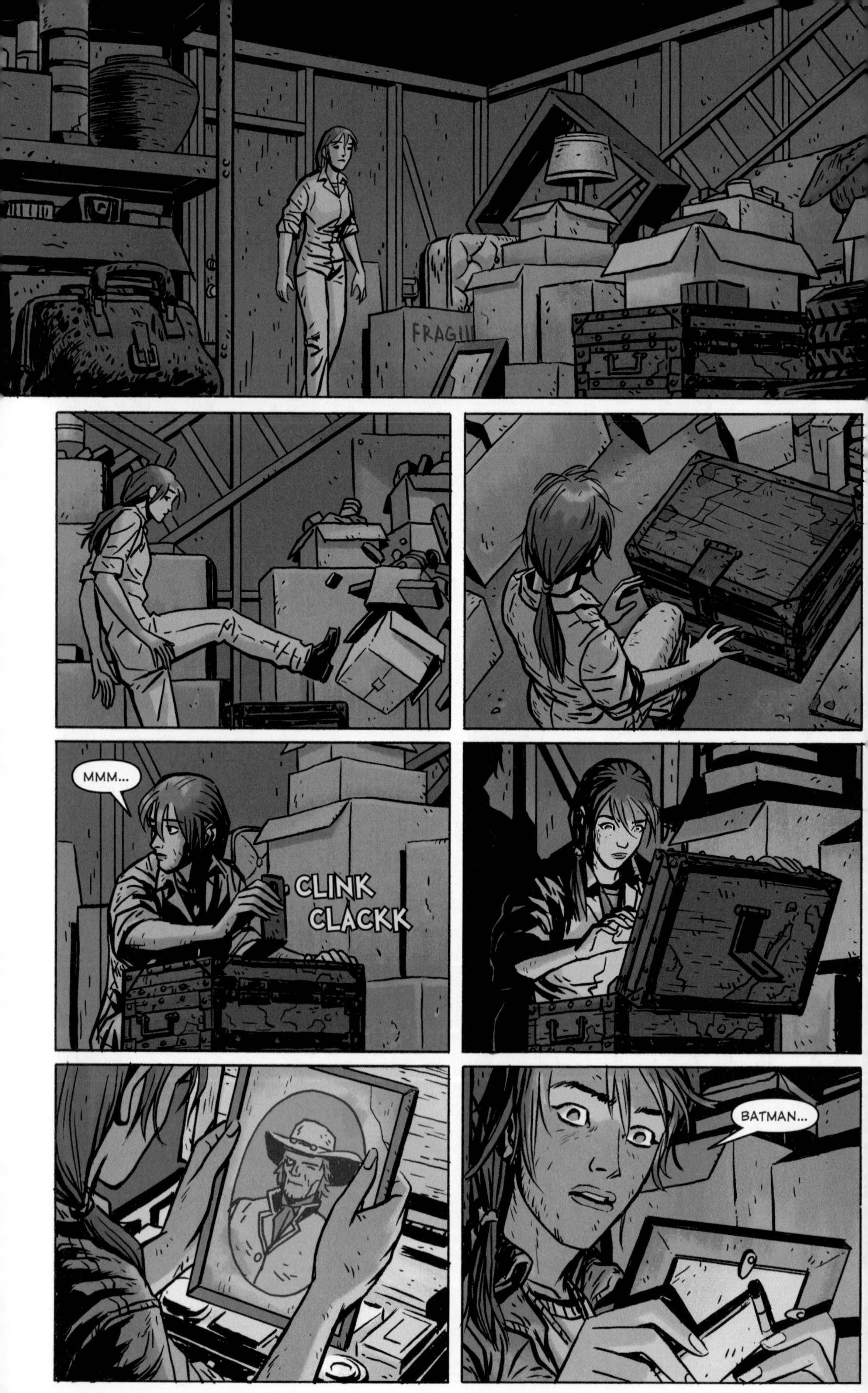
FRAGIL
MMM...
CLINK
CLACKK
BATMAN...

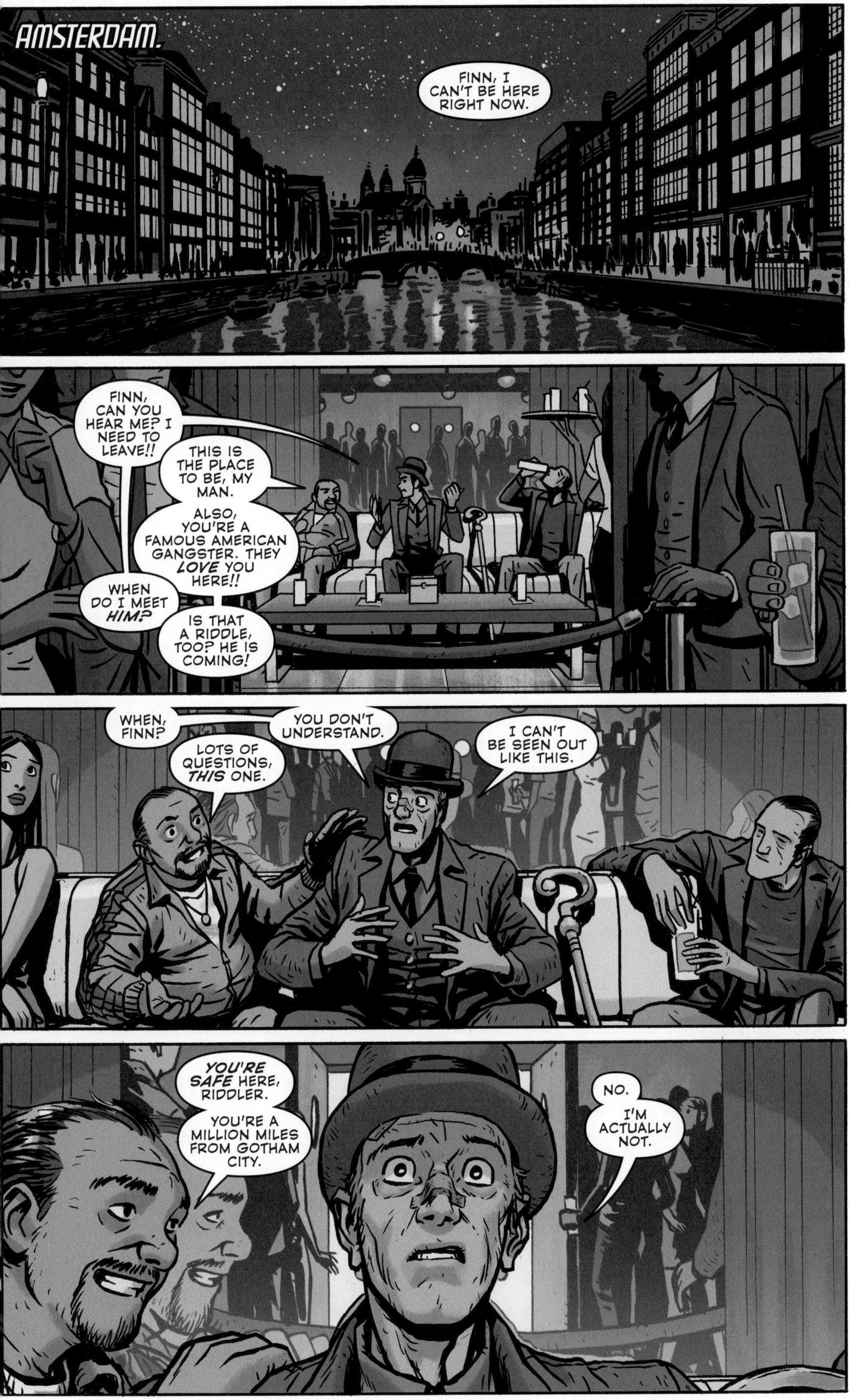
AMSTERDAM.
FINN, I CAN'T BE HERE RIGHT NOW.
FINN, CAN YOU HEAR ME? I NEED TO LEAVE!!
THIS IS THE PLACE TO BE, MY MAN.
ALSO, YOU'RE A FAMOUS AMERICAN GANGSTER. THEY LOVE YOU HERE!!
WHEN DO I MEET HIM?
IS THAT A RIDDLE, TOO? HE IS COMING!
WHEN, FINN?
LOTS OF QUESTIONS, THIS ONE.
YOU DON'T UNDERSTAND.
I CAN'T BE SEEN OUT LIKE THIS.
YOU'RE SAFE HERE, RIDDLER.
YOU'RE A MILLION MILES FROM GOTHAM CITY.
NO.
I'M ACTUALLY NOT.

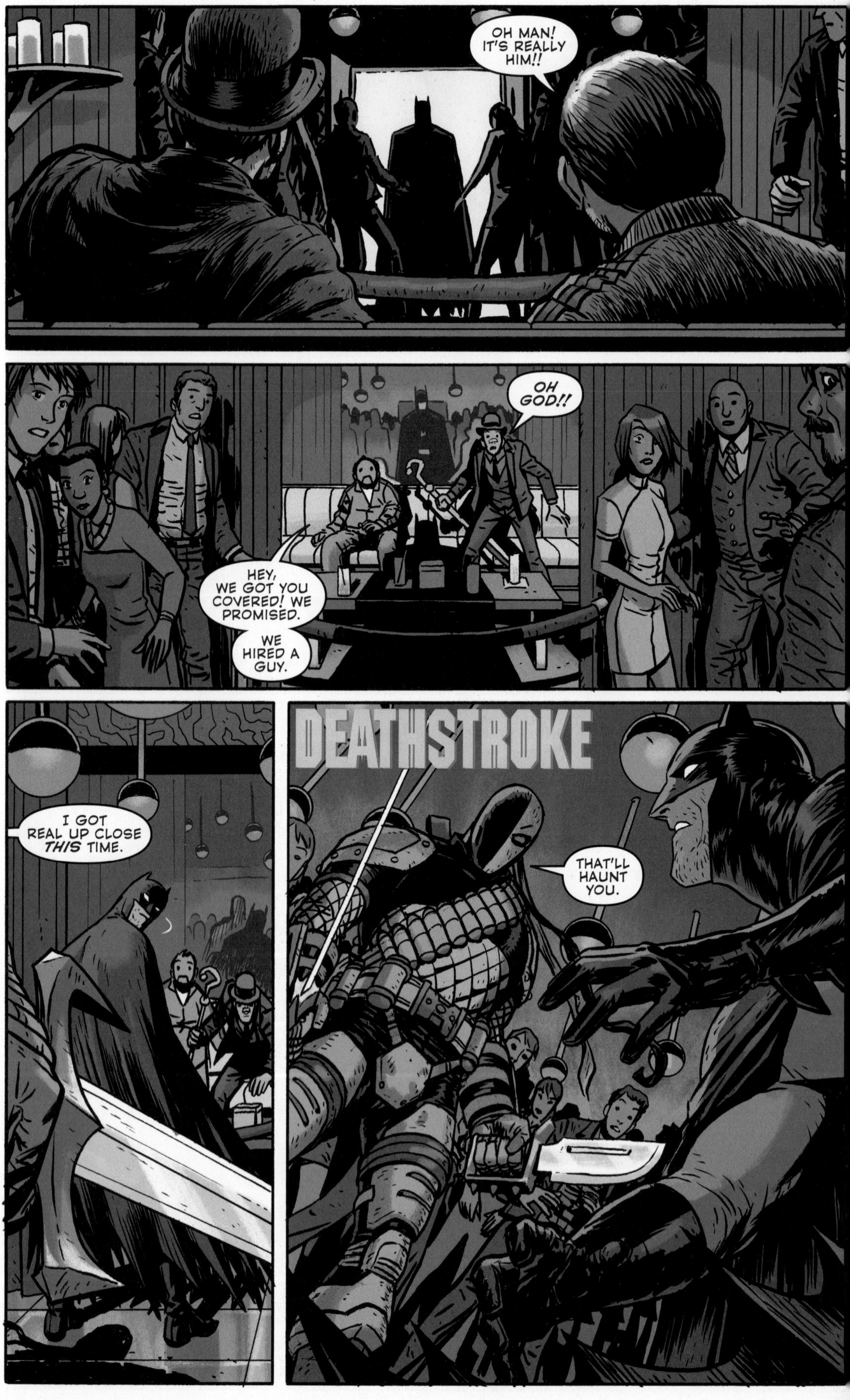
OH MAN! IT'S REALLY HIM!!
OH GOD!!
HEY, WE GOT YOU COVERED! WE PROMISED.
WE HIRED A GUY.
I GOT REAL UP CLOSE *THIS* TIME.
DEATHSTROKE
THAT'LL HAUNT YOU.

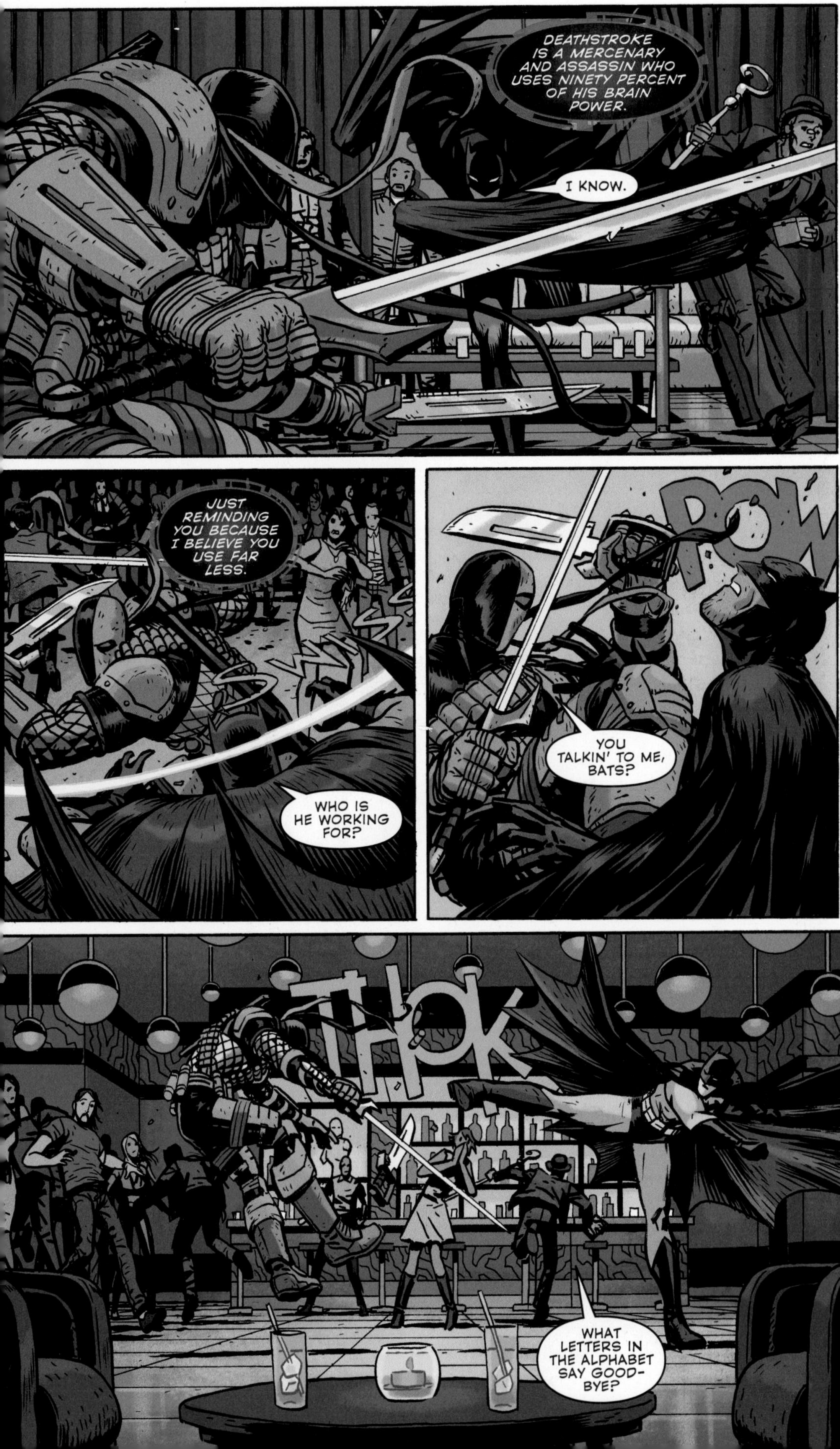
DEATHSTROKE IS A MERCENARY AND ASSASSIN WHO USES NINETY PERCENT OF HIS BRAIN POWER.
I KNOW.
JUST REMINDING YOU BECAUSE I BELIEVE YOU USE FAR LESS.
WHO IS HE WORKING FOR?
POW
YOU TALKIN' TO ME, BATS?
THOK
WHAT LETTERS IN THE ALPHABET SAY GOOD-BYE?

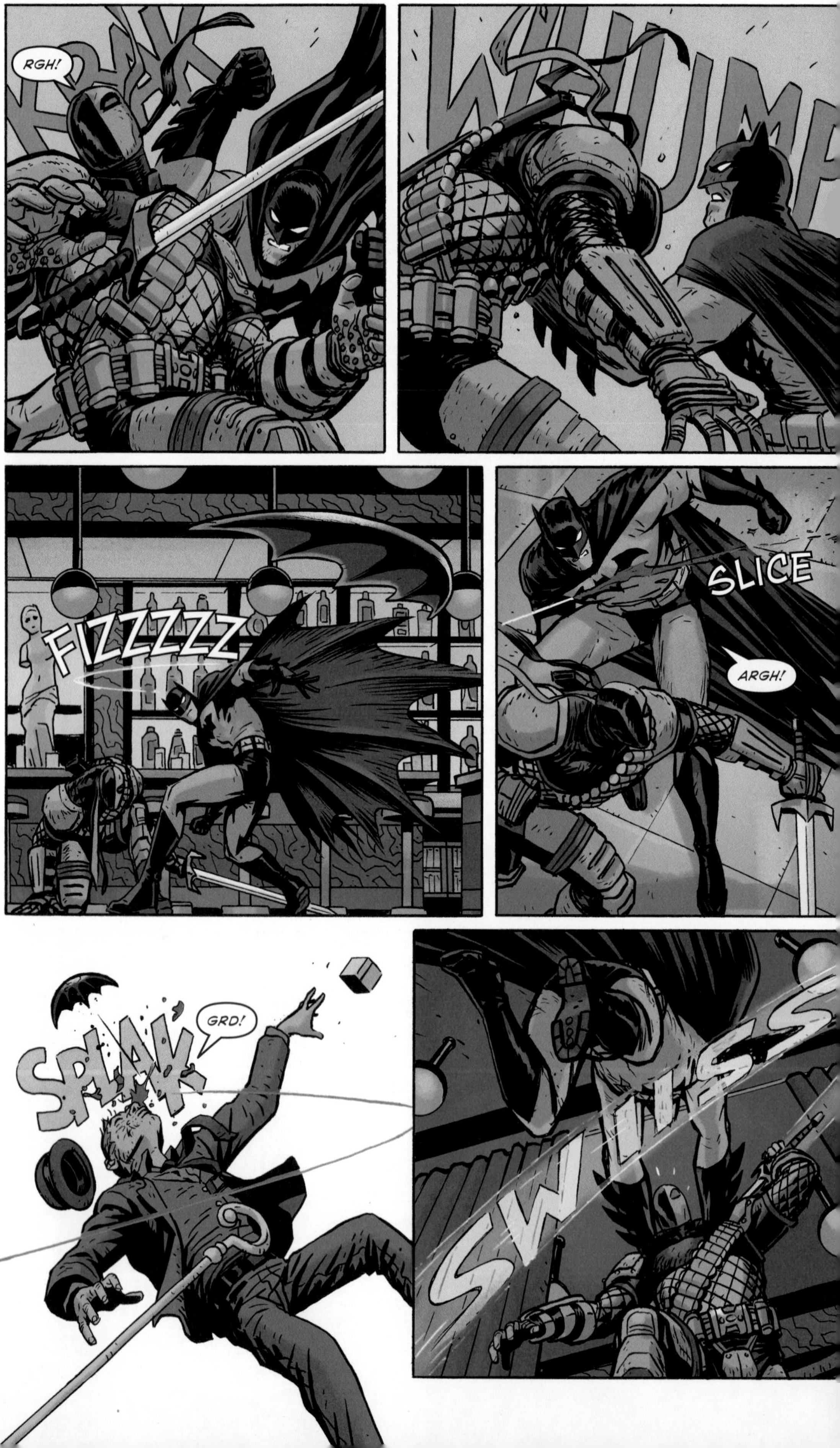

RGH!
FIZZZZZZ
SLICE
ARGH!
SPLAK
GRD!

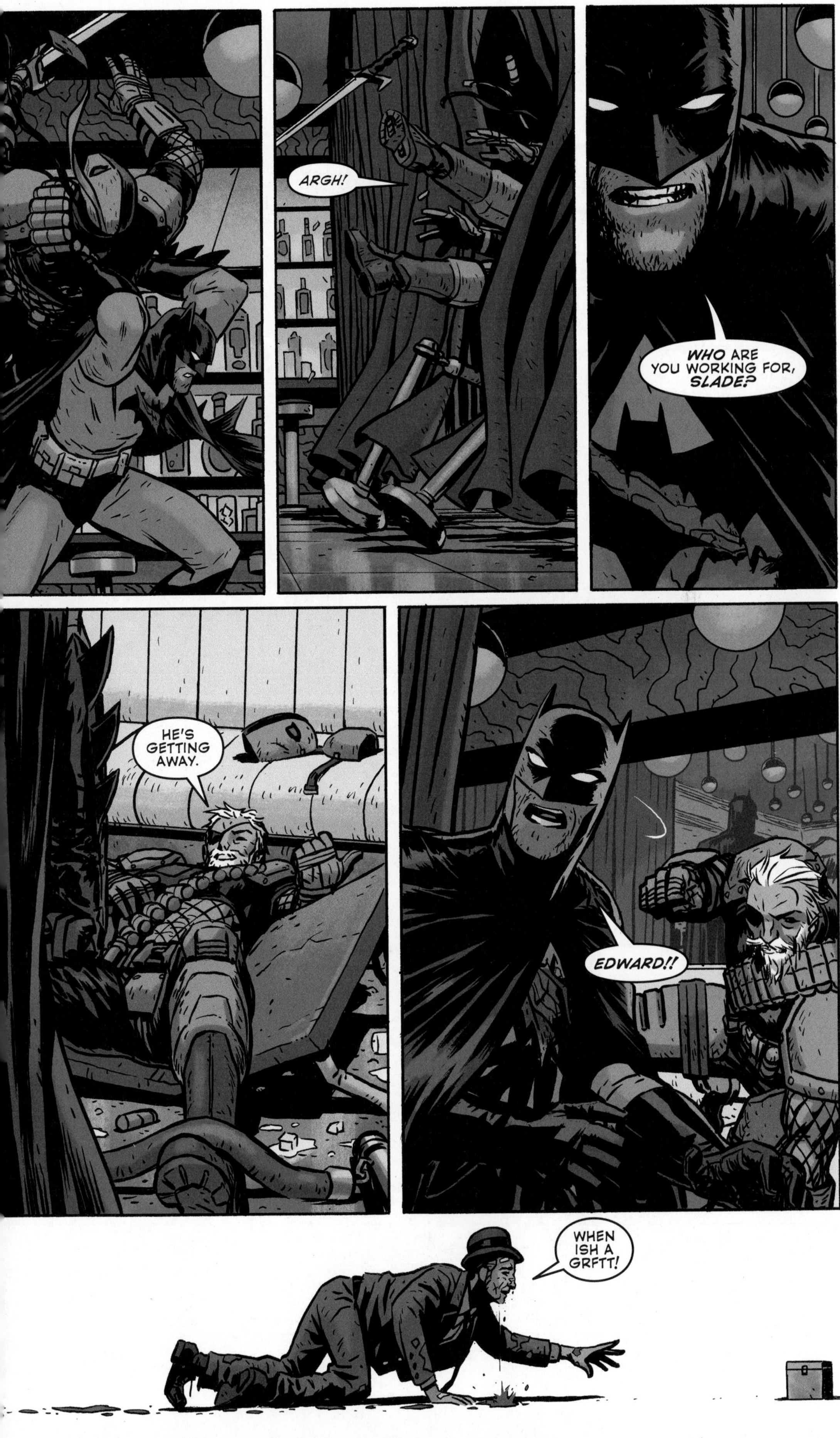

ARGH!
WHO ARE YOU WORKING FOR, SLADE?
HE'S GETTING AWAY.
EDWARD!!
WHEN ISH A GRFTT!

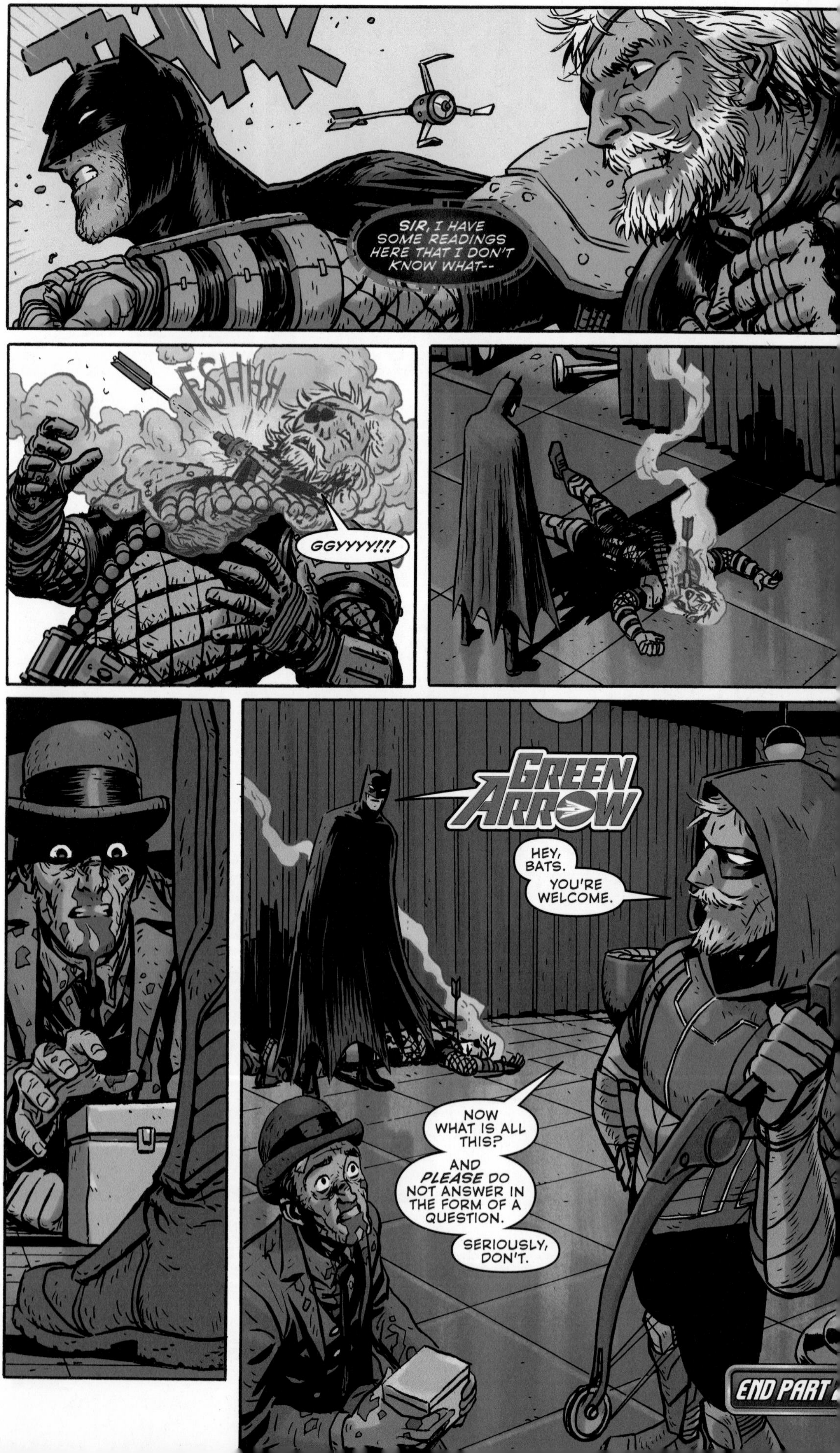
THAK
SIR, I HAVE SOME READINGS HERE THAT I DON'T KNOW WHAT--
FSHHH
GGYYYY!!!
GREEN ARROW
HEY, BATS.
YOU'RE WELCOME.
NOW WHAT IS ALL THIS?
AND PLEASE DO NOT ANSWER IN THE FORM OF A QUESTION.
SERIOUSLY, DON'T.
END PART

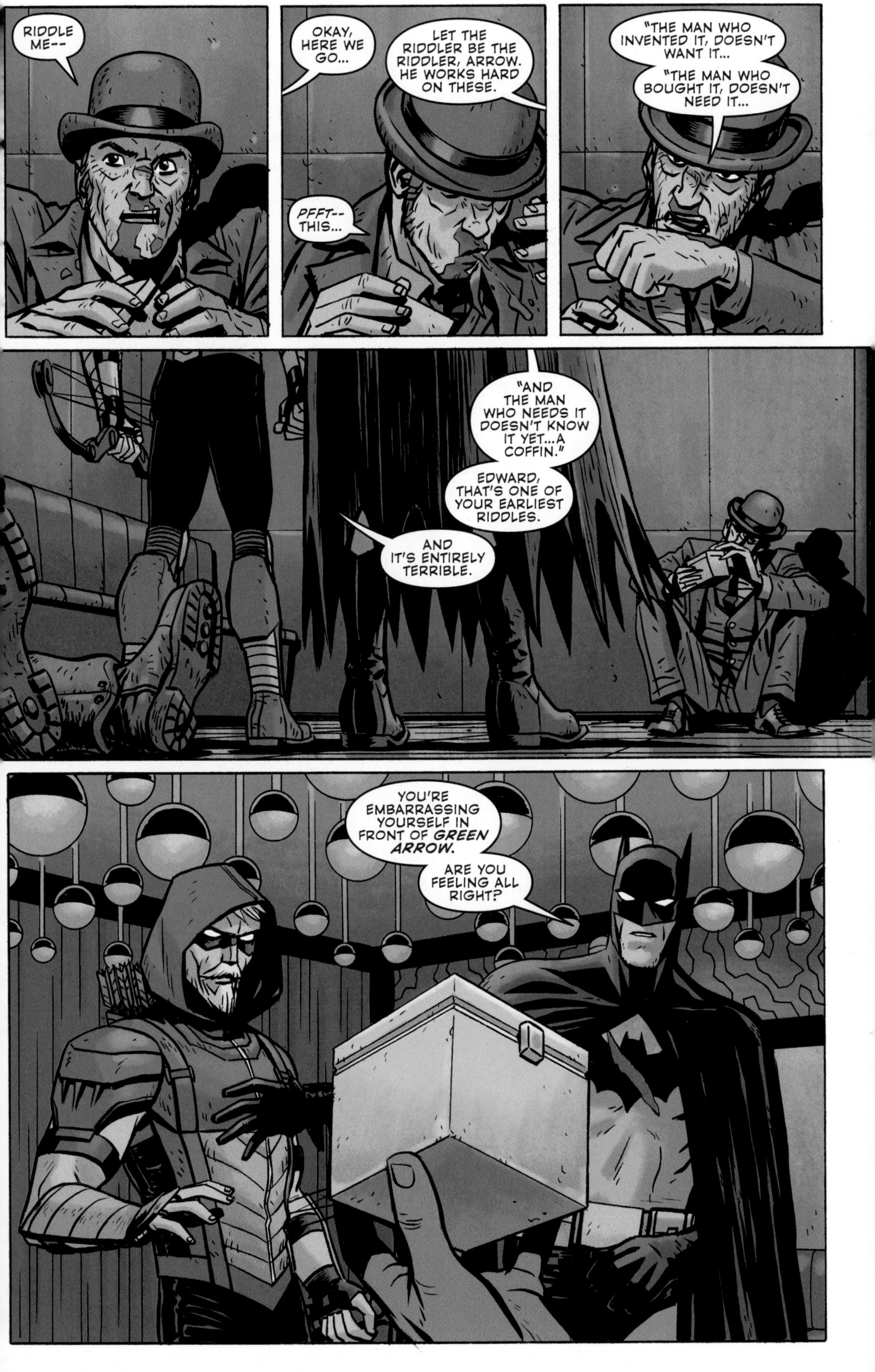
RIDDLE ME--
OKAY, HERE WE GO...
LET THE RIDDLER BE THE RIDDLER, ARROW. HE WORKS HARD ON THESE.
PFFT-- THIS...
"THE MAN WHO INVENTED IT, DOESN'T WANT IT...
"THE MAN WHO BOUGHT IT, DOESN'T NEED IT...
"AND THE MAN WHO NEEDS IT DOESN'T KNOW IT YET...A COFFIN."
EDWARD, THAT'S ONE OF YOUR EARLIEST RIDDLES.
AND IT'S ENTIRELY TERRIBLE.
YOU'RE EMBARRASSING YOURSELF IN FRONT OF GREEN ARROW.
ARE YOU FEELING ALL RIGHT?

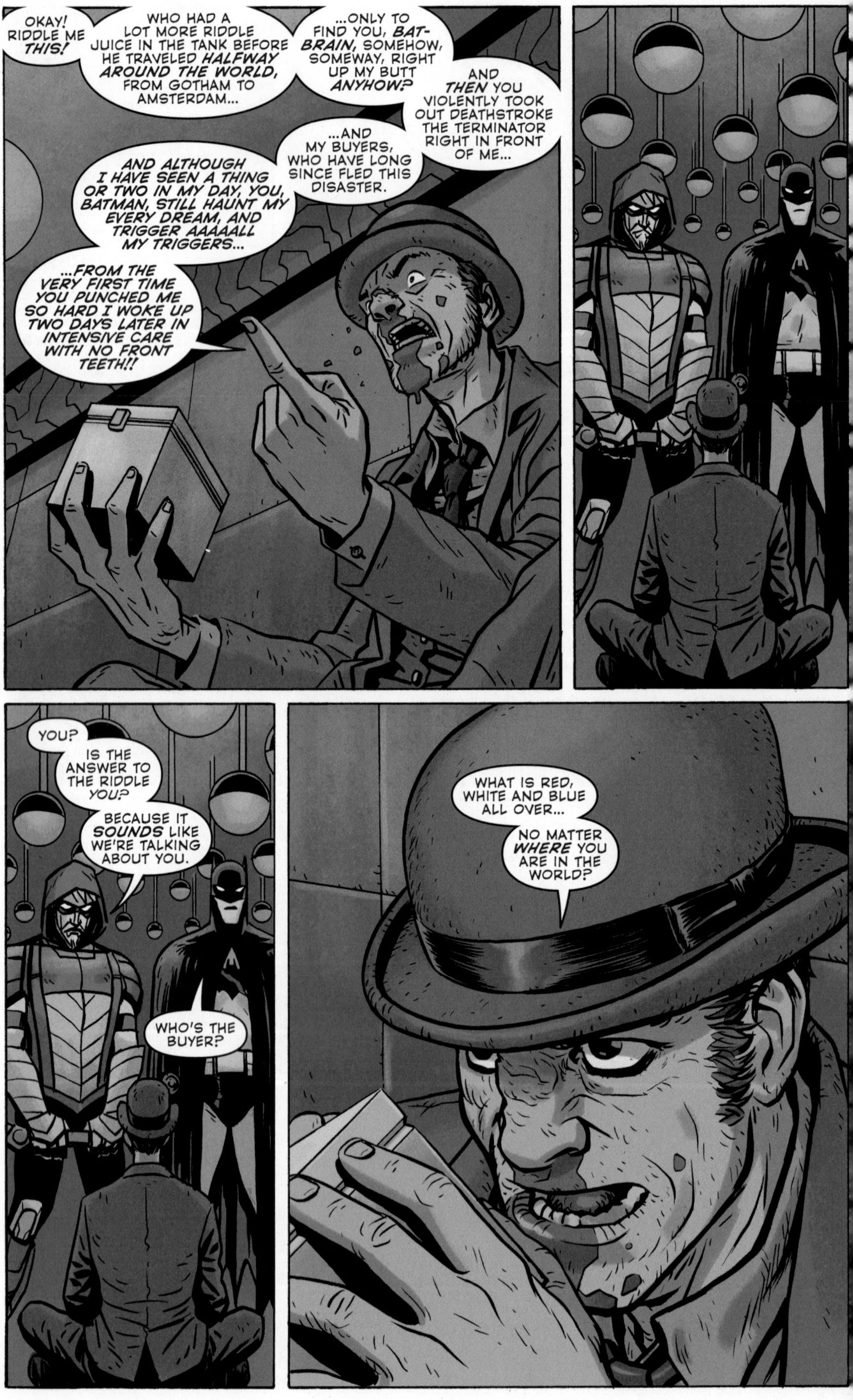
OKAY! RIDDLE ME THIS!
WHO HAD A LOT MORE RIDDLE JUICE IN THE TANK BEFORE HE TRAVELED HALFWAY AROUND THE WORLD, FROM GOTHAM TO AMSTERDAM...
...ONLY TO FIND YOU, BAT-BRAIN, SOMEHOW, SOMEWAY, RIGHT UP MY BUTT ANYHOW?
AND THEN YOU VIOLENTLY TOOK OUT DEATHSTROKE THE TERMINATOR RIGHT IN FRONT OF ME...
...AND MY BUYERS, WHO HAVE LONG SINCE FLED THIS DISASTER.
AND ALTHOUGH I HAVE SEEN A THING OR TWO IN MY DAY, YOU, BATMAN, STILL HAUNT MY EVERY DREAM, AND TRIGGER AAAAALL MY TRIGGERS...
...FROM THE VERY FIRST TIME YOU PUNCHED ME SO HARD I WOKE UP TWO DAYS LATER IN INTENSIVE CARE WITH NO FRONT TEETH!!
YOU?
IS THE ANSWER TO THE RIDDLE YOU?
BECAUSE IT SOUNDS LIKE WE'RE TALKING ABOUT YOU.
WHO'S THE BUYER?
WHAT IS RED, WHITE AND BLUE ALL OVER...
NO MATTER WHERE YOU ARE IN THE WORLD?

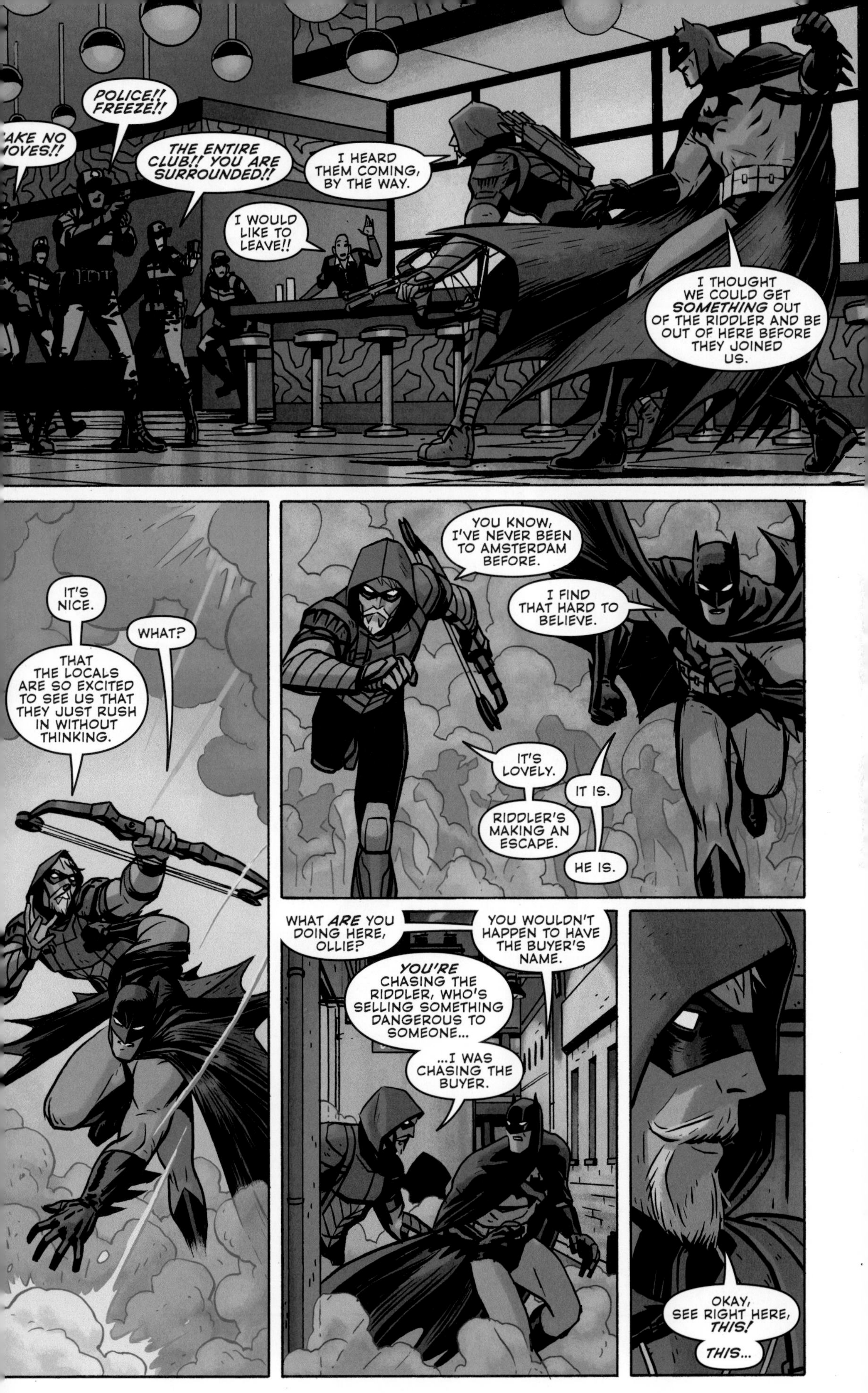
POLICE!! FREEZE!!
AKE NO
MOVES!!
THE ENTIRE CLUB!! YOU ARE SURROUNDED!!
I WOULD LIKE TO LEAVE!!
I HEARD THEM COMING, BY THE WAY.
I THOUGHT WE COULD GET SOMETHING OUT OF THE RIDDLER AND BE OUT OF HERE BEFORE THEY JOINED US.
IT'S NICE.
WHAT?
THAT THE LOCALS ARE SO EXCITED TO SEE US THAT THEY JUST RUSH IN WITHOUT THINKING.
YOU KNOW, I'VE NEVER BEEN TO AMSTERDAM BEFORE.
I FIND THAT HARD TO BELIEVE.
IT'S LOVELY.
IT IS.
RIDDLER'S MAKING AN ESCAPE.
HE IS.
WHAT ARE YOU DOING HERE, OLLIE?
YOU WOULDN'T HAPPEN TO HAVE THE BUYER'S NAME.
YOU'RE CHASING THE RIDDLER, WHO'S SELLING SOMETHING DANGEROUS TO SOMEONE...
...I WAS CHASING THE BUYER.
OKAY, SEE RIGHT HERE, THIS!
THIS...

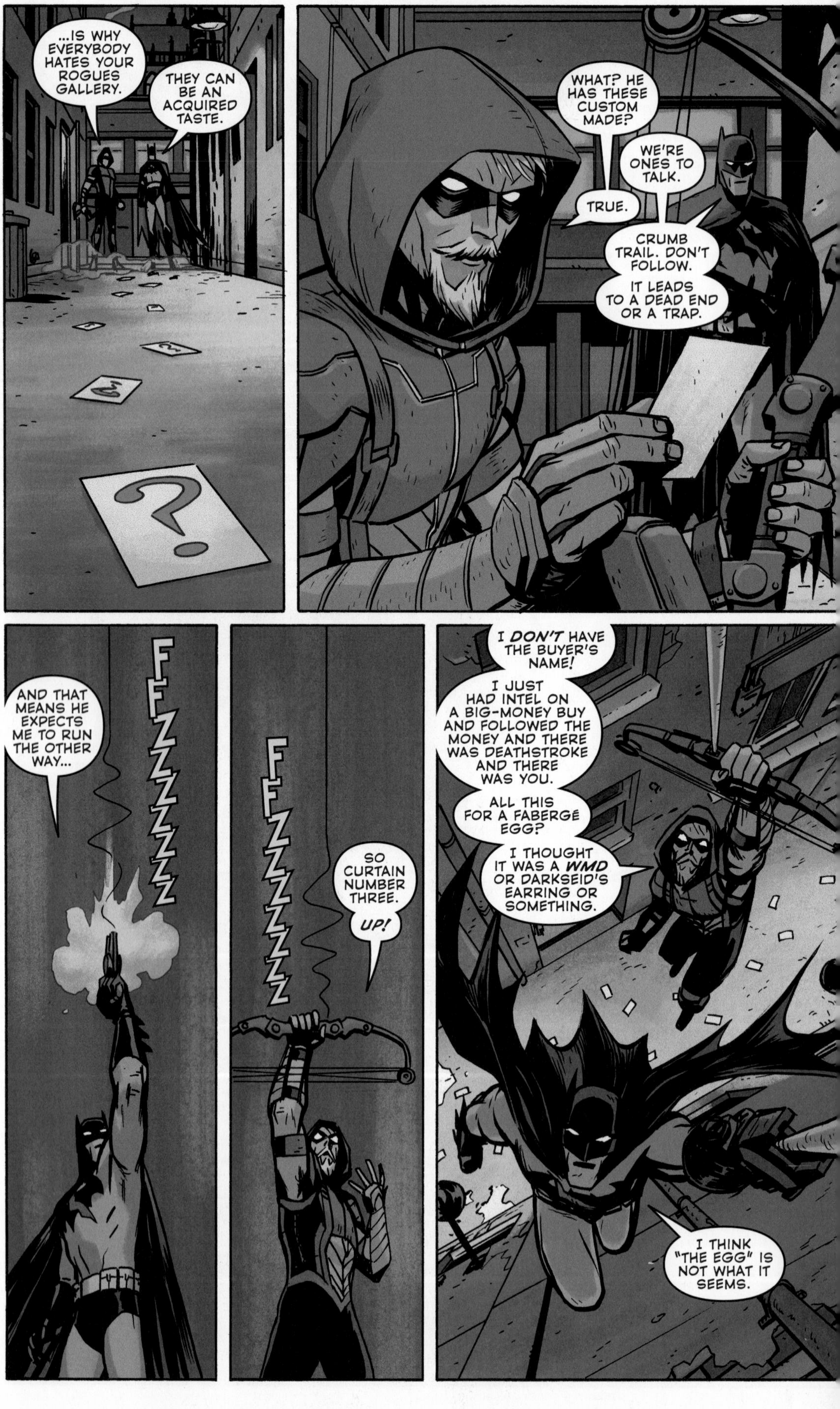
...IS WHY EVERYBODY HATES YOUR ROGUES GALLERY.
THEY CAN BE AN ACQUIRED TASTE.
WHAT? HE HAS THESE CUSTOM MADE?
WE'RE ONES TO TALK.
TRUE.
CRUMB TRAIL. DON'T FOLLOW.
IT LEADS TO A DEAD END OR A TRAP.
AND THAT MEANS HE EXPECTS ME TO RUN THE OTHER WAY...
FFZZZZZZZZ
FFZZZZZZZZ
SO CURTAIN NUMBER THREE.
UP!
I DON'T HAVE THE BUYER'S NAME!
I JUST HAD INTEL ON A BIG-MONEY BUY AND FOLLOWED THE MONEY AND THERE WAS DEATHSTROKE AND THERE WAS YOU.
ALL THIS FOR A FABERGÉ EGG?
I THOUGHT IT WAS A WMD OR DARKSEID'S EARRING OR SOMETHING.
I THINK "THE EGG" IS NOT WHAT IT SEEMS.

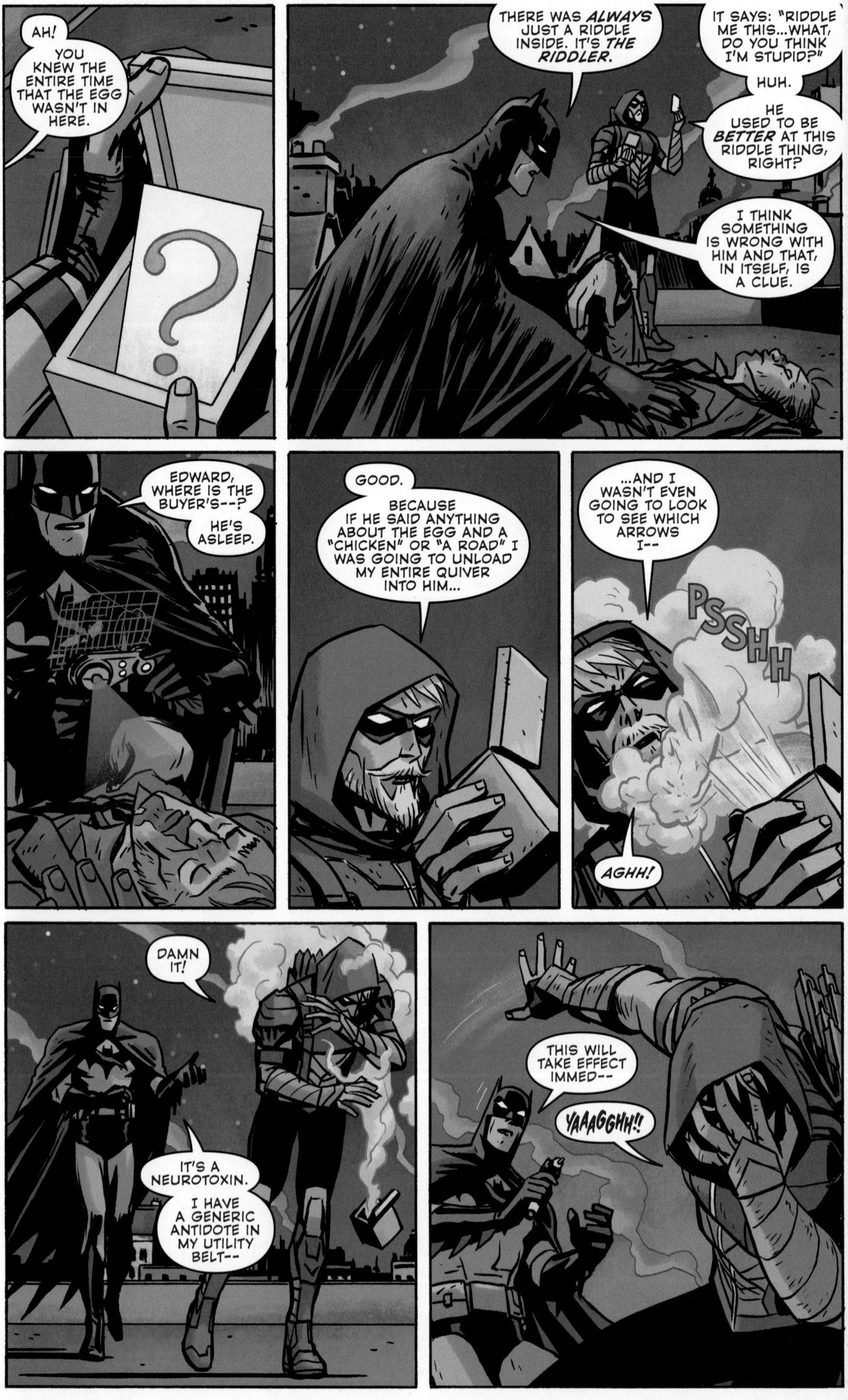
AH!
YOU KNEW THE ENTIRE TIME THAT THE EGG WASN'T IN HERE.
THERE WAS *ALWAYS* JUST A RIDDLE INSIDE. IT'S *THE RIDDLER*.
IT SAYS: "RIDDLE ME THIS...WHAT, DO YOU THINK I'M STUPID?"
HUH.
HE USED TO BE *BETTER* AT THIS RIDDLE THING, RIGHT?
I THINK SOMETHING IS WRONG WITH HIM AND THAT, IN ITSELF, IS A CLUE.
EDWARD, WHERE IS THE BUYER'S--?
HE'S ASLEEP.
GOOD.
BECAUSE IF HE SAID ANYTHING ABOUT THE EGG AND A "CHICKEN" OR "A ROAD" I WAS GOING TO UNLOAD MY ENTIRE QUIVER INTO HIM...
...AND I WASN'T EVEN GOING TO LOOK TO SEE WHICH ARROWS I--
PSSHH
AGHH!
DAMN IT!
IT'S A NEUROTOXIN.
I HAVE A GENERIC ANTIDOTE IN MY UTILITY BELT--
THIS WILL TAKE EFFECT IMMED--
YAAAGGHH!!

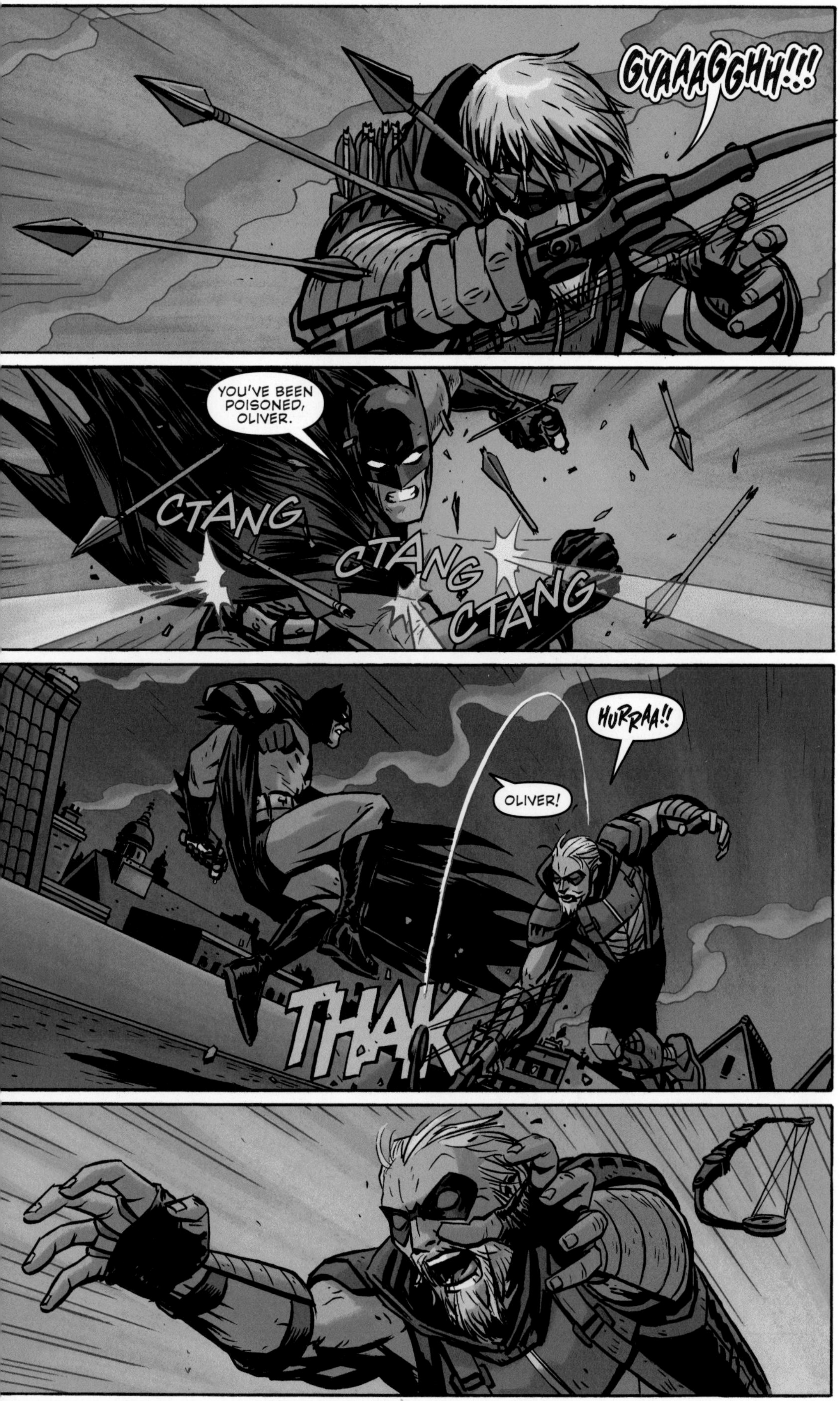
GYAAAGGHH!!!
YOU'VE BEEN POISONED, OLIVER.
CTANG
CTANG
CTANG
HURRAA!!
OLIVER!
THAK

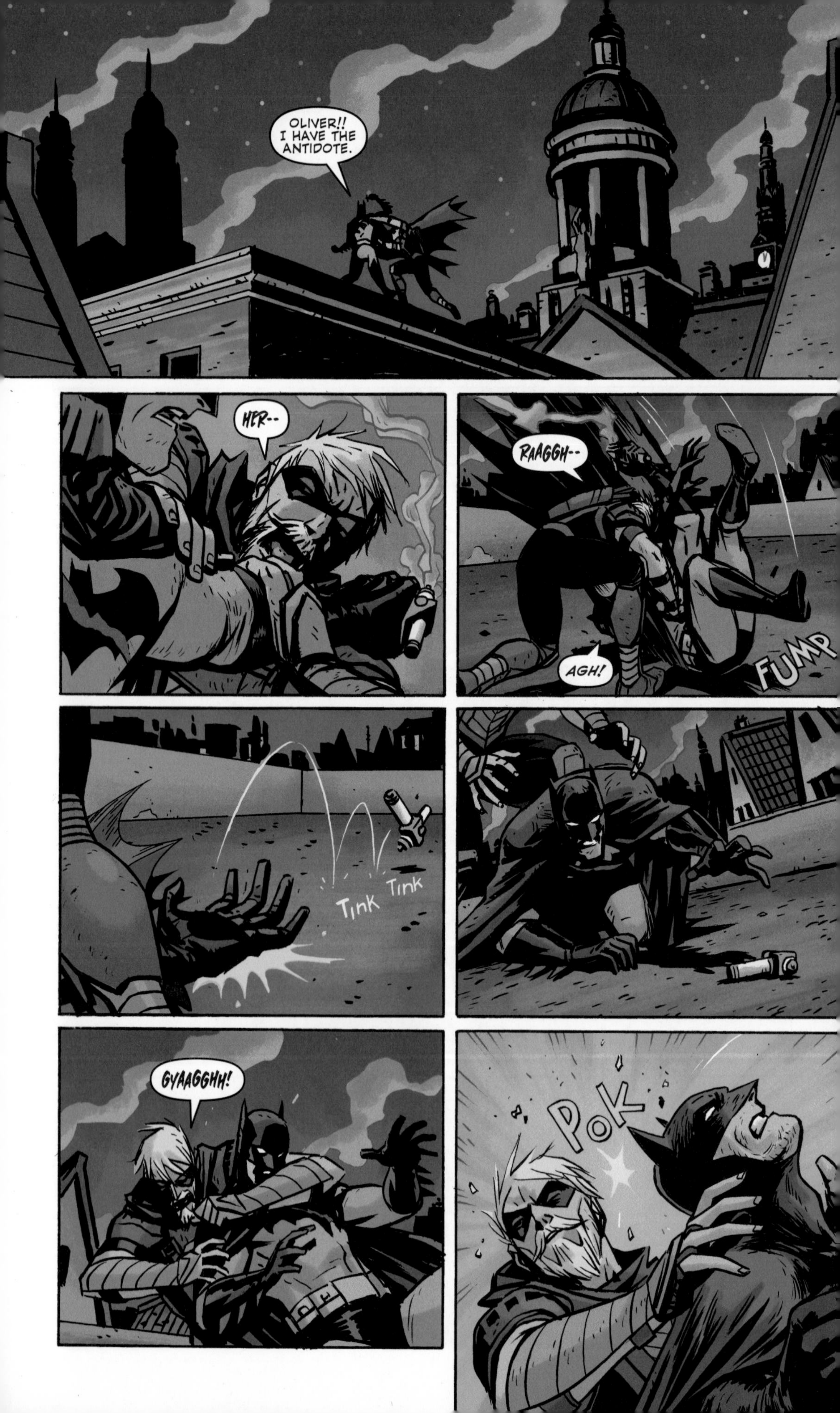
OLIVER!! I HAVE THE ANTIDOTE.
HRR--
RAAGGH--
AGH!
FUMP
TINK
TINK
GYAAGGHH!
POK

GUAAGGH!

OLLIE!

NYAAGGHH!

FOCUS! IT'S OKAY.

RRRRRI'M OKAY.

TAKE A DEEP BREATH.

OR FIVE.

SHEEZE... THIRSTY.

I HAVE SOMETHING FOR THAT, TOO.

THE RIDDLER ESCAPED.

I HAVE A TRACKER ON HIM NOW.

THAT IS SUCH A BATMAN THING TO DO.

YOU NEED A HOSPITAL.

DID I--DID I JUMP YOU BACK THERE?

DID I WIN?

YES.

OF COURSE.

I FEEL SHAME.

PLEASE DON'T TELL THE OTHERS...

"NOW RIDDLE ME THIS..."

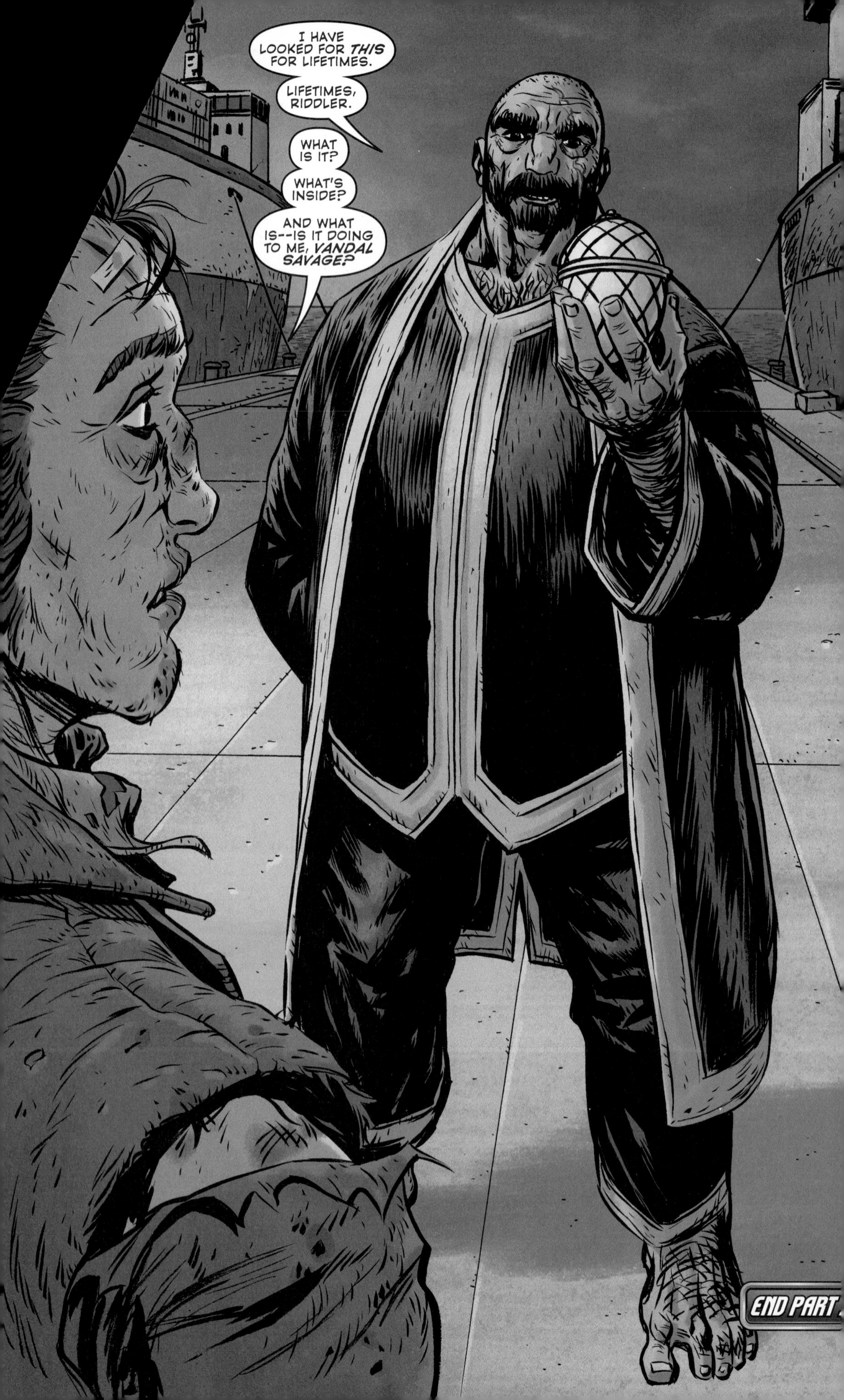
I HAVE LOOKED FOR *THIS* FOR LIFETIMES.
LIFETIMES, RIDDLER.
WHAT IS IT?
WHAT'S INSIDE?
AND WHAT IS--IS IT DOING TO ME, *VANDAL SAVAGE?*
END PART

THERE IS NO SIGN OF TRAUMA OR BRAIN DAMAGE OF ANY KIND.

WHICH, I WON'T LIE TO YOU, SIR, SURPRISED ME TO NO END.

SO WHATEVER THE RADIATION DID TO SCRAMBLE OUR BRAIN-WAVE PATTERNS...

IT WAS SEEMINGLY NOT PERMANENT.

DID THE BRAIN-WAVE ABNORMALITY HAPPEN TO GIVE YOU A SUDDEN SENSE OF PATERNAL INSTINCT OR THE DESIRE FOR A NORMAL LIFE?

COMPUTER, I THINK THIS RADIATION IS ALIEN IN ORIGIN.

CROSS-REFERENCE INTERGALACTIC SOURCES. TRY TO GET AHOLD OF GREEN LANTERN. ANY OF THEM.

MAYBE SETTLE DOWN AND HAVE SOME CHILDREN YOU DON'T TRAIN IN THE MARTIAL ARTS.

OKAY, CATALOG IT.

WITHOUT THE PROPER REFERENCE OR THE PROPER ANALYTICA TOOLS THERE'S NO MUCH THE RADIATIC SIGNATURE CAN TELL US.

WE ARE APPROACHING THE RIDDLER'S LOCATION.

OUTSTANDING JOB GETTING A TRACKER ON HIM DURING THE AMSTERDAM SCUFFLE.

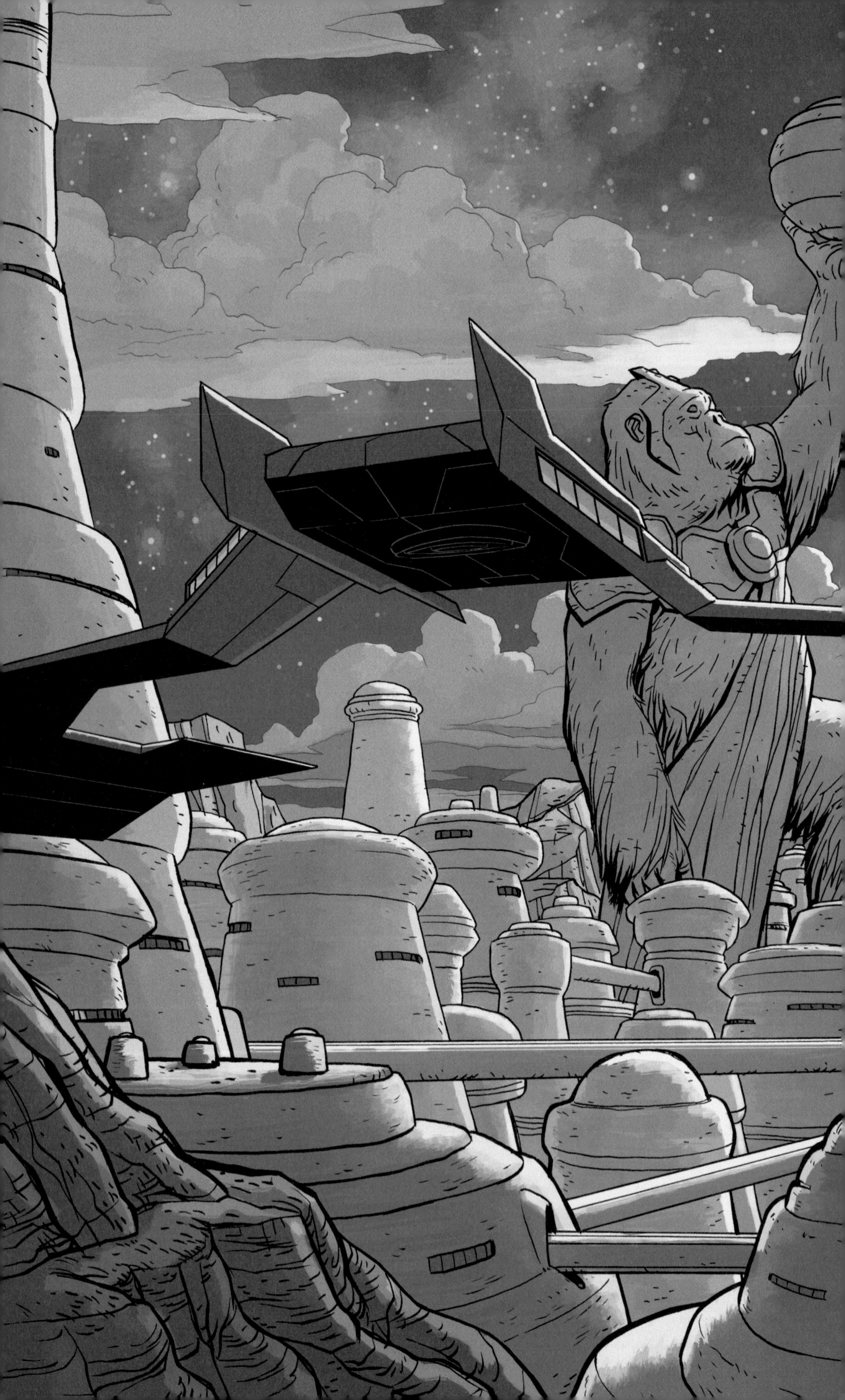

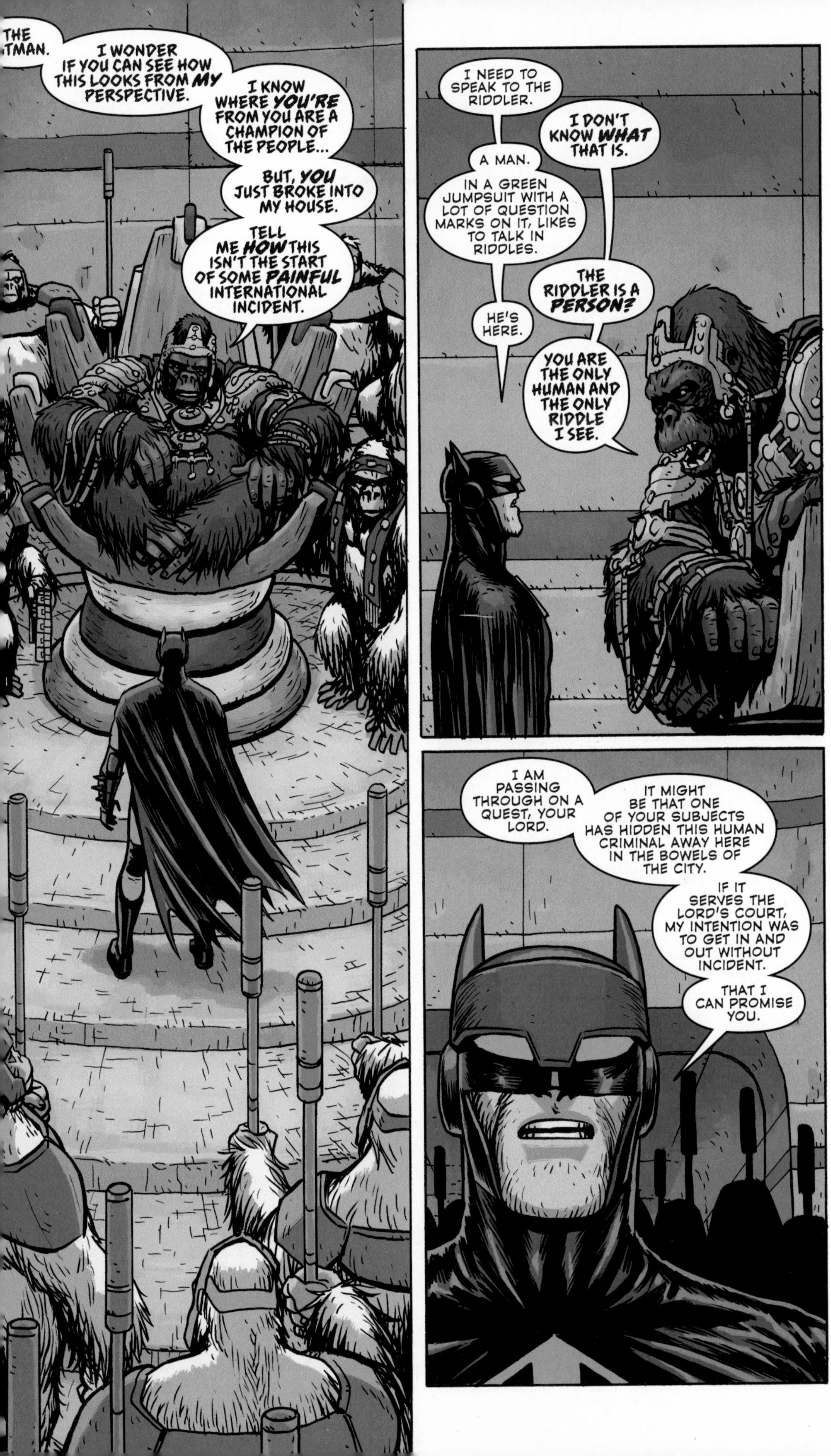
THE
I WONDER IF YOU CAN SEE HOW THIS LOOKS FROM MY PERSPECTIVE.
I KNOW WHERE YOU'RE FROM YOU ARE A CHAMPION OF THE PEOPLE...
BUT, YOU JUST BROKE INTO MY HOUSE.
TELL ME HOW THIS ISN'T THE START OF SOME PAINFUL INTERNATIONAL INCIDENT.
I NEED TO SPEAK TO THE RIDDLER.
I DON'T KNOW WHAT THAT IS.
A MAN.
IN A GREEN JUMPSUIT WITH A LOT OF QUESTION MARKS ON IT, LIKES TO TALK IN RIDDLES.
HE'S HERE.
THE RIDDLER IS A PERSON?
YOU ARE THE ONLY HUMAN AND THE ONLY RIDDLE I SEE.
I AM PASSING THROUGH ON A QUEST, YOUR LORD.
IT MIGHT BE THAT ONE OF YOUR SUBJECTS HAS HIDDEN THIS HUMAN CRIMINAL AWAY HERE IN THE BOWELS OF THE CITY.
IF IT SERVES THE LORD'S COURT, MY INTENTION WAS TO GET IN AND OUT WITHOUT INCIDENT.
THAT I CAN PROMISE YOU.

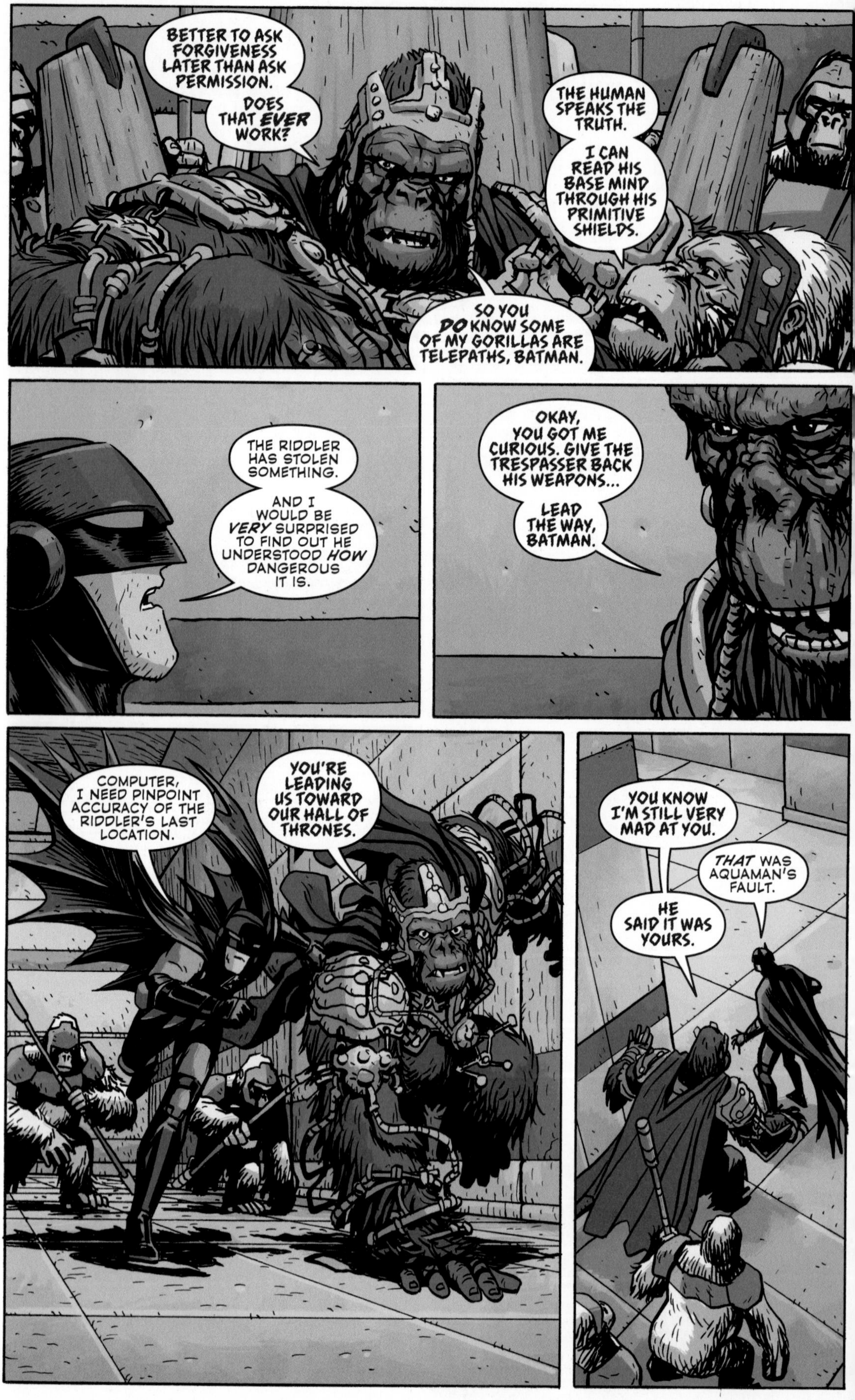
BETTER TO ASK FORGIVENESS LATER THAN ASK PERMISSION.
DOES THAT EVER WORK?
THE HUMAN SPEAKS THE TRUTH.
I CAN READ HIS BASE MIND THROUGH HIS PRIMITIVE SHIELDS.
SO YOU DO KNOW SOME OF MY GORILLAS ARE TELEPATHS, BATMAN.
THE RIDDLER HAS STOLEN SOMETHING.
AND I WOULD BE VERY SURPRISED TO FIND OUT HE UNDERSTOOD HOW DANGEROUS IT IS.
OKAY, YOU GOT ME CURIOUS. GIVE THE TRESPASSER BACK HIS WEAPONS...
LEAD THE WAY, BATMAN.
COMPUTER, I NEED PINPOINT ACCURACY OF THE RIDDLER'S LAST LOCATION.
YOU'RE LEADING US TOWARD OUR HALL OF THRONES.
YOU KNOW I'M STILL VERY MAD AT YOU.
THAT WAS AQUAMAN'S FAULT.
HE SAID IT WAS YOURS.

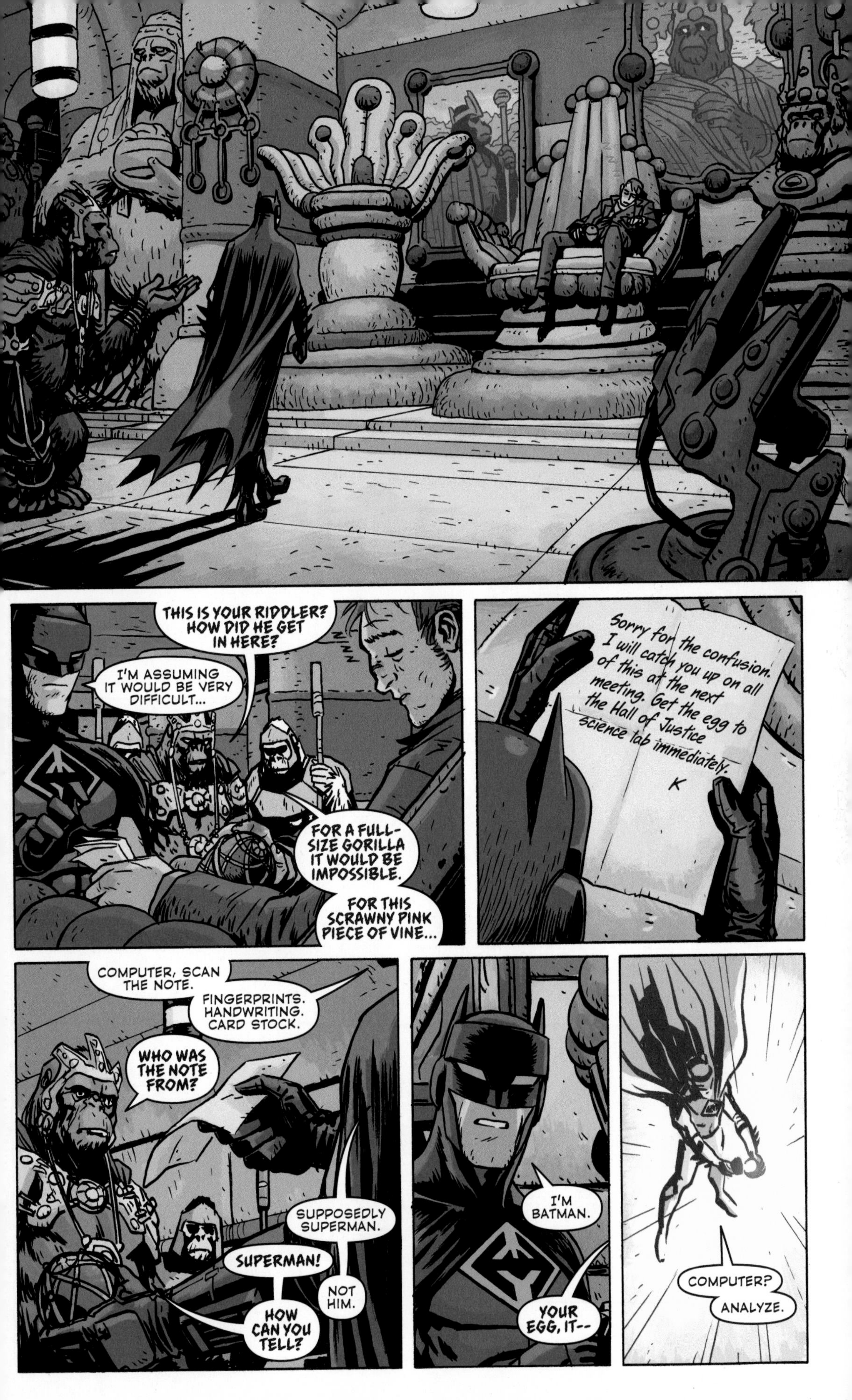
THIS IS YOUR RIDDLER? HOW DID HE GET IN HERE?
I'M ASSUMING IT WOULD BE VERY DIFFICULT...
FOR A FULL-SIZE GORILLA IT WOULD BE IMPOSSIBLE.
FOR THIS SCRAWNY PINK PIECE OF VINE...
Sorry for the confusion. I will catch you up on all of this at the next meeting. Get the egg to the Hall of Justice science lab immediately.
K
COMPUTER, SCAN THE NOTE.
FINGERPRINTS. HANDWRITING. CARD STOCK.
WHO WAS THE NOTE FROM?
SUPPOSEDLY SUPERMAN.
SUPERMAN!
NOT HIM.
HOW CAN YOU TELL?
I'M BATMAN.
YOUR EGG, IT--
COMPUTER?
ANALYZE.

END PART 4

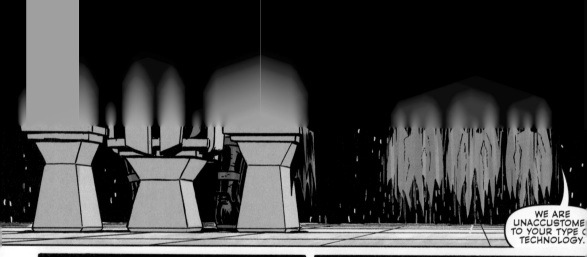

WE ARE UNACCUSTOME TO YOUR TYPE C TECHNOLOGY.

AH. I APPEAR TO BE A THREAT TO YOU.

A STRANGER WHO SUDDENLY APPEARED OUT OF NOWHERE ARMED TO THE TEETH.

ENTIRELY.

I'M ACTUALLY A GOOD FRIEND OF KATAR HOL.

HE CAN VOUCH FOR ME.

REALLY?

OKAY.

ALSO, I WAS CLOSE WITH SHAYERA THAL.

REALLY?

SHAYERA THAL.

WE WERE TEAMMATES.

YOU'RE TEAMMATES WITH KATAR HOL, THE IMPERIAL PRINCE OF THANAGAR?

UH-HUH.

WHAT A TREAT FOR US.

THE COWL, PLEASE...

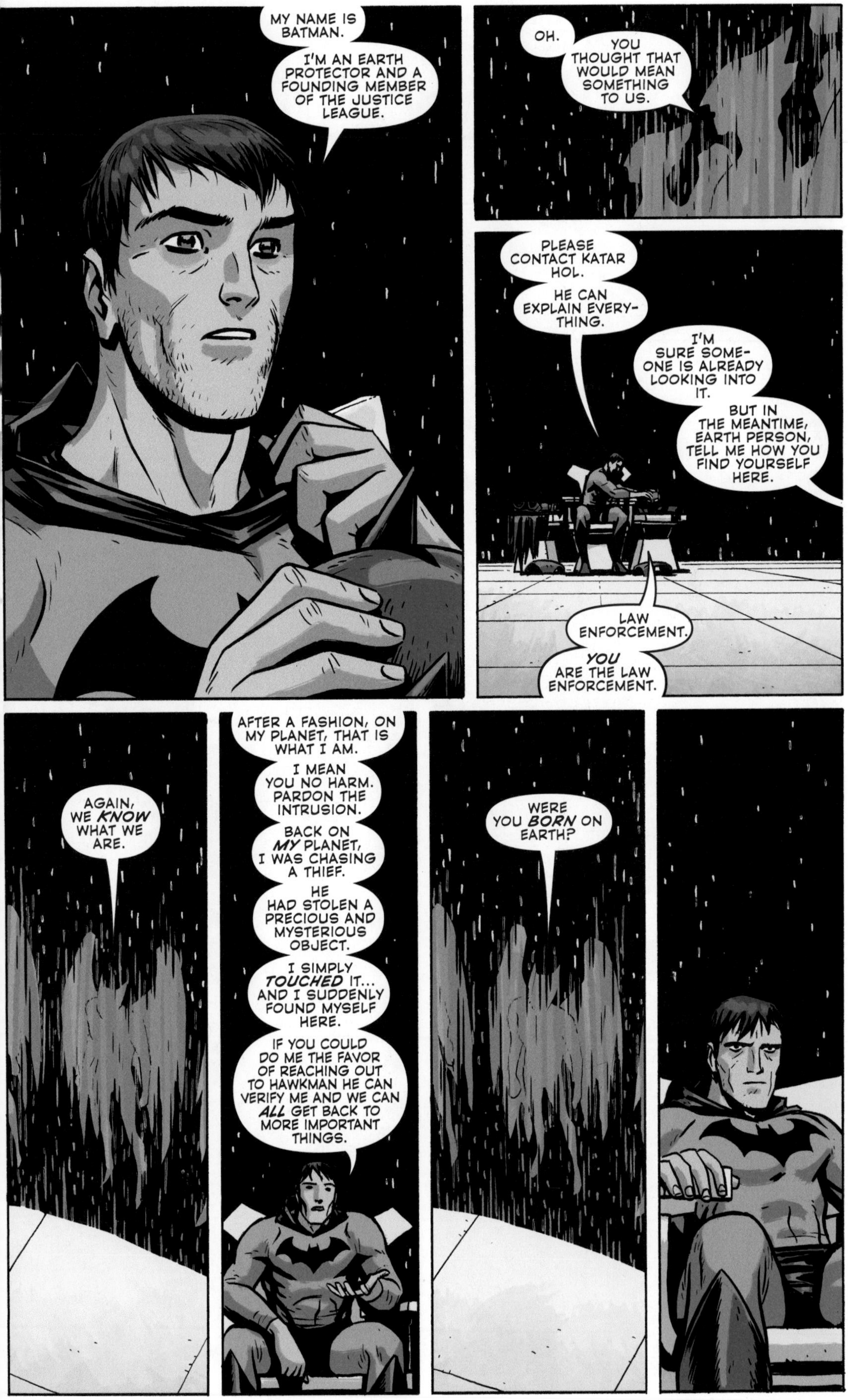
MY NAME IS BATMAN.
I'M AN EARTH PROTECTOR AND A FOUNDING MEMBER OF THE JUSTICE LEAGUE.
OH.
YOU THOUGHT THAT WOULD MEAN SOMETHING TO US.
PLEASE CONTACT KATAR HOL.
HE CAN EXPLAIN EVERY-THING.
I'M SURE SOME-ONE IS ALREADY LOOKING INTO IT.
BUT IN THE MEANTIME, EARTH PERSON, TELL ME HOW YOU FIND YOURSELF HERE.
LAW ENFORCEMENT.
YOU ARE THE LAW ENFORCEMENT.
AGAIN, WE KNOW WHAT WE ARE.
AFTER A FASHION, ON MY PLANET, THAT IS WHAT I AM.
I MEAN YOU NO HARM. PARDON THE INTRUSION.
BACK ON MY PLANET, I WAS CHASING A THIEF.
HE HAD STOLEN A PRECIOUS AND MYSTERIOUS OBJECT.
I SIMPLY TOUCHED IT... AND I SUDDENLY FOUND MYSELF HERE.
IF YOU COULD DO ME THE FAVOR OF REACHING OUT TO HAWKMAN HE CAN VERIFY ME AND WE CAN ALL GET BACK TO MORE IMPORTANT THINGS.
WERE YOU BORN ON EARTH?

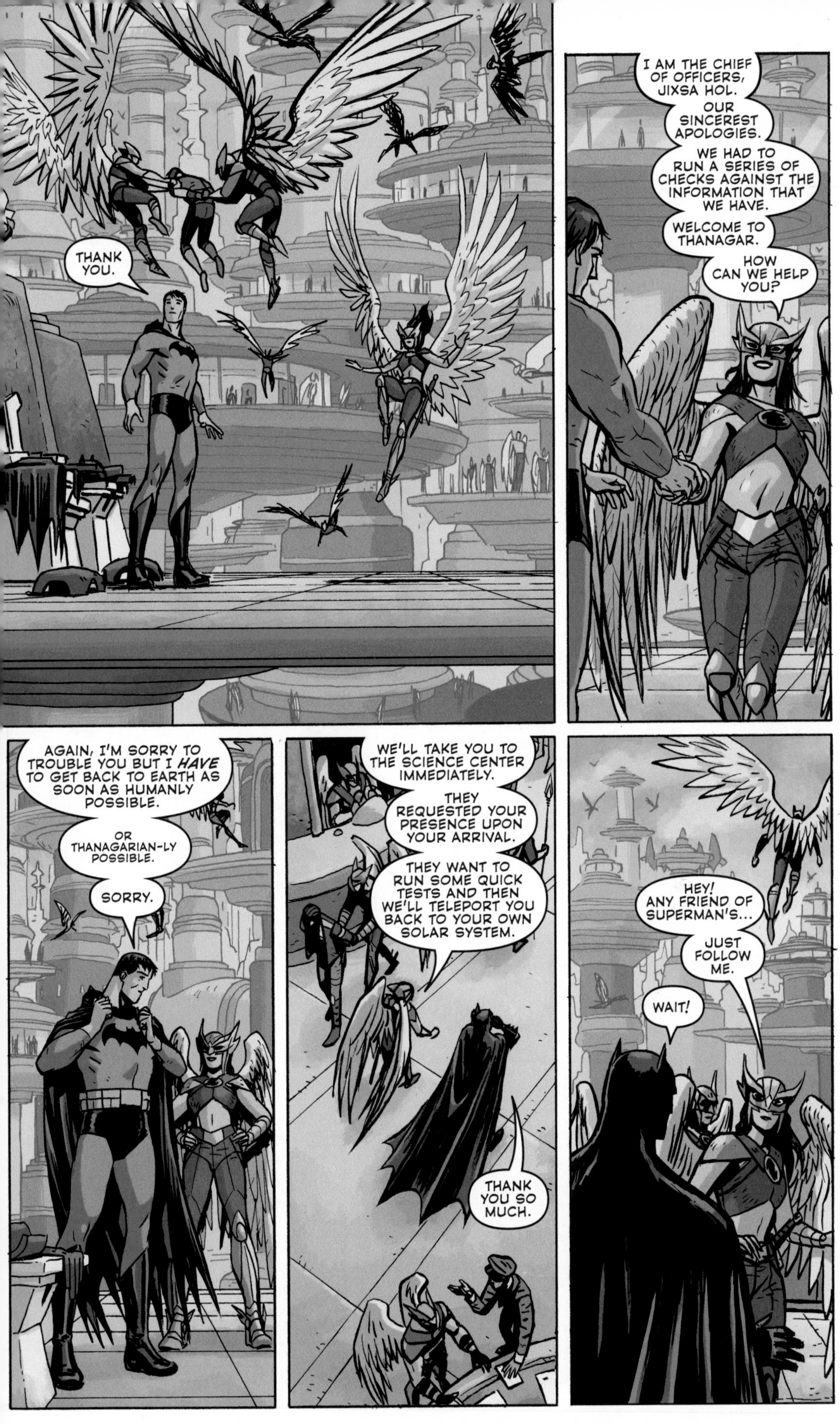
THANK YOU.
I AM THE CHIEF OF OFFICERS, JIXSA HOL.
OUR SINCEREST APOLOGIES.
WE HAD TO RUN A SERIES OF CHECKS AGAINST THE INFORMATION THAT WE HAVE.
WELCOME TO THANAGAR.
HOW CAN WE HELP YOU?
AGAIN, I'M SORRY TO TROUBLE YOU BUT I *HAVE* TO GET BACK TO EARTH AS SOON AS HUMANLY POSSIBLE.
OR THANAGARIAN-LY POSSIBLE.
SORRY.
WE'LL TAKE YOU TO THE SCIENCE CENTER IMMEDIATELY.
THEY REQUESTED YOUR PRESENCE UPON YOUR ARRIVAL.
THEY WANT TO RUN SOME QUICK TESTS AND THEN WE'LL TELEPORT YOU BACK TO YOUR OWN SOLAR SYSTEM.
THANK YOU SO MUCH.
HEY! ANY FRIEND OF SUPERMAN'S...
JUST FOLLOW ME.
WAIT!

CAPTAIN, I'M VERY CONCERNED ABOUT THE TECHNOLOGY THAT BROUGHT ME HERE.

THAT KIND OF POWER SHOULD NOT BE ON THE PLANET EARTH IN THE BEST OF SITUATIONS.

ALSO, TELEPORTATION TECHNOLOGY ITSELF IS VERY TEMPERAMENTAL AND DOESN'T ALWAYS--

THAT I CAN COMPLETELY UNDERSTAND.

IT SOUNDS LIKE AN UNSTABLE QUANTUM CORE.

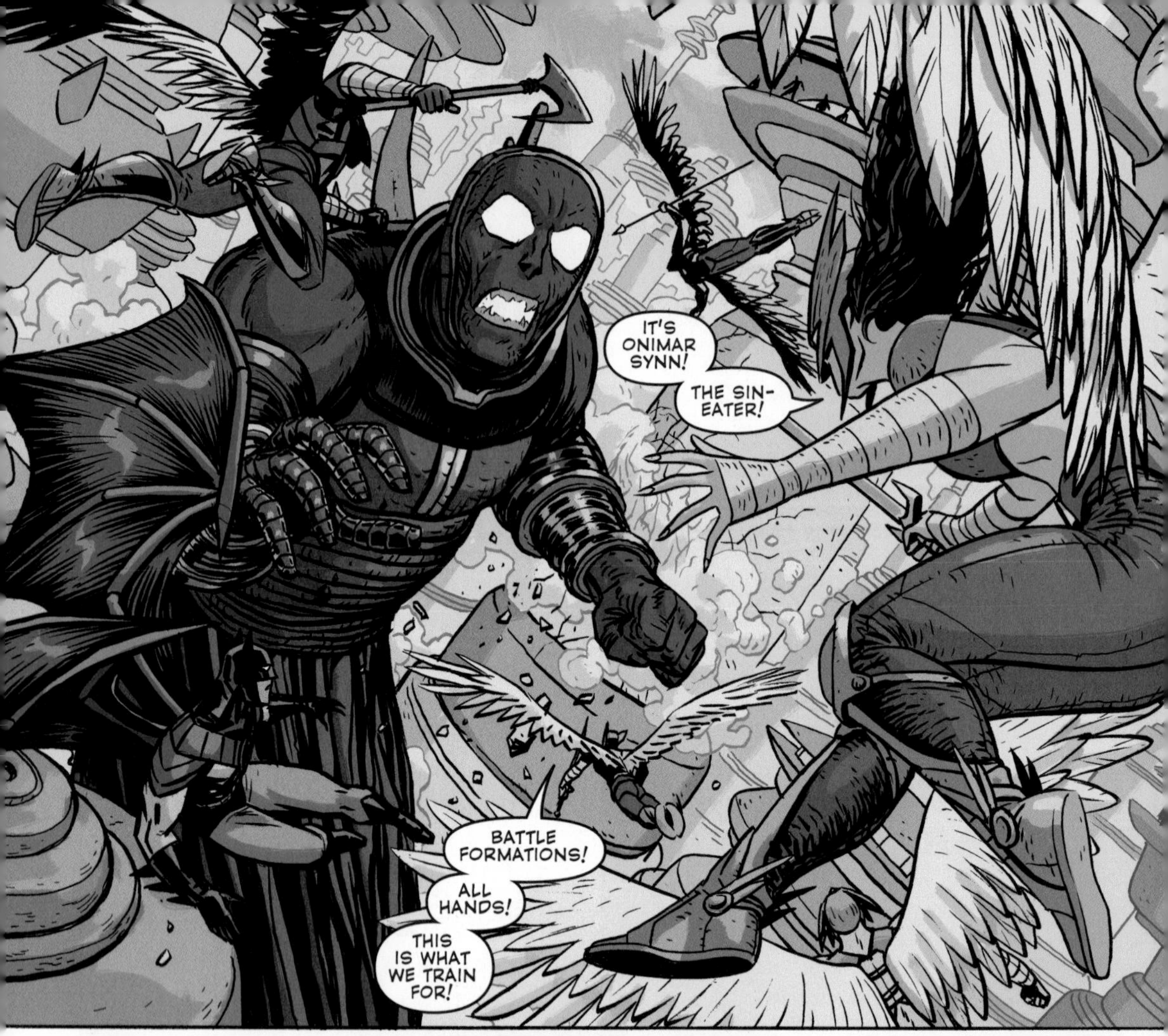
IT'S ONIMAR SYNN!
THE SIN-EATER!
BATTLE FORMATIONS!
ALL HANDS!
THIS IS WHAT WE TRAIN FOR!

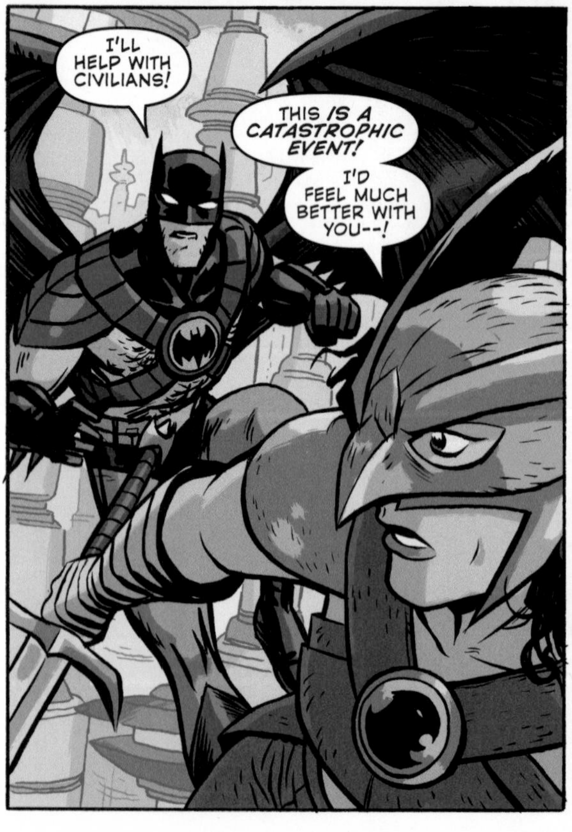
I'LL HELP WITH CIVILIANS!
THIS *IS A CATASTROPHIC EVENT!*
I'D FEEL MUCH BETTER WITH YOU--!

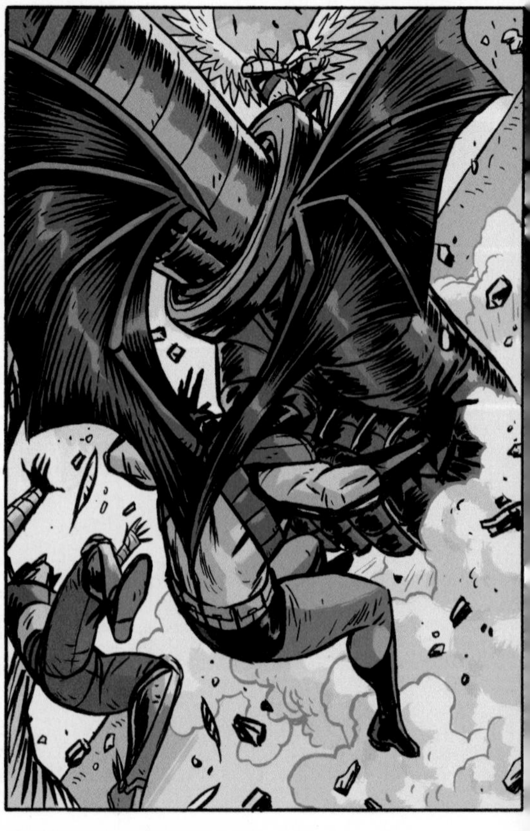

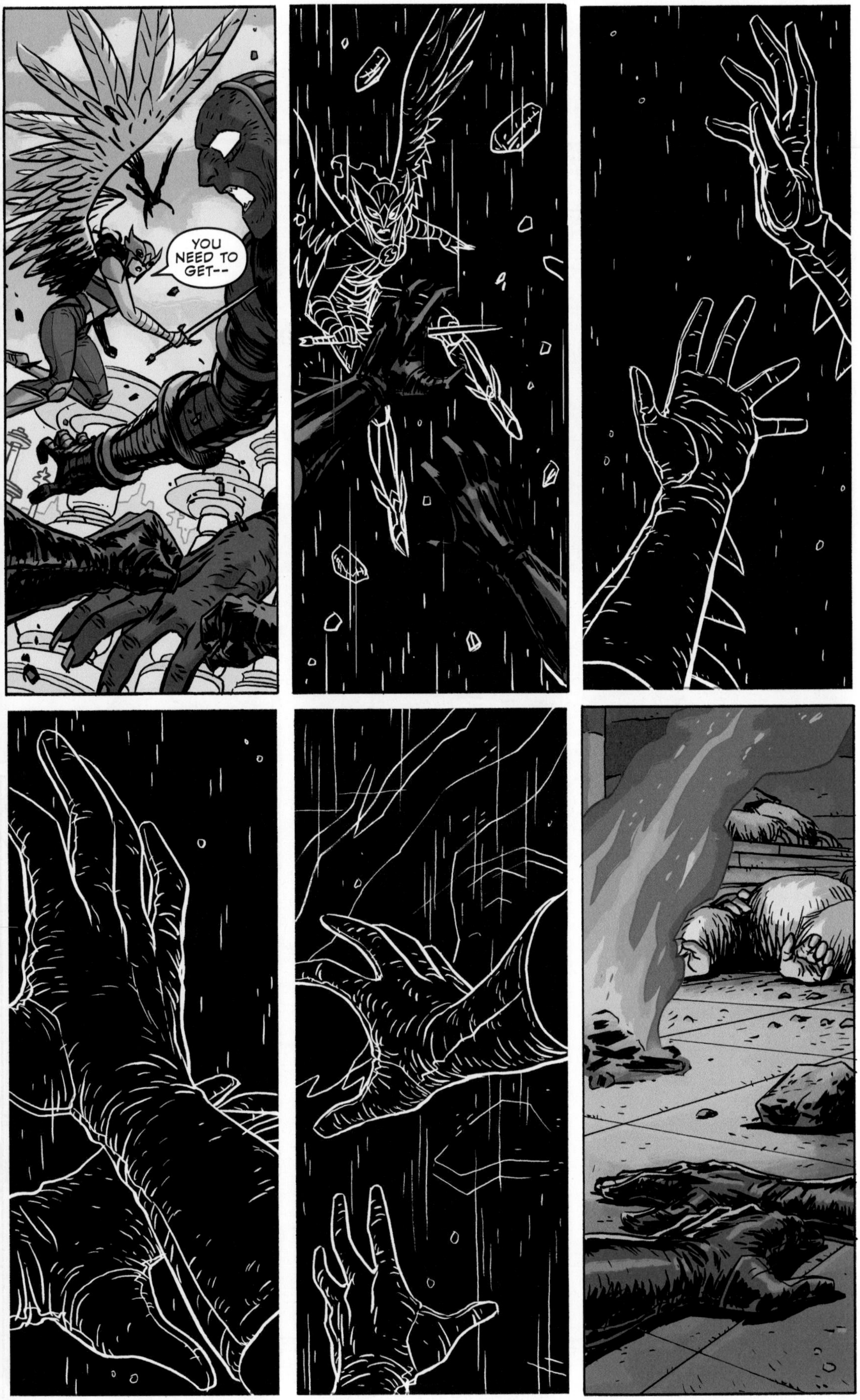
YOU NEED TO GET--

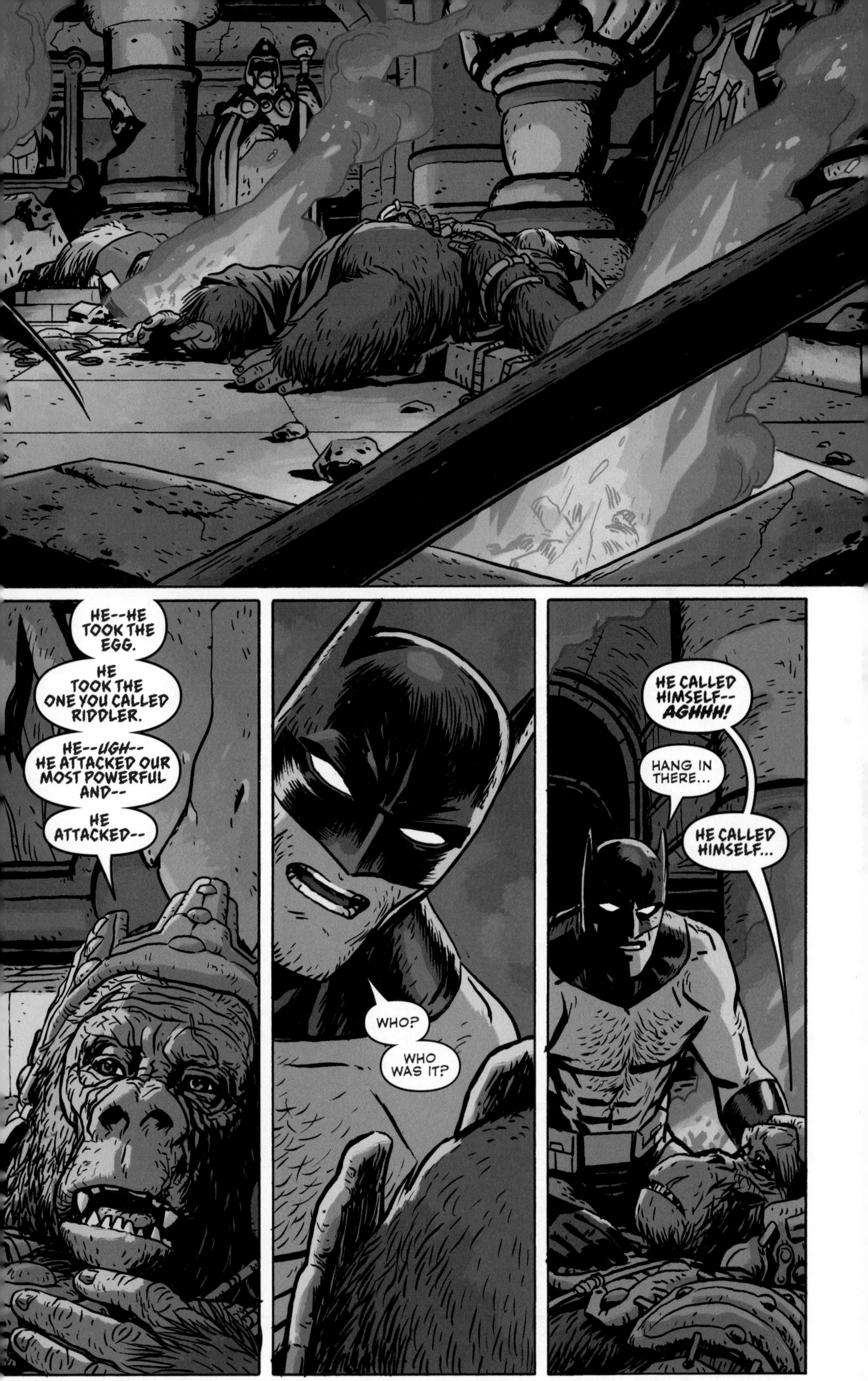
HE--HE TOOK THE EGG.
HE TOOK THE ONE YOU CALLED RIDDLER.
HE--UGH-- HE ATTACKED OUR MOST POWERFUL AND--
HE ATTACKED--
WHO?
WHO WAS IT?
HE CALLED HIMSELF-- AGHHH!
HANG IN THERE...
HE CALLED HIMSELF...

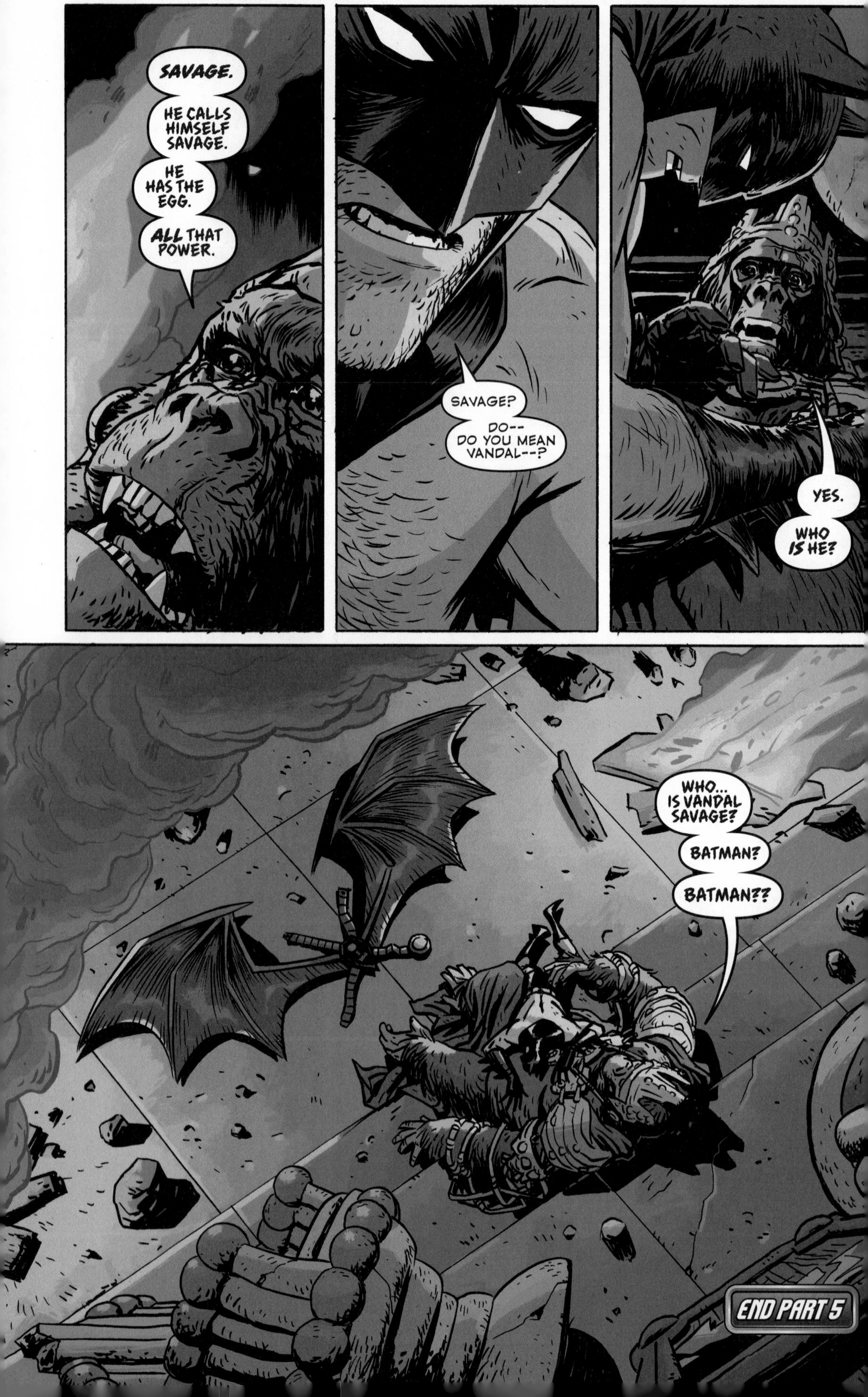
SAVAGE.
HE CALLS HIMSELF SAVAGE.
HE HAS THE EGG.
ALL THAT POWER.
SAVAGE?
DO-- DO YOU MEAN VANDAL--?
YES.
WHO IS HE?
WHO... IS VANDAL SAVAGE?
BATMAN?
BATMAN??
END PART 5

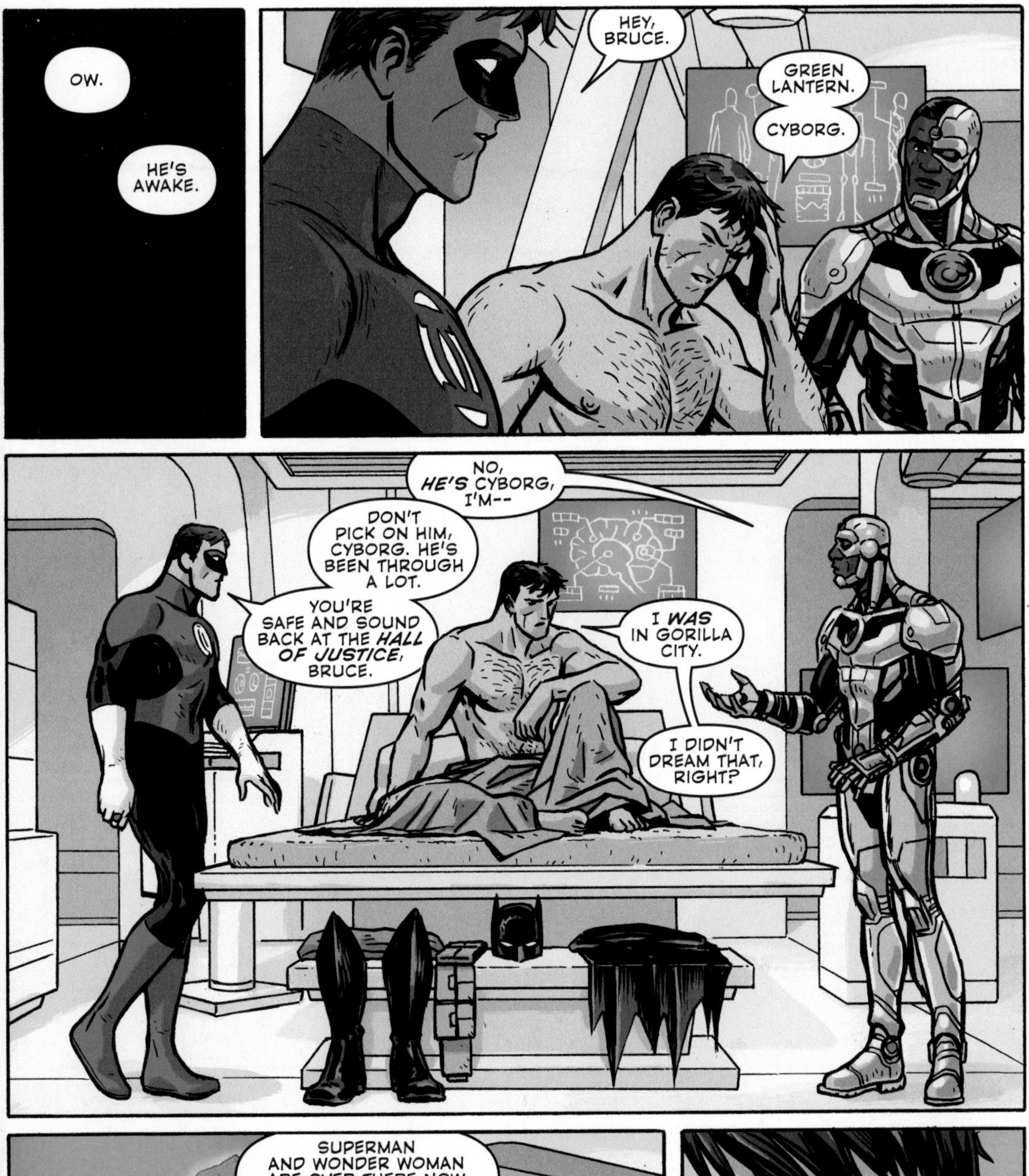
OW.
HE'S AWAKE.
HEY, BRUCE.
GREEN LANTERN.
CYBORG.
NO, *HE'S* CYBORG, I'M--
DON'T PICK ON HIM, CYBORG. HE'S BEEN THROUGH A LOT.
YOU'RE SAFE AND SOUND BACK AT THE *HALL OF JUSTICE*, BRUCE.
I *WAS* IN GORILLA CITY.
I DIDN'T DREAM THAT, RIGHT?
SUPERMAN AND WONDER WOMAN ARE OVER THERE NOW SMOOTHING THINGS OVER DIPLOMATICALLY.
THE GORILLA KING UNDERSTANDS THAT NOBODY WAS TO BLAME FOR THIS BUT--
VANDAL SAVAGE.

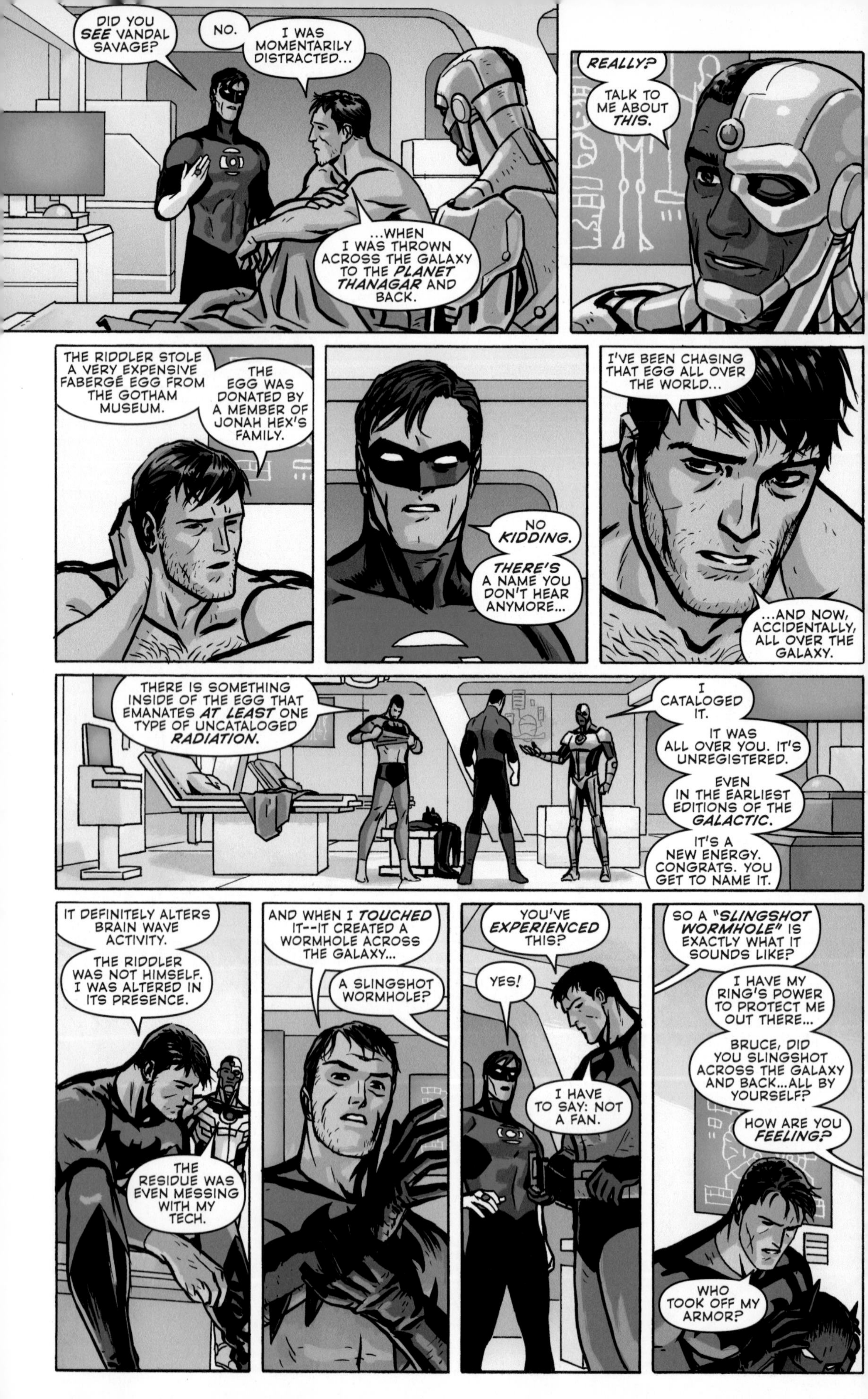
DID YOU SEE VANDAL SAVAGE?
NO.
I WAS MOMENTARILY DISTRACTED...
...WHEN I WAS THROWN ACROSS THE GALAXY TO THE PLANET THANAGAR AND BACK.
REALLY?
TALK TO ME ABOUT THIS.
THE RIDDLER STOLE A VERY EXPENSIVE FABERGÉ EGG FROM THE GOTHAM MUSEUM.
THE EGG WAS DONATED BY A MEMBER OF JONAH HEX'S FAMILY.
NO KIDDING.
THERE'S A NAME YOU DON'T HEAR ANYMORE...
I'VE BEEN CHASING THAT EGG ALL OVER THE WORLD...
...AND NOW, ACCIDENTALLY, ALL OVER THE GALAXY.
THERE IS SOMETHING INSIDE OF THE EGG THAT EMANATES AT LEAST ONE TYPE OF UNCATALOGED RADIATION.
I CATALOGED IT.
IT WAS ALL OVER YOU. IT'S UNREGISTERED.
EVEN IN THE EARLIEST EDITIONS OF THE GALACTIC.
IT'S A NEW ENERGY. CONGRATS. YOU GET TO NAME IT.
IT DEFINITELY ALTERS BRAIN WAVE ACTIVITY.
THE RIDDLER WAS NOT HIMSELF. I WAS ALTERED IN ITS PRESENCE.
THE RESIDUE WAS EVEN MESSING WITH MY TECH.
AND WHEN I TOUCHED IT--IT CREATED A WORMHOLE ACROSS THE GALAXY...
A SLINGSHOT WORMHOLE?
YOU'VE EXPERIENCED THIS?
YES!
I HAVE TO SAY: NOT A FAN.
SO A "SLINGSHOT WORMHOLE" IS EXACTLY WHAT IT SOUNDS LIKE?
I HAVE MY RING'S POWER TO PROTECT ME OUT THERE...
BRUCE, DID YOU SLINGSHOT ACROSS THE GALAXY AND BACK...ALL BY YOURSELF?
HOW ARE YOU FEELING?
WHO TOOK OFF MY ARMOR?

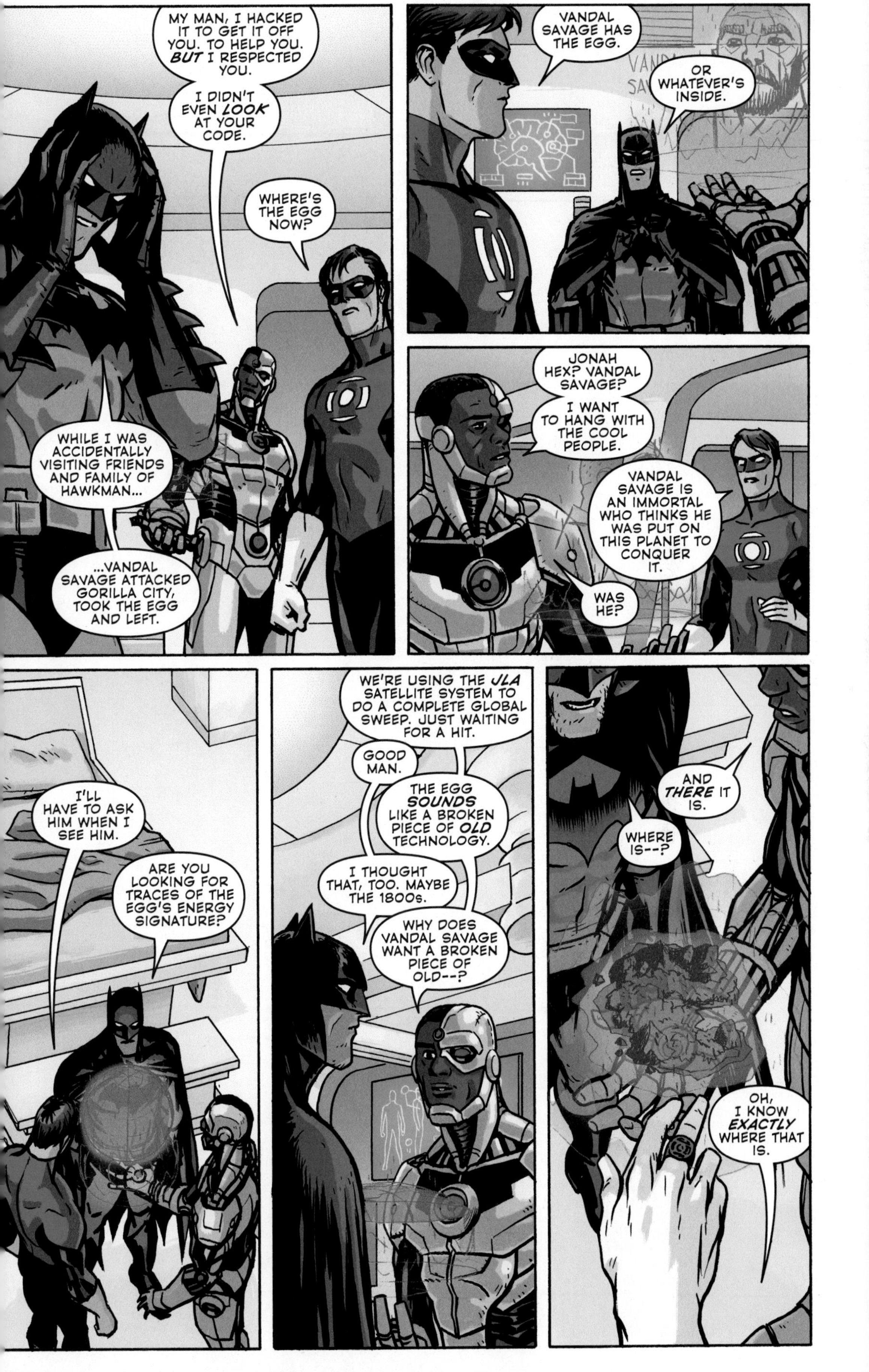
MY MAN, I HACKED IT TO GET IT OFF YOU. TO HELP YOU. BUT I RESPECTED YOU.
I DIDN'T EVEN LOOK AT YOUR CODE.
WHERE'S THE EGG NOW?
WHILE I WAS ACCIDENTALLY VISITING FRIENDS AND FAMILY OF HAWKMAN...
...VANDAL SAVAGE ATTACKED GORILLA CITY, TOOK THE EGG AND LEFT.
VANDAL SAVAGE HAS THE EGG.
OR WHATEVER'S INSIDE.
JONAH HEX? VANDAL SAVAGE?
I WANT TO HANG WITH THE COOL PEOPLE.
VANDAL SAVAGE IS AN IMMORTAL WHO THINKS HE WAS PUT ON THIS PLANET TO CONQUER IT.
WAS HE?
I'LL HAVE TO ASK HIM WHEN I SEE HIM.
ARE YOU LOOKING FOR TRACES OF THE EGG'S ENERGY SIGNATURE?
WE'RE USING THE JLA SATELLITE SYSTEM TO DO A COMPLETE GLOBAL SWEEP. JUST WAITING FOR A HIT.
GOOD MAN.
THE EGG SOUNDS LIKE A BROKEN PIECE OF OLD TECHNOLOGY.
I THOUGHT THAT, TOO. MAYBE THE 1800s.
WHY DOES VANDAL SAVAGE WANT A BROKEN PIECE OF OLD--?
AND THERE IT IS.
WHERE IS--?
OH, I KNOW EXACTLY WHERE THAT IS.

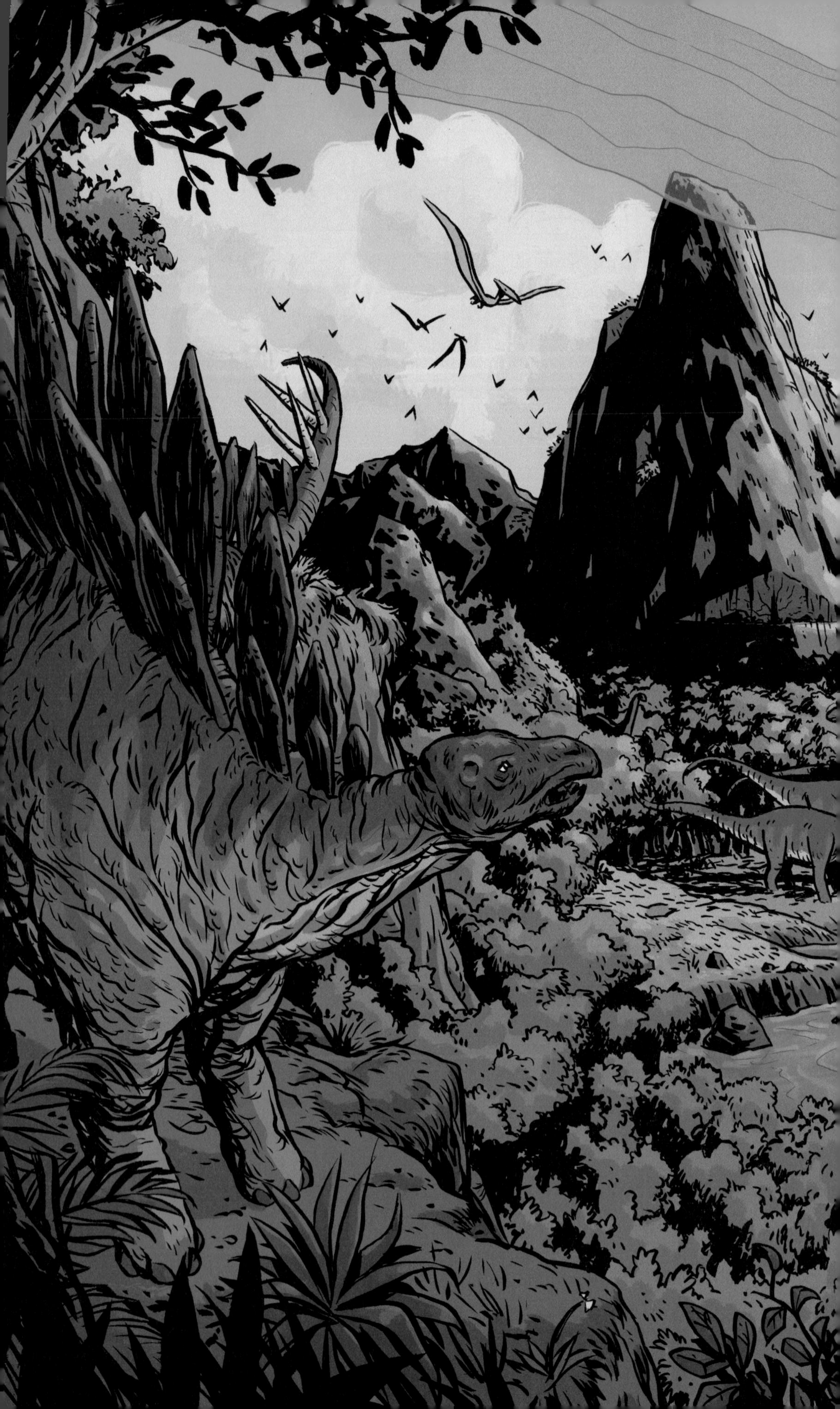

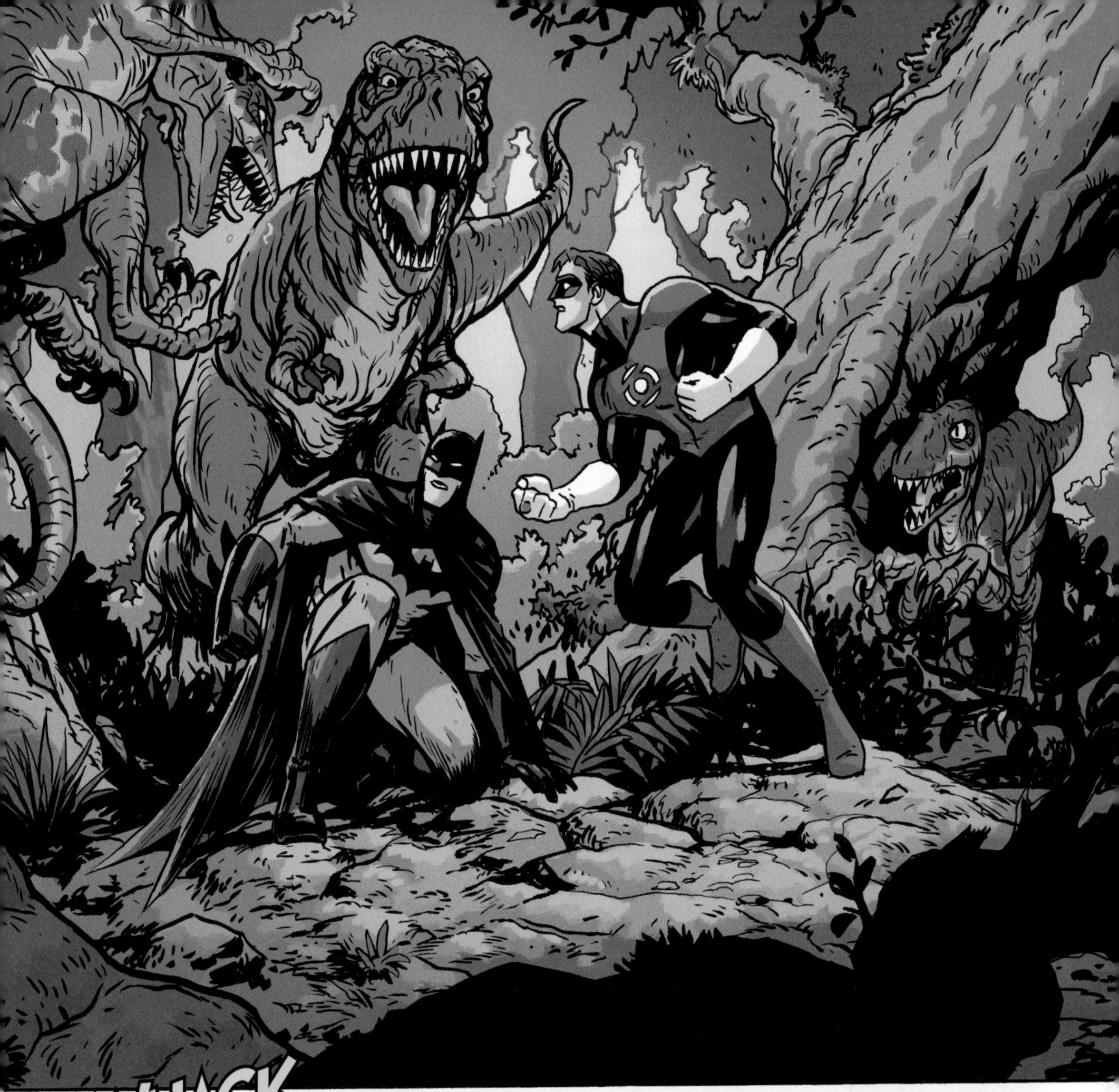

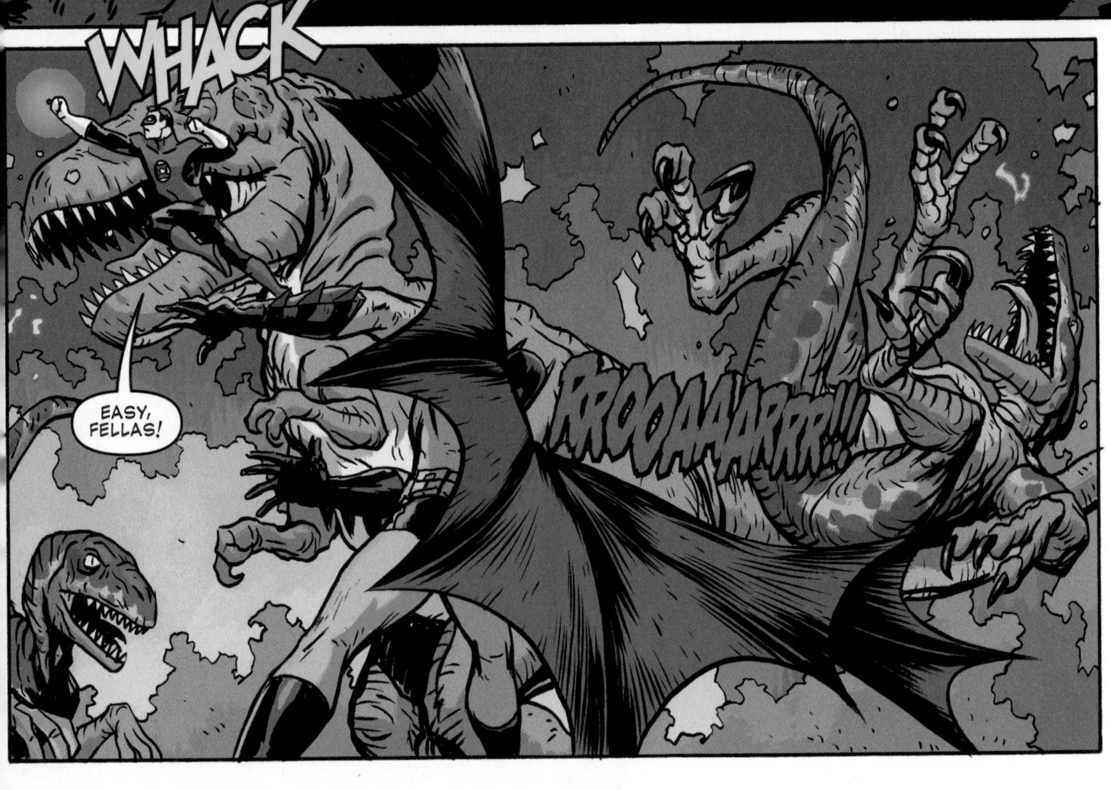
WHACK
EASY, FELLAS!
RROOAAARRR!!!

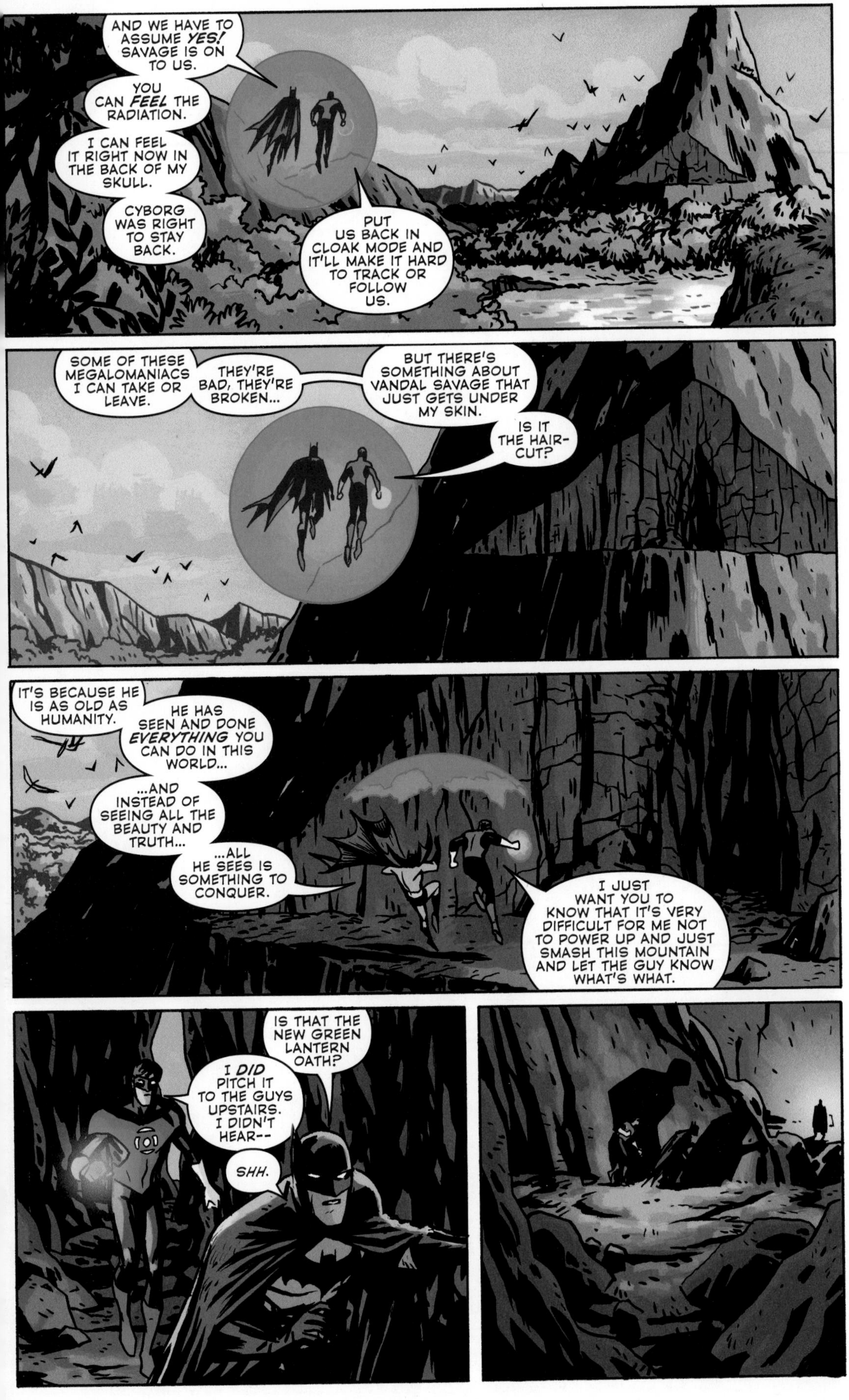
AND WE HAVE TO ASSUME *YES!* SAVAGE IS ON TO US.
YOU CAN *FEEL* THE RADIATION.
I CAN FEEL IT RIGHT NOW IN THE BACK OF MY SKULL.
CYBORG WAS RIGHT TO STAY BACK.
PUT US BACK IN CLOAK MODE AND IT'LL MAKE IT HARD TO TRACK OR FOLLOW US.
SOME OF THESE MEGALOMANIACS I CAN TAKE OR LEAVE.
THEY'RE BAD, THEY'RE BROKEN...
BUT THERE'S SOMETHING ABOUT VANDAL SAVAGE THAT JUST GETS UNDER MY SKIN.
IS IT THE HAIR-CUT?
IT'S BECAUSE HE IS AS OLD AS HUMANITY.
HE HAS SEEN AND DONE *EVERYTHING* YOU CAN DO IN THIS WORLD...
...AND INSTEAD OF SEEING ALL THE BEAUTY AND TRUTH...
...ALL HE SEES IS SOMETHING TO CONQUER.
I JUST WANT YOU TO KNOW THAT IT'S VERY DIFFICULT FOR ME NOT TO POWER UP AND JUST SMASH THIS MOUNTAIN AND LET THE GUY KNOW WHAT'S WHAT.
IS THAT THE NEW GREEN LANTERN OATH?
I *DID* PITCH IT TO THE GUYS UPSTAIRS. I DIDN'T HEAR--
SHH.

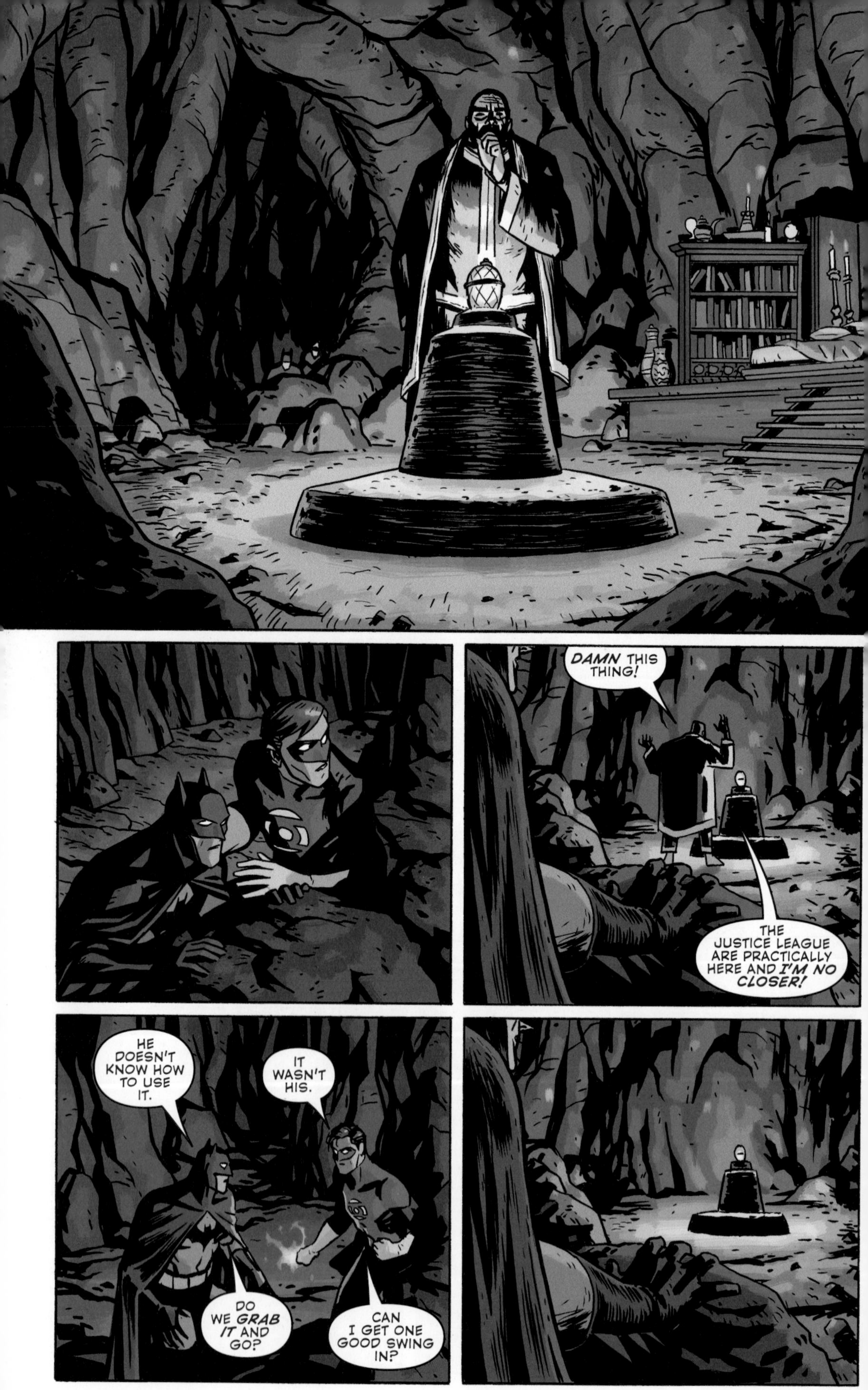
DAMN THIS THING!
THE JUSTICE LEAGUE ARE PRACTICALLY HERE AND I'M NO CLOSER!
HE DOESN'T KNOW HOW TO USE IT.
IT WASN'T HIS.
DO WE GRAB IT AND GO?
CAN I GET ONE GOOD SWING IN?

END PART 6

JONAH HEX, MY NAME IS--

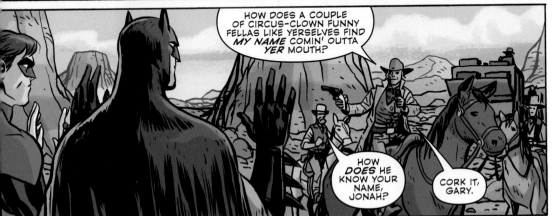

HOW DOES A COUPLE OF CIRCUS-CLOWN FUNNY FELLAS LIKE YERSELVES FIND *MY NAME* COMIN' OUTTA *YER* MOUTH?

HOW *DOES* HE KNOW YOUR NAME, JONAH?

CORK IT, GARY.

ARE WE TAKING OFF OUR MASKS?

OF COURSE, HAL.

IN THIS CULTURE, MASKS ARE FOR ROBBERS AND CRIMINALS.

TRUE.

AND MINE WAS DESIGNED TO STRIKE *FEAR* INTO THE HEARTS OF CRIMINALS, SO--

NAH.

JUST THINK YA LOOK *OVER-HEATED.*

YA OVER-HEATED?

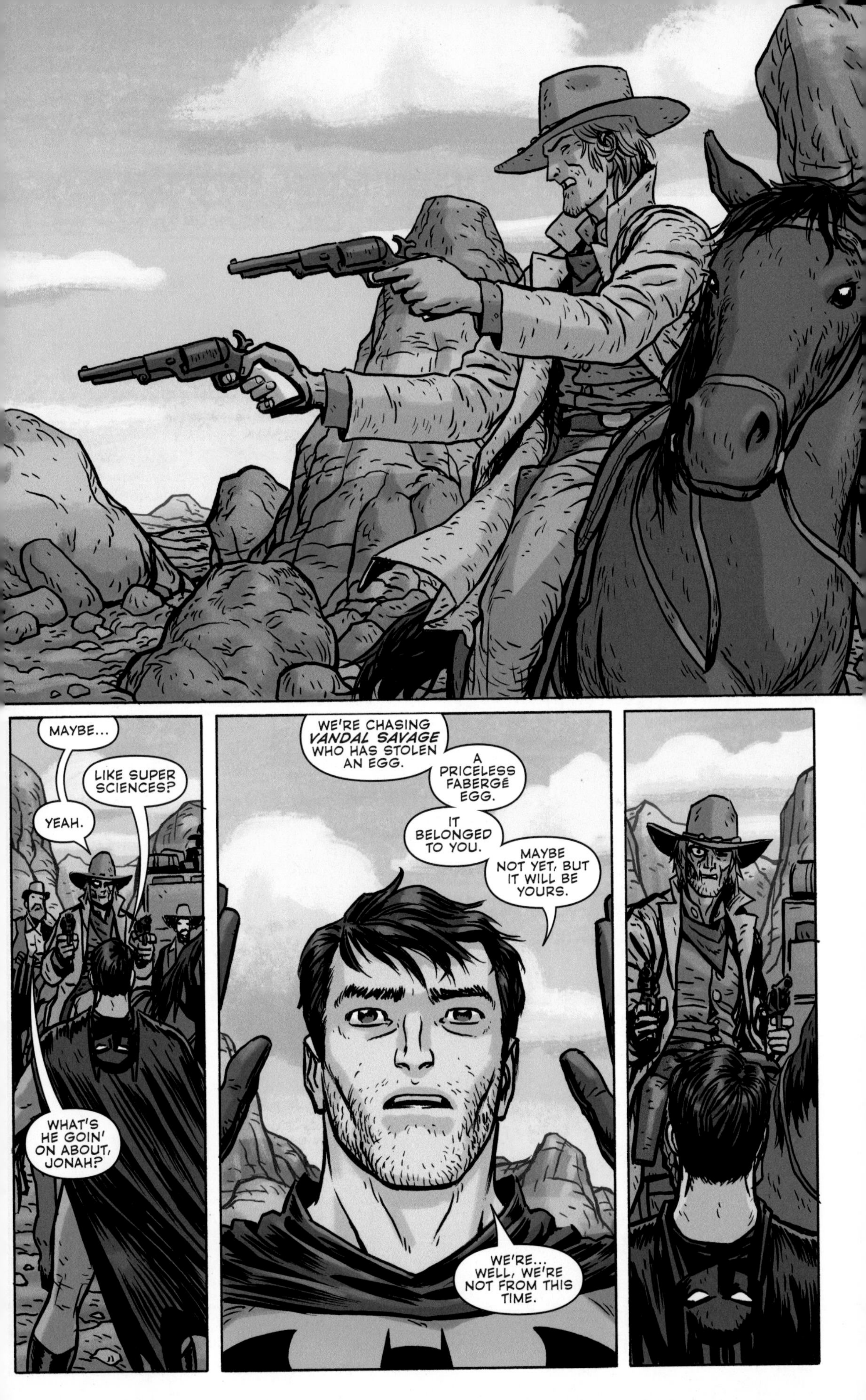
MAYBE...
LIKE SUPER SCIENCES?
YEAH.
WHAT'S HE GOIN' ON ABOUT, JONAH?
WE'RE CHASING VANDAL SAVAGE WHO HAS STOLEN AN EGG.
A PRICELESS FABERGÉ EGG.
IT BELONGED TO YOU.
MAYBE NOT YET, BUT IT WILL BE YOURS.
WE'RE... WELL, WE'RE NOT FROM THIS TIME.

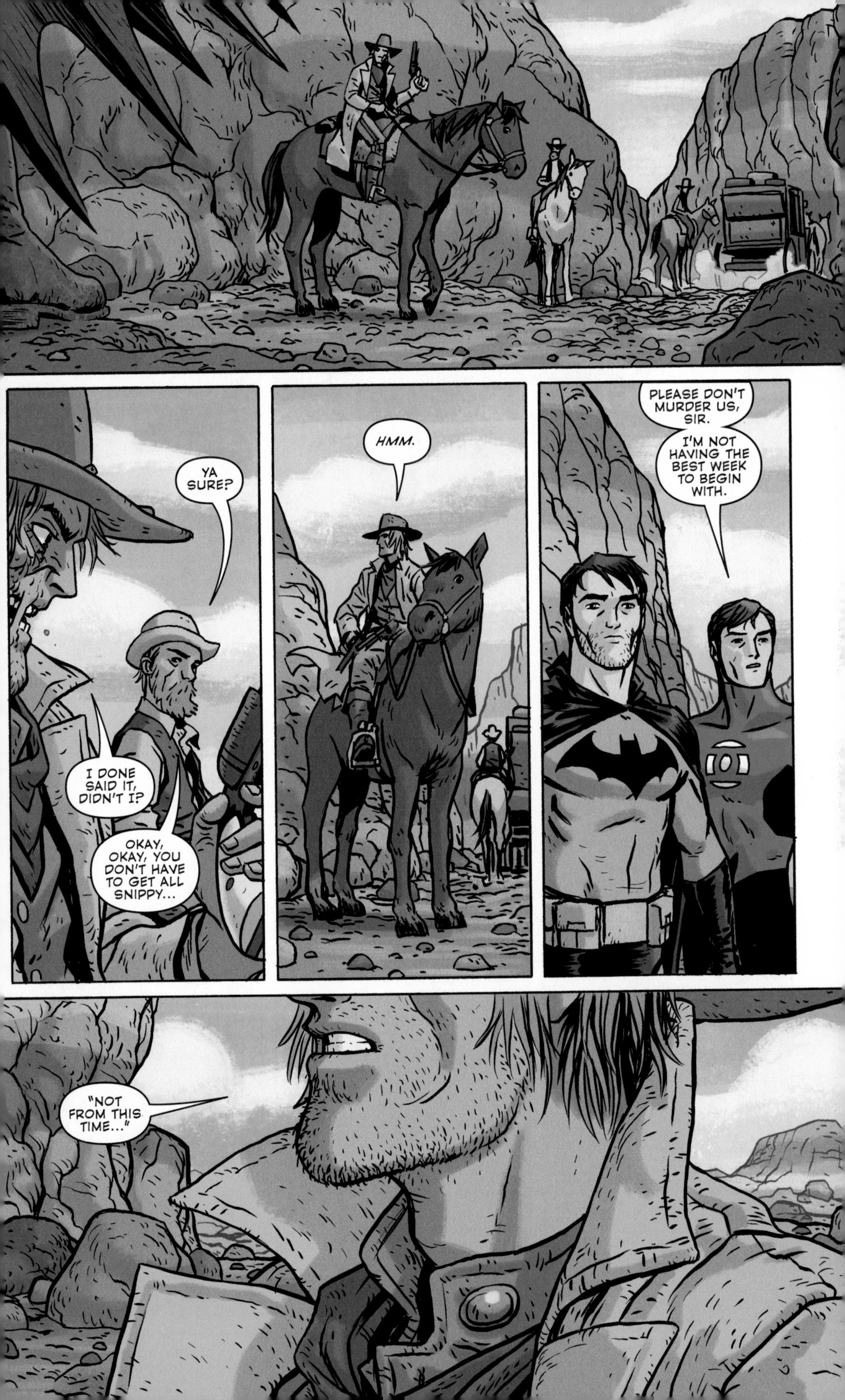
YA SURE?
I DONE SAID IT, DIDN'T I?
OKAY, OKAY, YOU DON'T HAVE TO GET ALL SNIPPY...
HMM.
PLEASE DON'T MURDER US, SIR.
I'M NOT HAVING THE BEST WEEK TO BEGIN WITH.
"NOT FROM THIS TIME..."

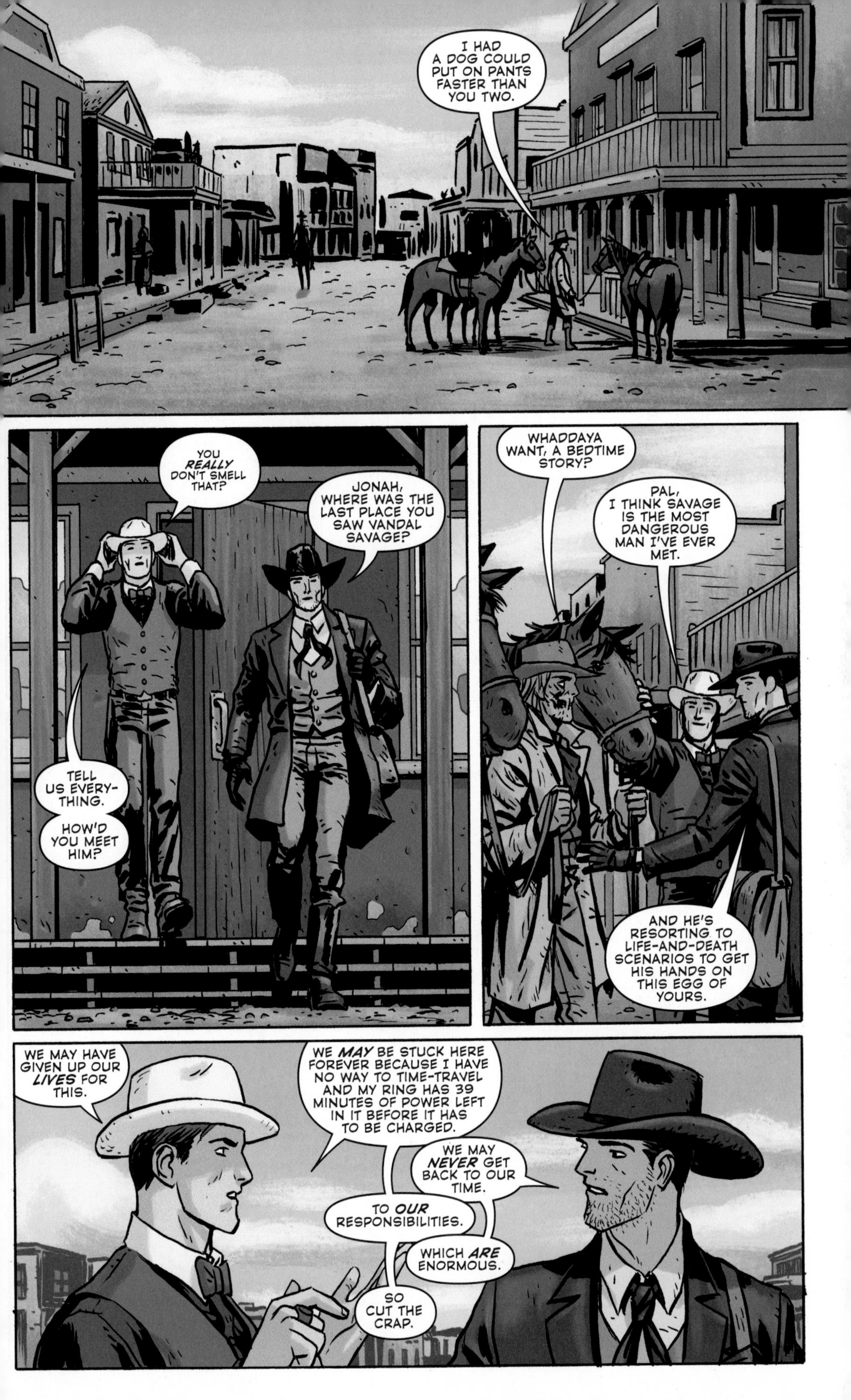
I HAD A DOG COULD PUT ON PANTS FASTER THAN YOU TWO.
YOU *REALLY* DON'T SMELL THAT?
JONAH, WHERE WAS THE LAST PLACE YOU SAW VANDAL SAVAGE?
TELL US EVERY-THING.
HOW'D YOU MEET HIM?
WHADDAYA WANT, A BEDTIME STORY?
PAL, I THINK SAVAGE IS THE MOST DANGEROUS MAN I'VE EVER MET.
AND HE'S RESORTING TO LIFE-AND-DEATH SCENARIOS TO GET HIS HANDS ON THIS EGG OF YOURS.
WE MAY HAVE GIVEN UP OUR *LIVES* FOR THIS.
WE *MAY* BE STUCK HERE FOREVER BECAUSE I HAVE NO WAY TO TIME-TRAVEL AND MY RING HAS 39 MINUTES OF POWER LEFT IN IT BEFORE IT HAS TO BE CHARGED.
WE MAY *NEVER* GET BACK TO OUR TIME.
TO *OUR* RESPONSIBILITIES.
WHICH *ARE* ENORMOUS.
SO CUT THE CRAP.

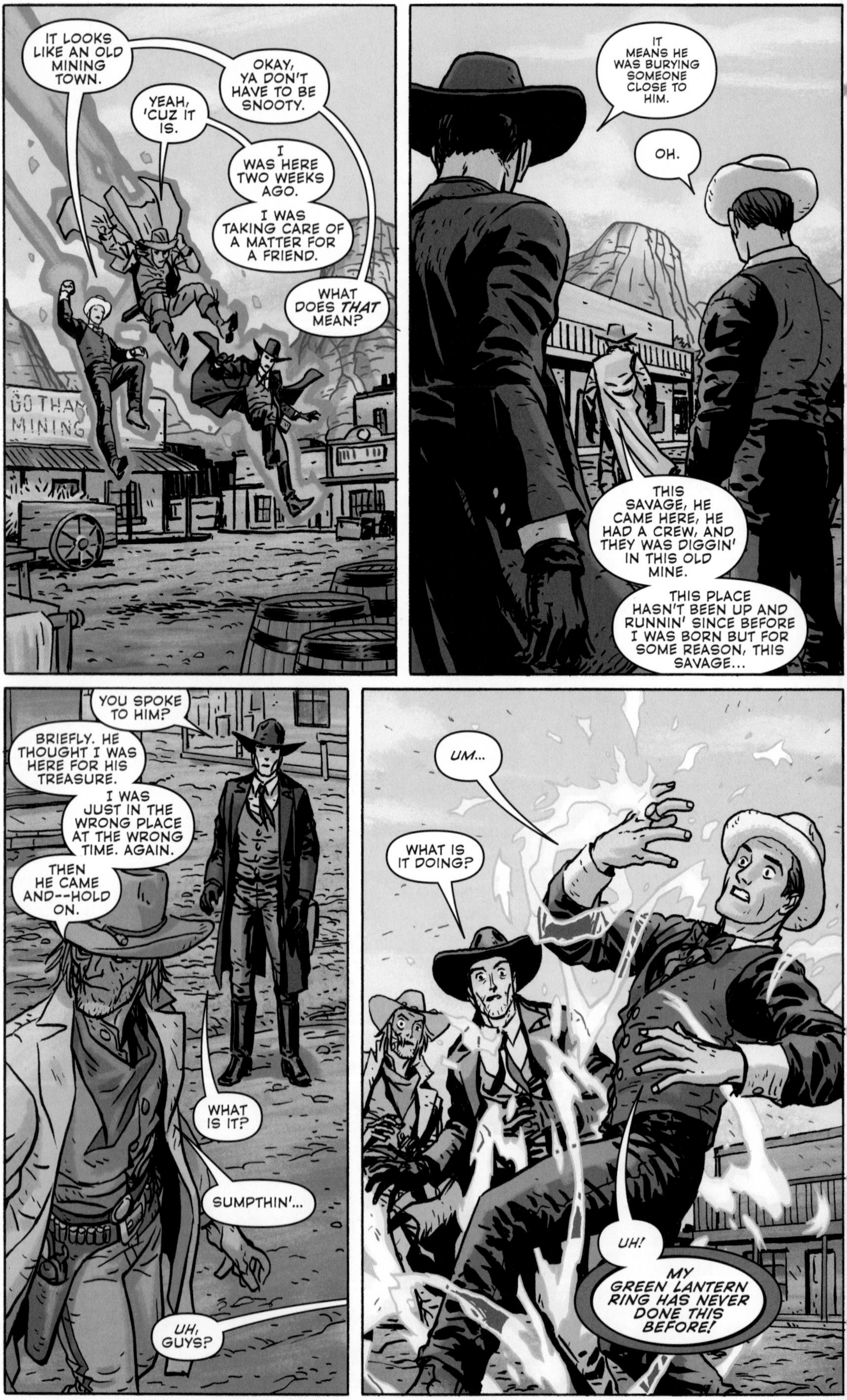
IT LOOKS LIKE AN OLD MINING TOWN.
YEAH, 'CUZ IT IS.
OKAY, YA DON'T HAVE TO BE SNOOTY.
I WAS HERE TWO WEEKS AGO.
I WAS TAKING CARE OF A MATTER FOR A FRIEND.
WHAT DOES *THAT* MEAN?
GOTHAM MINING
IT MEANS HE WAS BURYING SOMEONE CLOSE TO HIM.
OH.
THIS SAVAGE, HE CAME HERE, HE HAD A CREW, AND THEY WAS DIGGIN' IN THIS OLD MINE.
THIS PLACE HASN'T BEEN UP AND RUNNIN' SINCE BEFORE I WAS BORN BUT FOR SOME REASON, THIS SAVAGE...
YOU SPOKE TO HIM?
BRIEFLY. HE THOUGHT I WAS HERE FOR HIS TREASURE.
I WAS JUST IN THE WRONG PLACE AT THE WRONG TIME. AGAIN.
THEN HE CAME AND--HOLD ON.
WHAT IS IT?
SUMPTHIN'...
UH, GUYS?
UM...
WHAT IS IT DOING?
UH!
MY GREEN LANTERN RING HAS NEVER DONE THIS BEFORE!

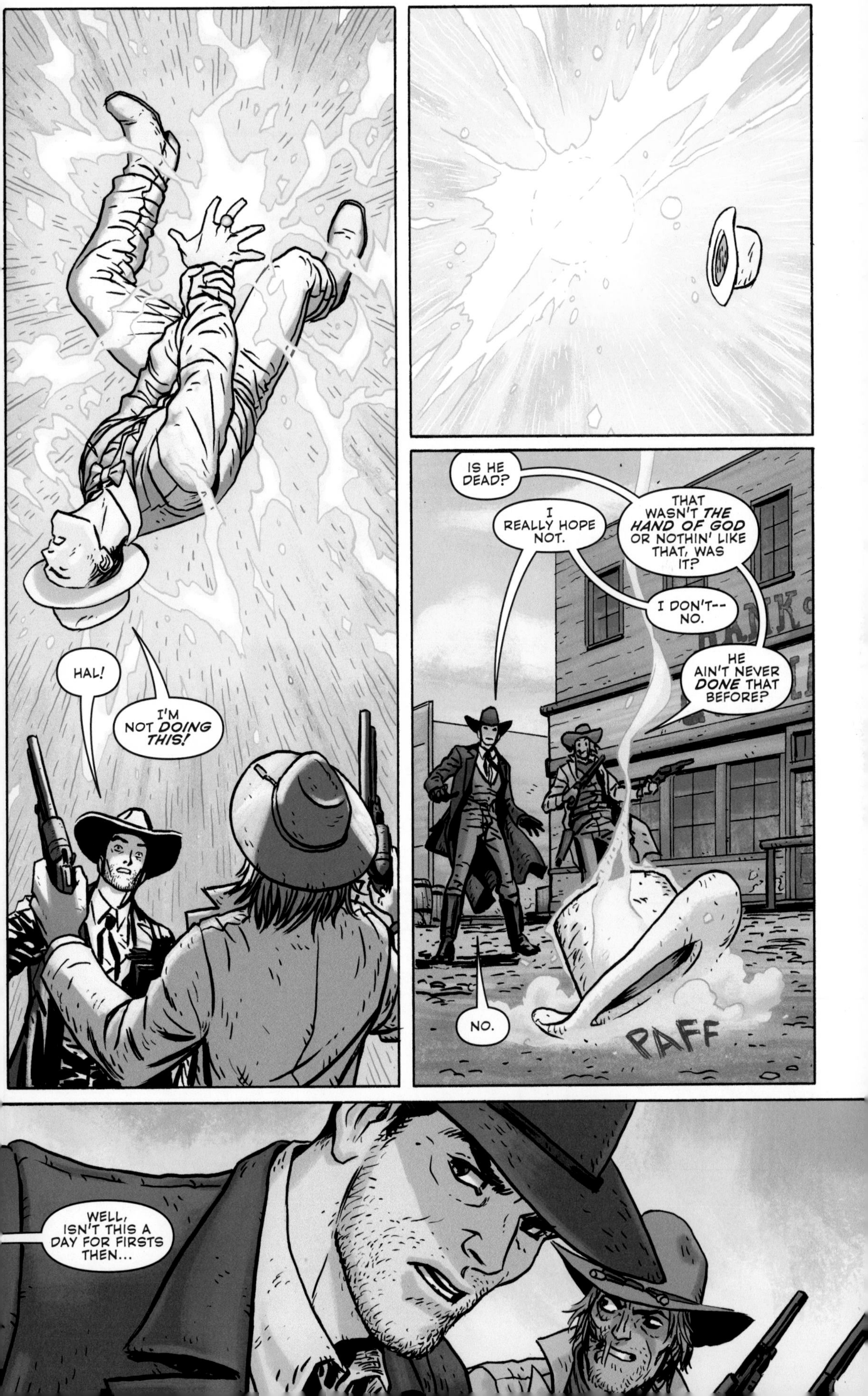
HAL!
I'M NOT DOING THIS!
IS HE DEAD?
I REALLY HOPE NOT.
NO.
THAT WASN'T THE HAND OF GOD OR NOTHIN' LIKE THAT, WAS IT?
I DON'T-- NO.
HE AIN'T NEVER DONE THAT BEFORE?
PAFF
WELL, ISN'T THIS A DAY FOR FIRSTS THEN...

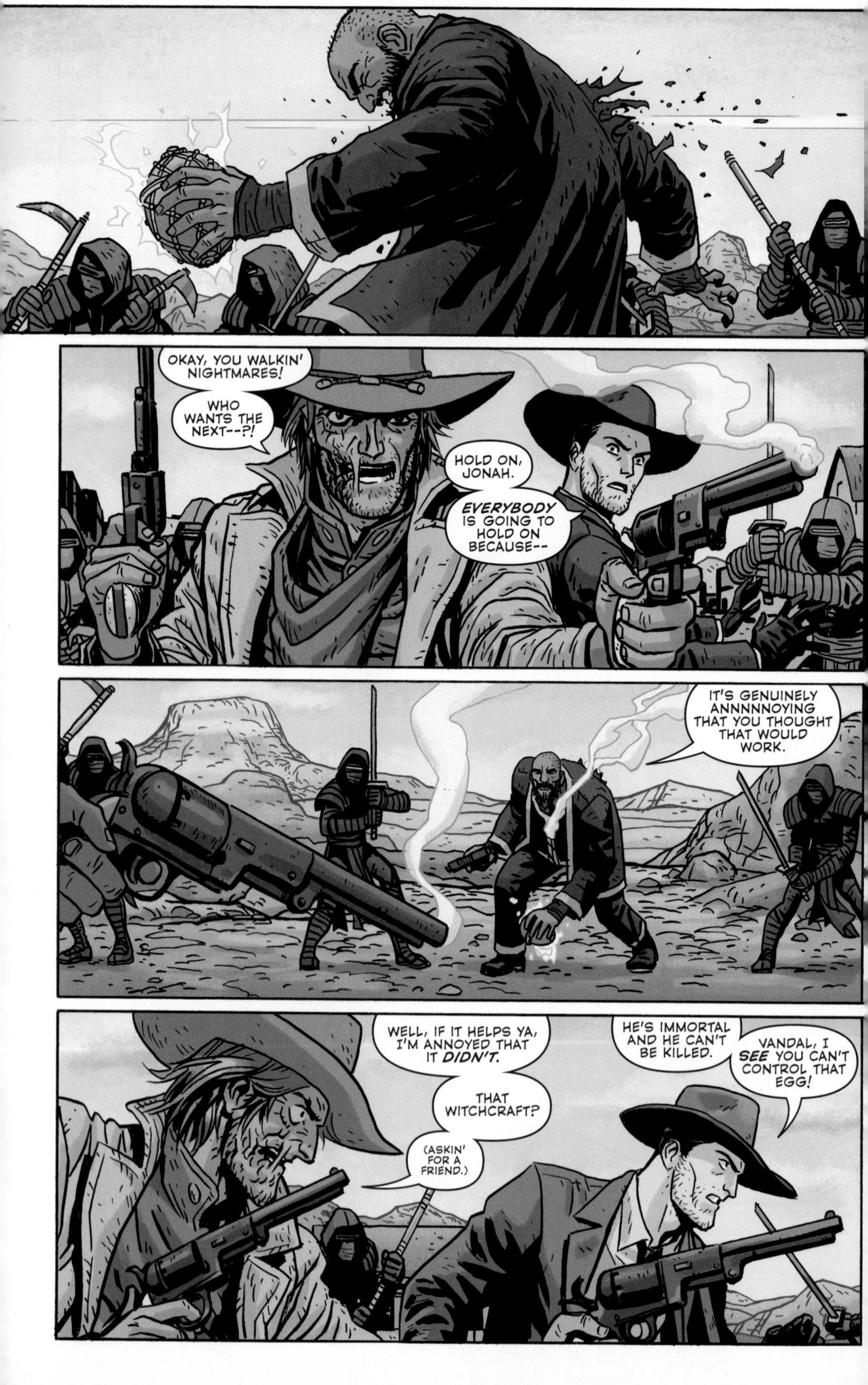

OKAY, YOU WALKIN' NIGHTMARES!
WHO WANTS THE NEXT--?!
HOLD ON, JONAH.
EVERYBODY IS GOING TO HOLD ON BECAUSE--
IT'S GENUINELY ANNNNNOYING THAT YOU THOUGHT THAT WOULD WORK.
WELL, IF IT HELPS YA, I'M ANNOYED THAT IT DIDN'T.
THAT WITCHCRAFT?
(ASKIN' FOR A FRIEND.)
HE'S IMMORTAL AND HE CAN'T BE KILLED.
VANDAL, I SEE YOU CAN'T CONTROL THAT EGG!

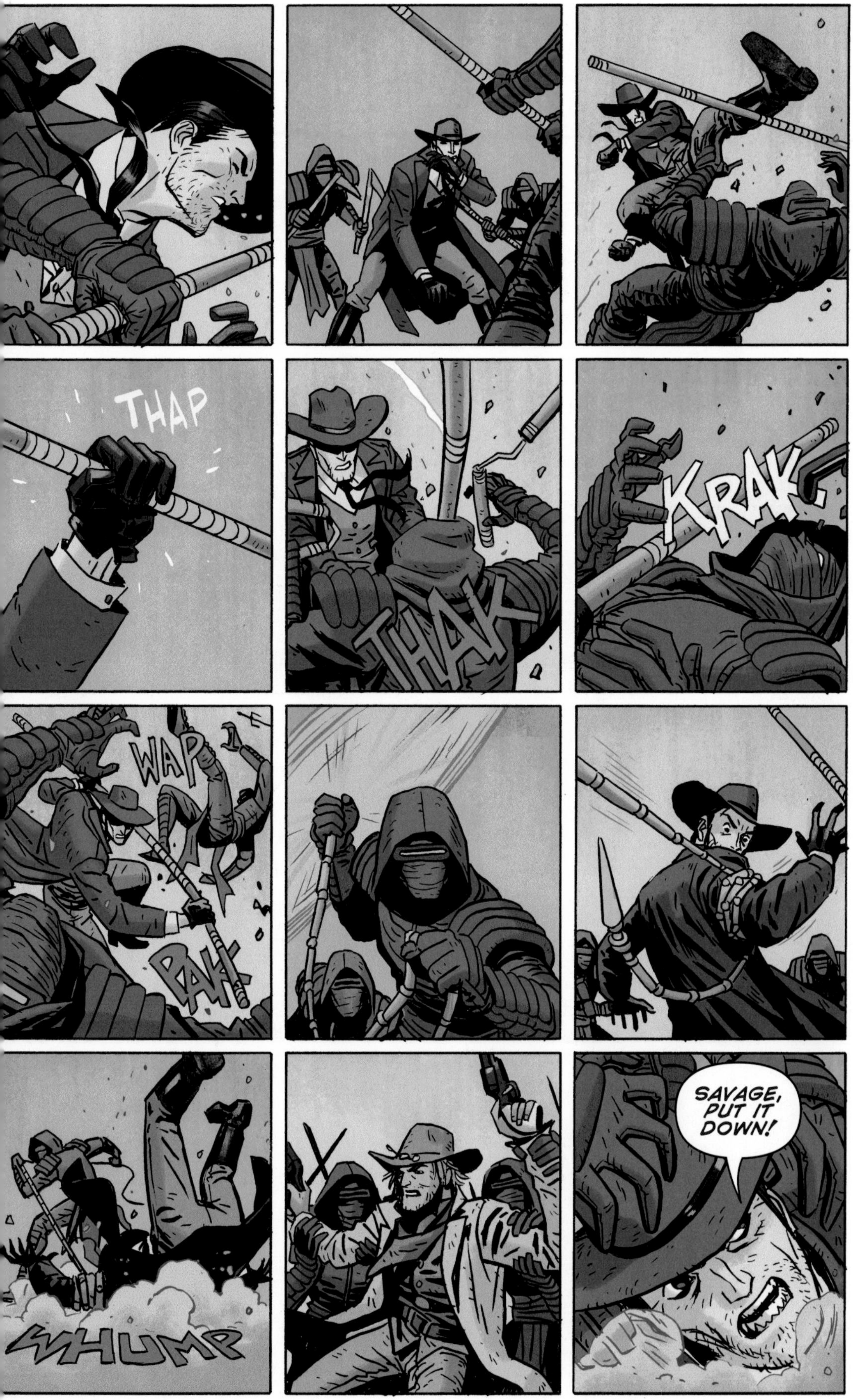
THAP
THAK
KRAK
WAP
PAK
WHUMP
SAVAGE, PUT IT DOWN!

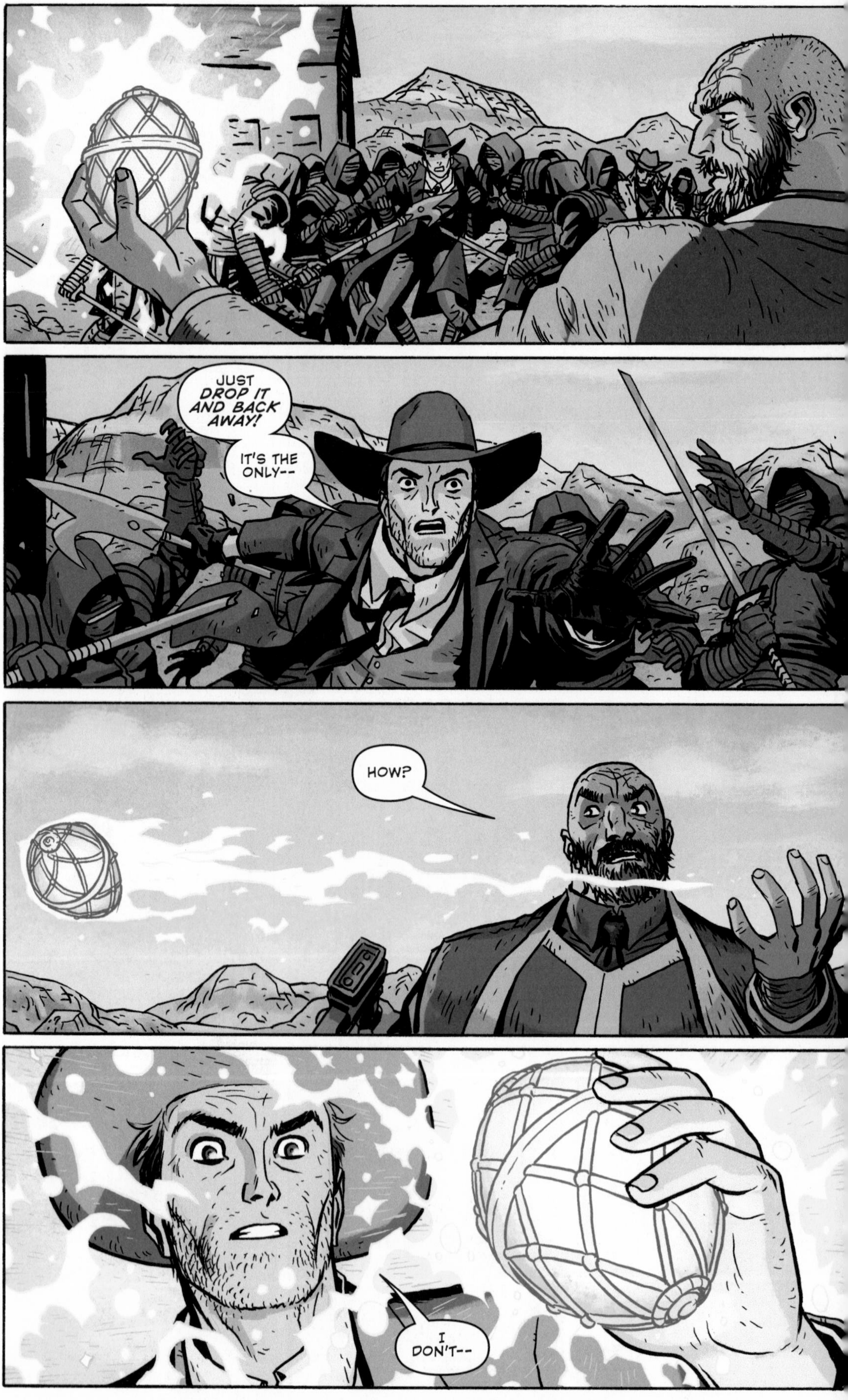
JUST *DROP IT AND BACK AWAY!*
IT'S THE ONLY--
HOW?
I DON'T--

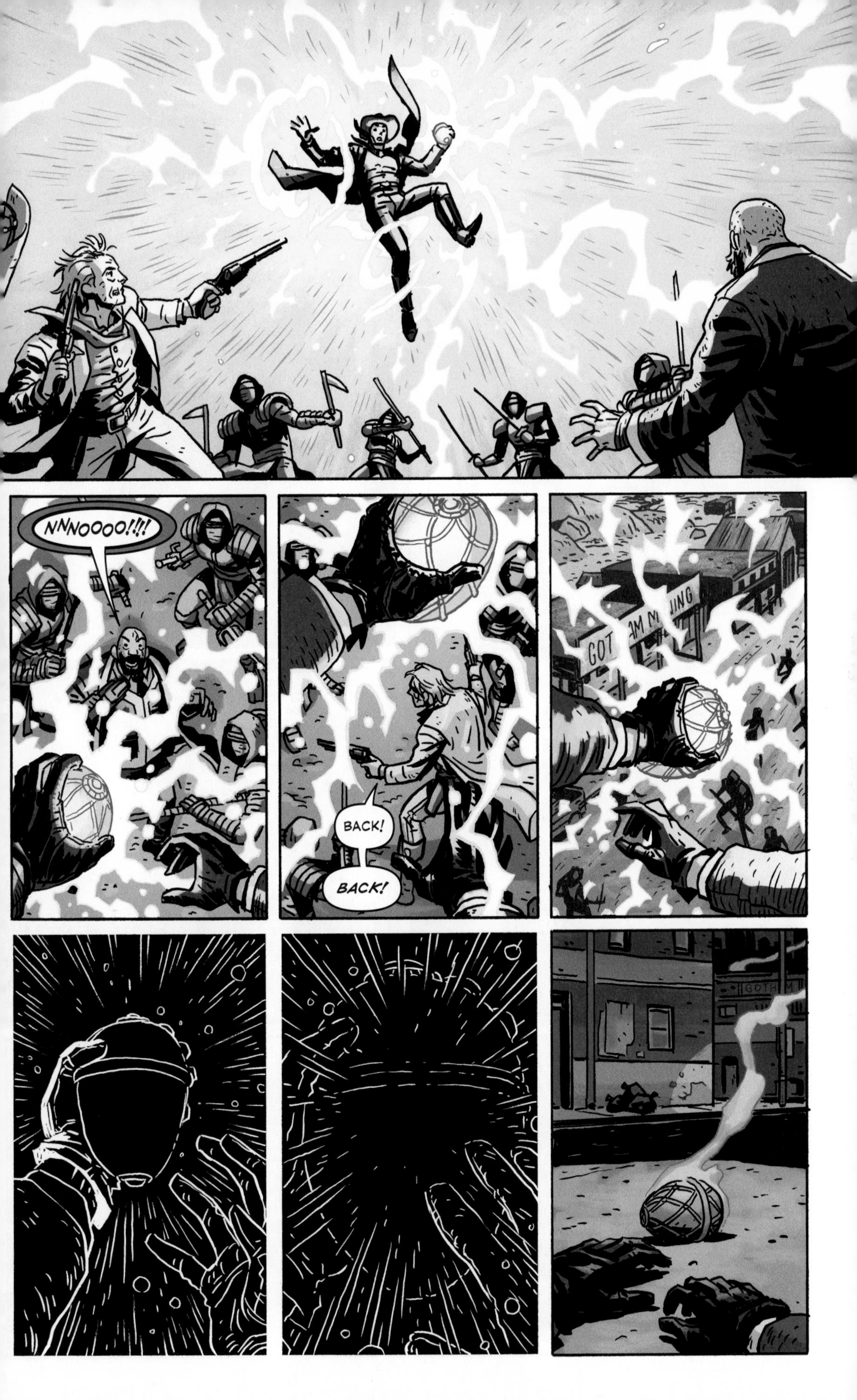
NNNOOOO!!!!
BACK!
BACK!

OH. GREAT.

CRIME ALLEY.

THE PLACE MY PARENTS WERE MURDERED. THE PLACE WHERE BATMAN WAS BORN.

MONARC THEAT

PLEASE BE MODERN DAY.

I REALLY DON'T NEED TO RELIVE THAT MO--

MASTER BRUCE?

ALFRED?

YOU HAVE RETURNED TO US!

PLEASE, PLEASE, PLEASE, PICK ME UP.

THE BAT-COMPUTER HAS YOUR LOCATION AND...OH, WE TALKED ABOUT YOU GOING BACK THERE--

IT WAS NOT MY IDEA.

ALFRED, I DON'T HAVE MY ARMOR. I ONLY HAVE MY EAR WIG COMM.

YOU LOST ALL OF YOUR ARMOR?

IN THE OLD WEST.

I'M SORRY?

AND VANDAL SAVAGE MAY HAVE SEEN MY FACE.

THAT'S-- THAT'S OFF-PUTTING.

END PART

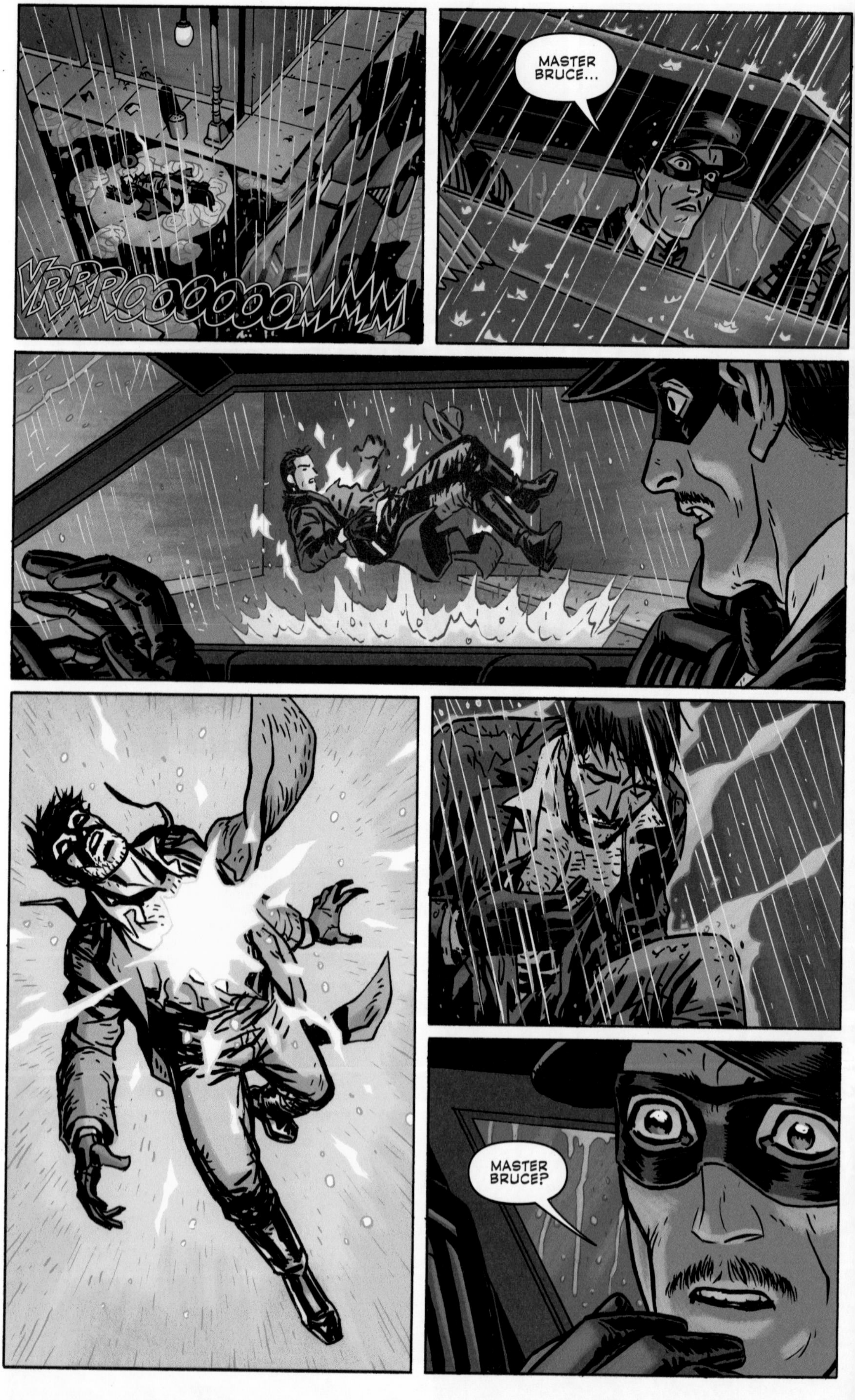
VRRROOOOOOOMMM
MASTER BRUCE...
MASTER BRUCE?

OKAY.

OKAY.

MA'AM.

THANKS FOR THE LIFT, ALFRED.

I WAS UNDER THE IMPRESSION THAT YOU WERE DEAD IN AN ALLEY...NOT TURNING INTO A DISNEY-THEMED COWBOY PRINCESS.

TODAY, I *AM* AN ACTUAL COWBOY.

YOU *SMELL* LIKE AN ACTUAL COWBOY.

THE OLD WEST ACTUALLY SMELLS AS BAD AS YOU THINK.

DID YOU ALMOST ACTUALLY DIE?

I BELIEVE I DID DIE AND I WAS... *SPARED.*

BY THE EGG THE RIDDLER STOLE OUT OF THE GOTHAM MUSEUM, WHICH YOU HAVE BEEN CHASING ALL OVER?

WE HAVE A LOT OF WORK TO DO.

HAVE YOU 'EARD FROM *GREEN LANTERN?*

GREEN LANTERN? WHAT DOES HE HAVE TO DO WITH THIS?

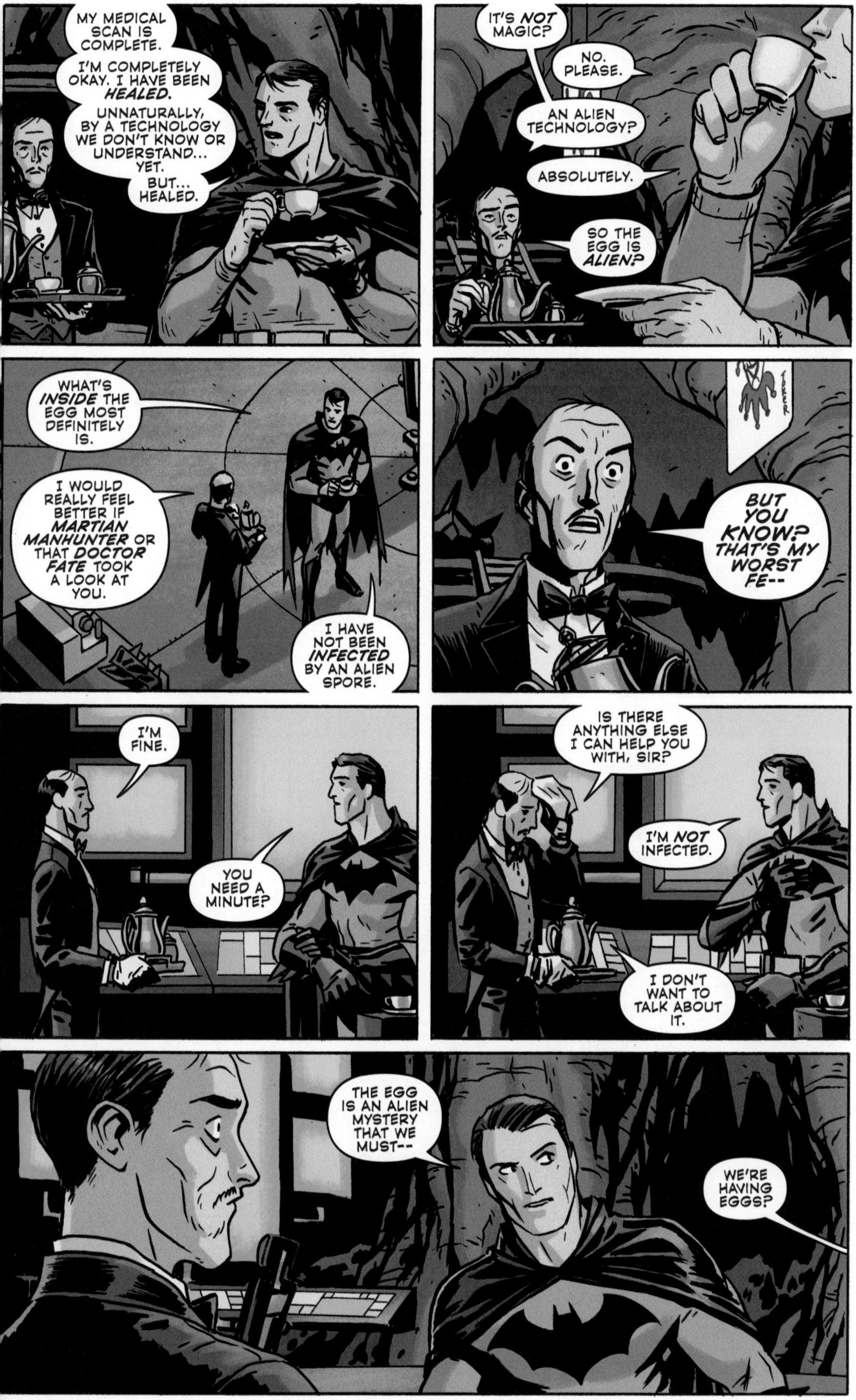
MY MEDICAL SCAN IS COMPLETE.
I'M COMPLETELY OKAY. I HAVE BEEN *HEALED.*
UNNATURALLY, BY A TECHNOLOGY WE DON'T KNOW OR UNDERSTAND... YET.
BUT... HEALED.
IT'S *NOT* MAGIC?
NO. PLEASE.
AN ALIEN TECHNOLOGY?
ABSOLUTELY.
SO THE EGG IS *ALIEN?*
WHAT'S *INSIDE* THE EGG MOST DEFINITELY IS.
I WOULD REALLY FEEL BETTER IF *MARTIAN MANHUNTER* OR THAT *DOCTOR FATE* TOOK A LOOK AT YOU.
I HAVE NOT BEEN *INFECTED* BY AN ALIEN SPORE.
BUT YOU KNOW? THAT'S MY WORST FE--
I'M FINE.
YOU NEED A MINUTE?
IS THERE ANYTHING ELSE I CAN HELP YOU WITH, SIR?
I'M *NOT* INFECTED.
I DON'T WANT TO TALK ABOUT IT.
THE EGG IS AN ALIEN MYSTERY THAT WE MUST--
WE'RE HAVING EGGS?

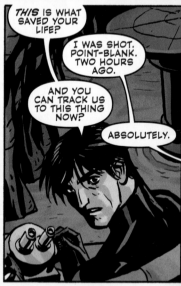

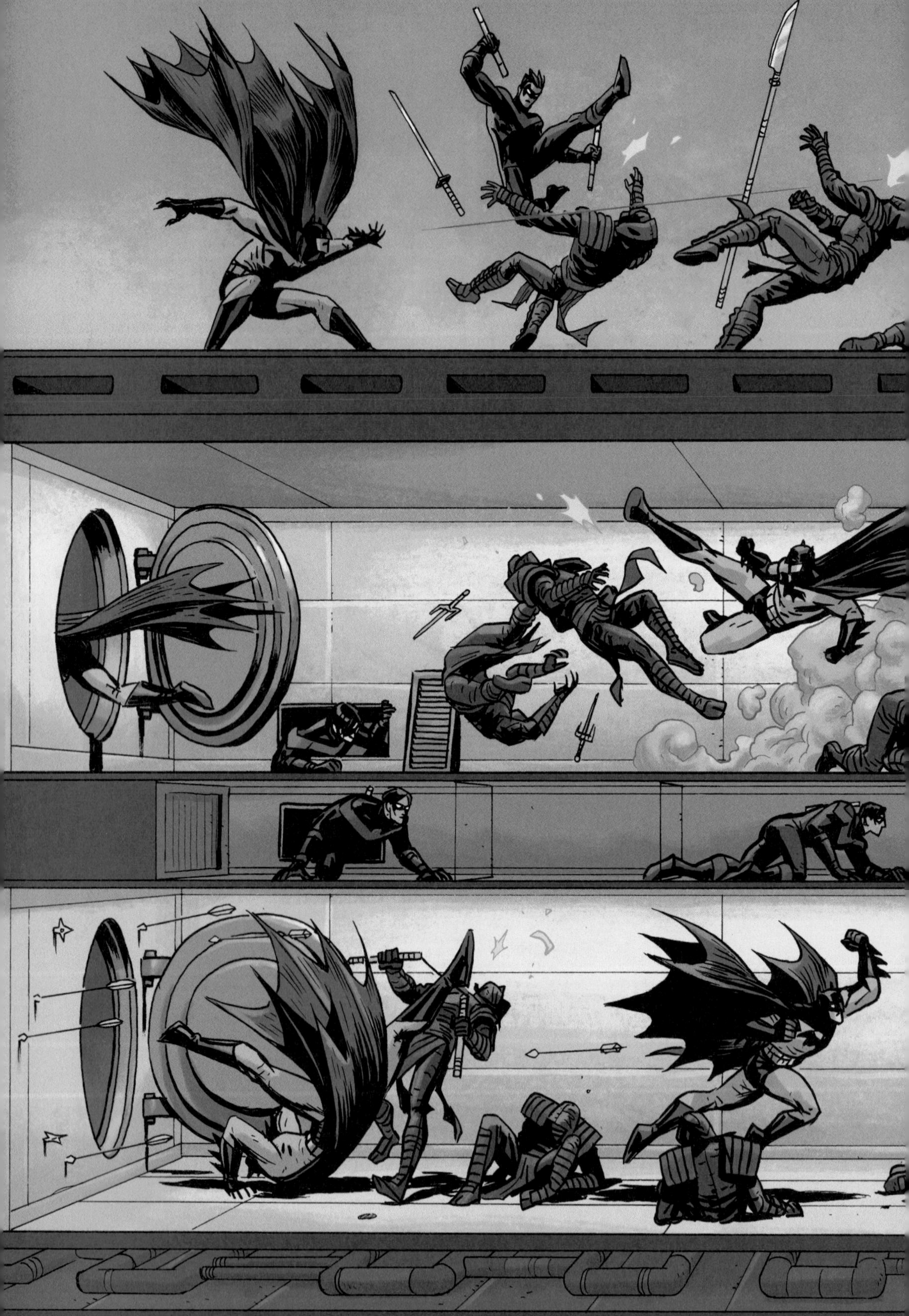

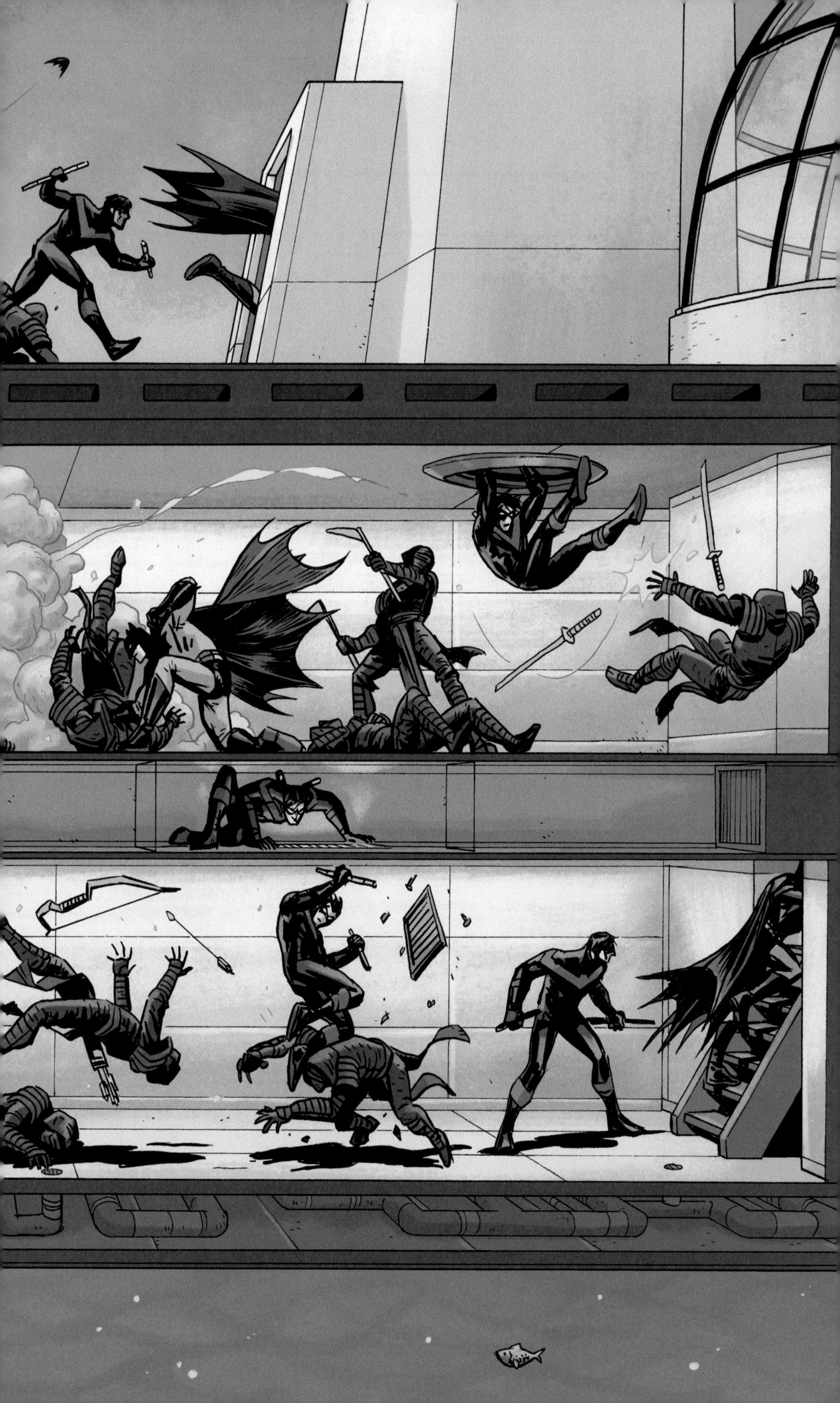

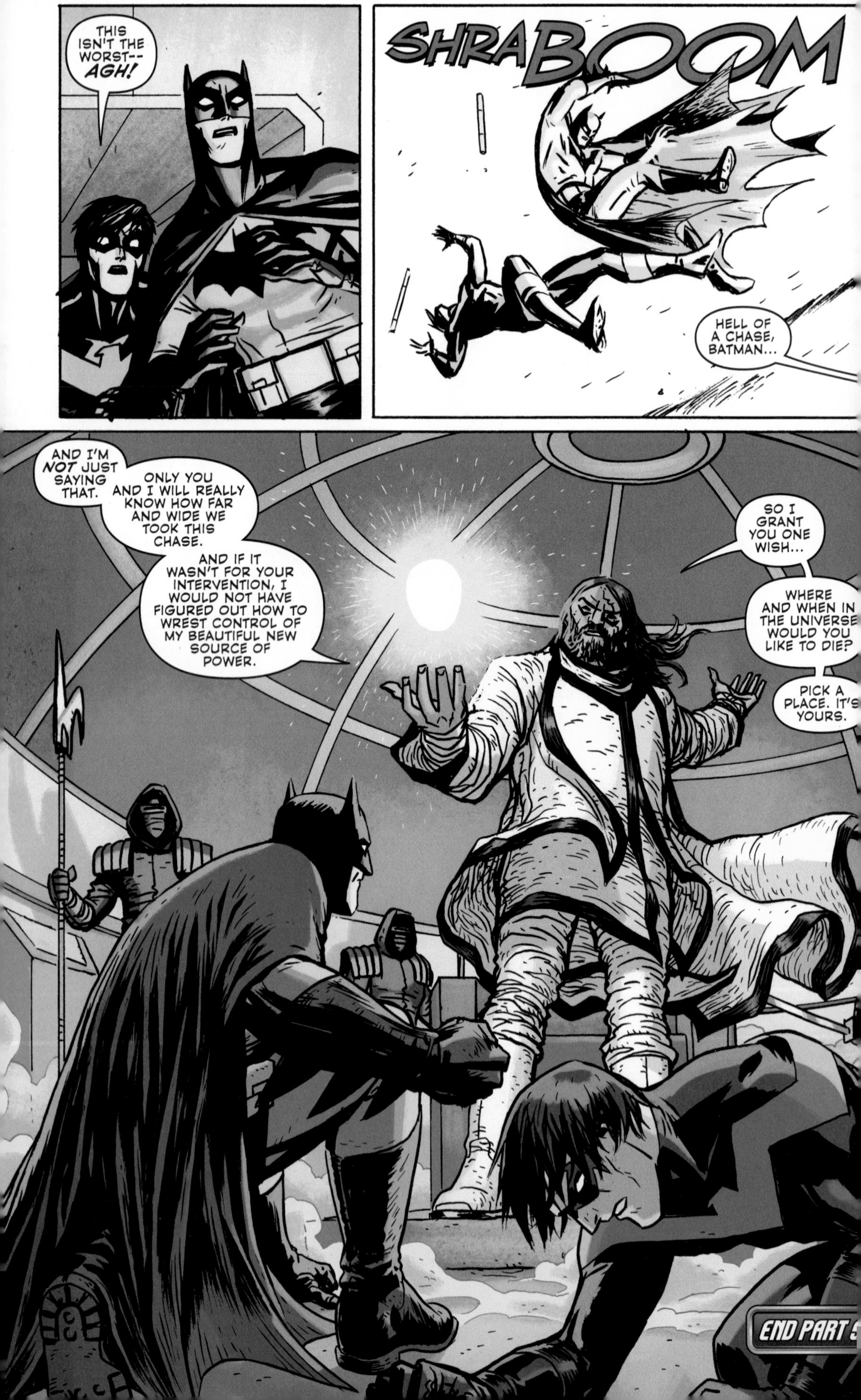
THIS ISN'T THE WORST-- AGH!
SHRABOOOM
HELL OF A CHASE, BATMAN...
AND I'M NOT JUST SAYING THAT.
ONLY YOU AND I WILL REALLY KNOW HOW FAR AND WIDE WE TOOK THIS CHASE.
AND IF IT WASN'T FOR YOUR INTERVENTION, I WOULD NOT HAVE FIGURED OUT HOW TO WREST CONTROL OF MY BEAUTIFUL NEW SOURCE OF POWER.
SO I GRANT YOU ONE WISH...
WHERE AND WHEN IN THE UNIVERSE WOULD YOU LIKE TO DIE?
PICK A PLACE. IT'S YOURS.
END PART

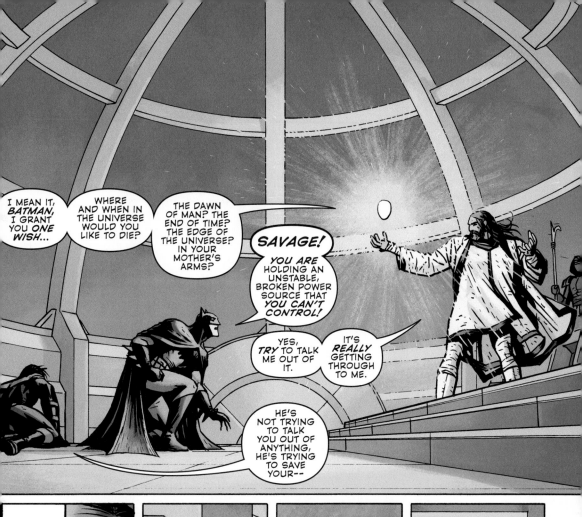

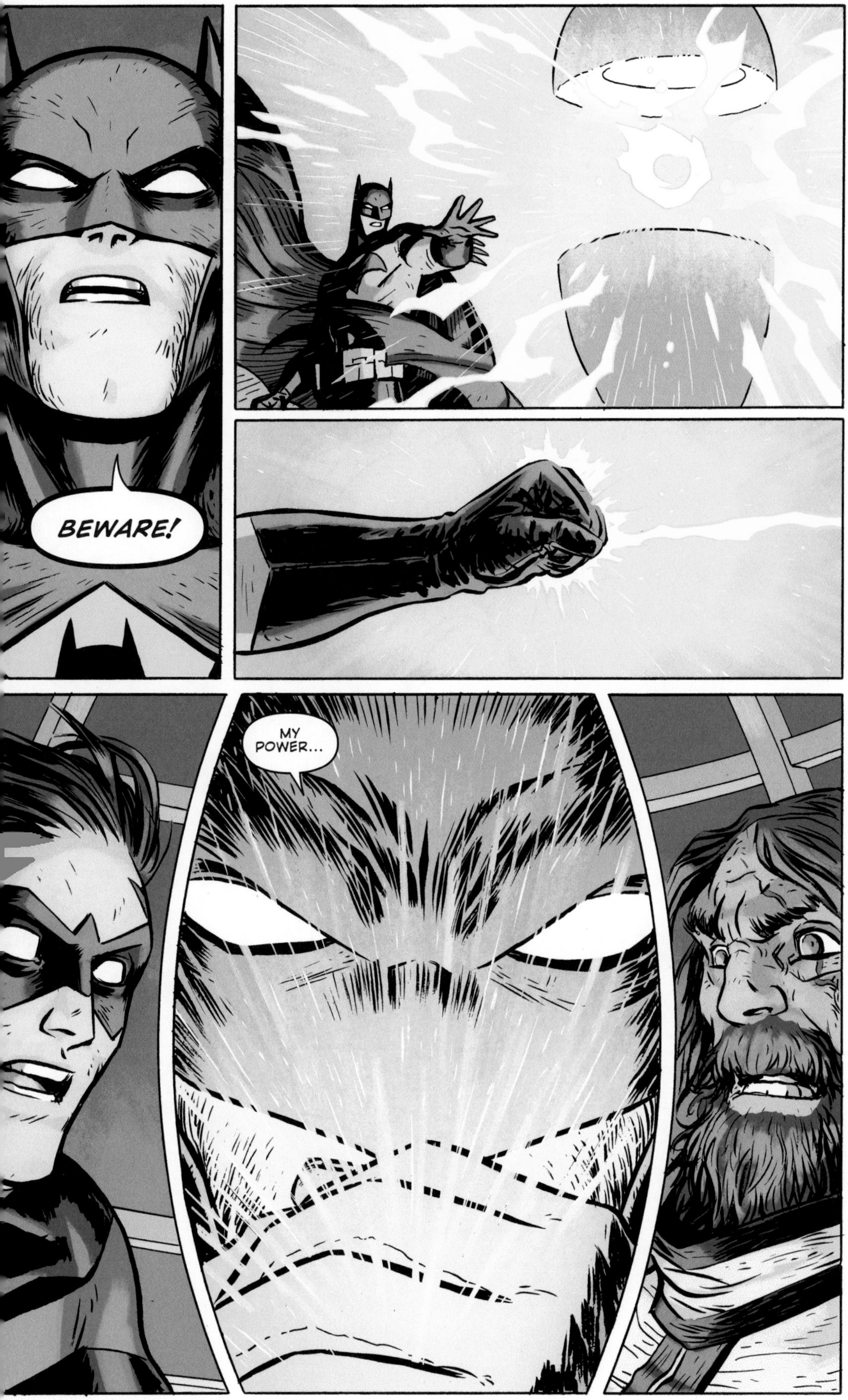
BEWARE!
MY POWER...

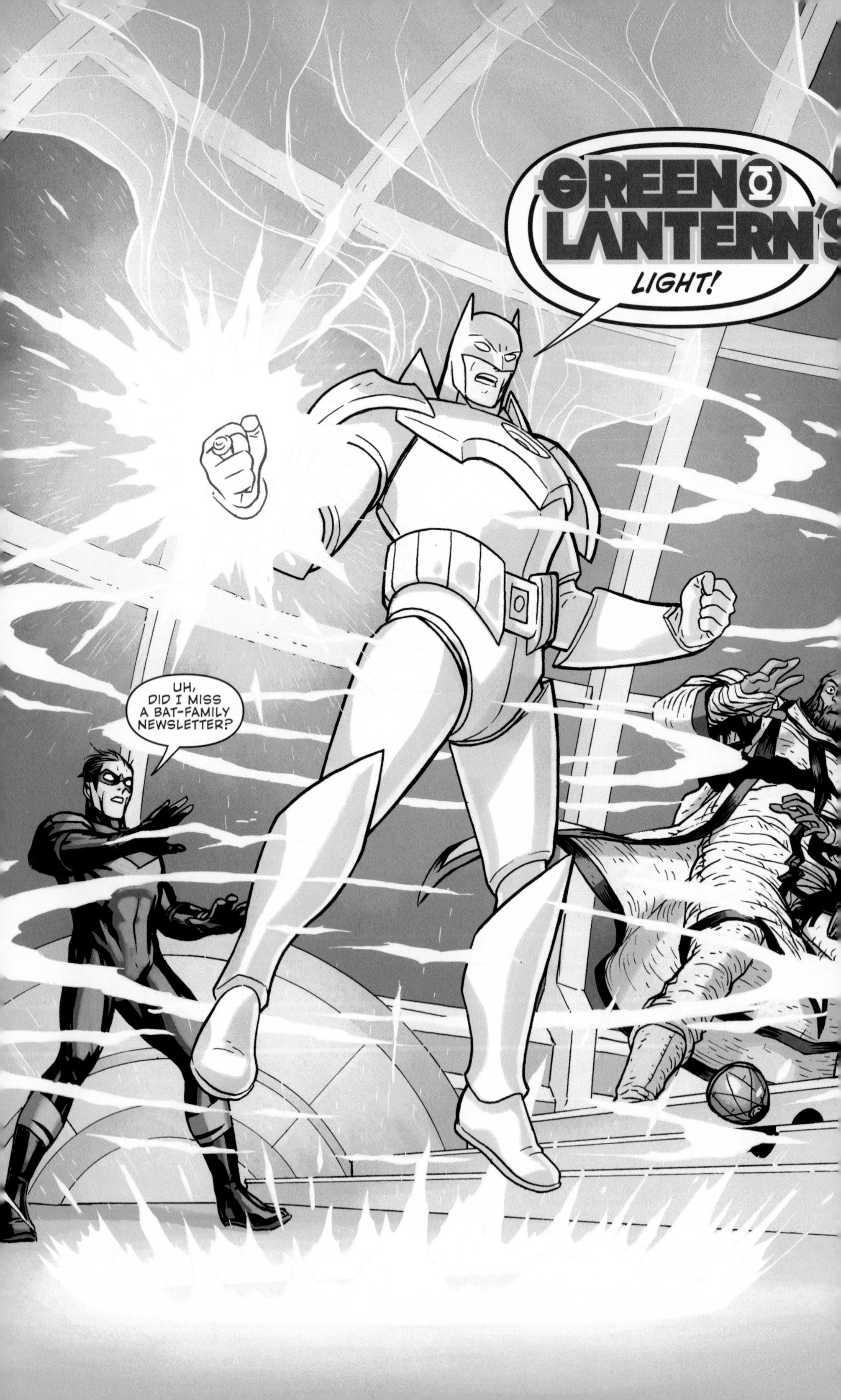

GREEN LANTERN'S
LIGHT!
UH, DID I MISS A BAT-FAMILY NEWSLETTER?

I'VE CHASED IT FOR CENTURIES!

WHY?

WHY DOES THE ANCIENT POWER RING PICK YOU?

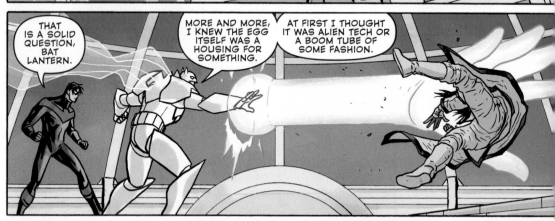

THAT IS A SOLID QUESTION, BAT LANTERN.

MORE AND MORE, I KNEW THE EGG ITSELF WAS A HOUSING FOR SOMETHING.

AT FIRST I THOUGHT IT WAS ALIEN TECH OR A BOOM TUBE OF SOME FASHION.

OMEGA ROD.

ACTUALLY, AT FIRST I WAS THINKING ZETA BEAMS FROM PLANET RANN.

OR A PIECE OF THE SOURCE WALL.

I THOUGHT THAT, TOO, BUT AFTER A RUN-IN WITH OUR GREEN LANTERN I WAS WITNESS TO SOME...BEHAVIOR FROM INSIDE THE EGG.

THAT'S WHEN IT SEEMED TO REALLY MISFIRE.

BUT THERE WAS A PATTERN. TO PROTECT.

I KNEW THE POWER SOURCE INSIDE WAS UNSTABLE AND THE PROGRAMMING FAULTY AND DANGEROUS.

IT WAS EITHER ANCIENT OR BROKEN OR BOTH.

BUT THIS--

THIS IS--

MORE THAN I THOUGHT.

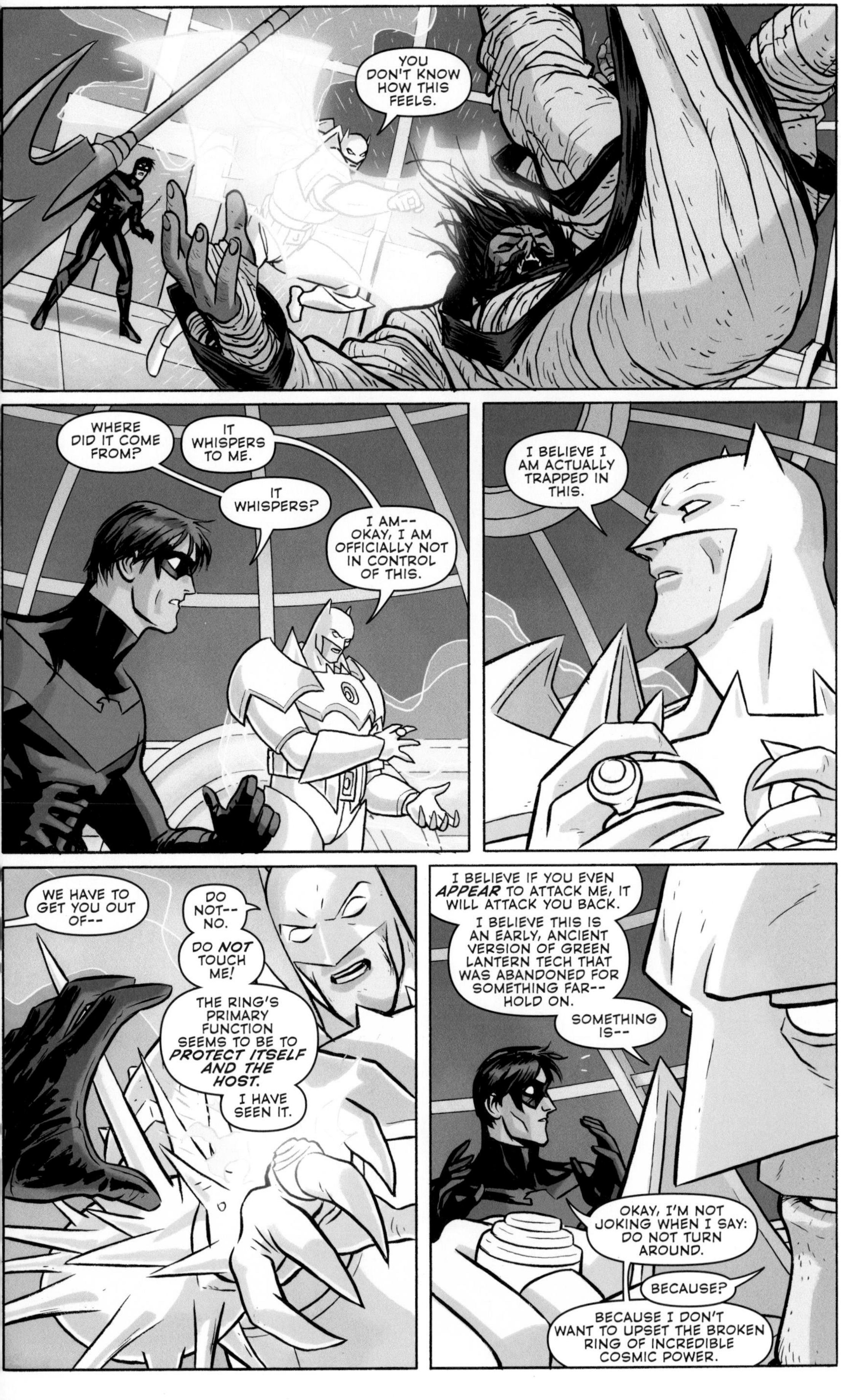
YOU DON'T KNOW HOW THIS FEELS.
WHERE DID IT COME FROM?
IT WHISPERS TO ME.
IT WHISPERS?
I AM-- OKAY, I AM OFFICIALLY NOT IN CONTROL OF THIS.
I BELIEVE I AM ACTUALLY TRAPPED IN THIS.
WE HAVE TO GET YOU OUT OF--
DO NOT-- NO.
DO NOT TOUCH ME!
THE RING'S PRIMARY FUNCTION SEEMS TO BE TO PROTECT ITSELF AND THE HOST.
I HAVE SEEN IT.
I BELIEVE IF YOU EVEN APPEAR TO ATTACK ME, IT WILL ATTACK YOU BACK.
I BELIEVE THIS IS AN EARLY, ANCIENT VERSION OF GREEN LANTERN TECH THAT WAS ABANDONED FOR SOMETHING FAR--
HOLD ON.
SOMETHING IS--
OKAY, I'M NOT JOKING WHEN I SAY: DO NOT TURN AROUND.
BECAUSE?
BECAUSE I DON'T WANT TO UPSET THE BROKEN RING OF INCREDIBLE COSMIC POWER.

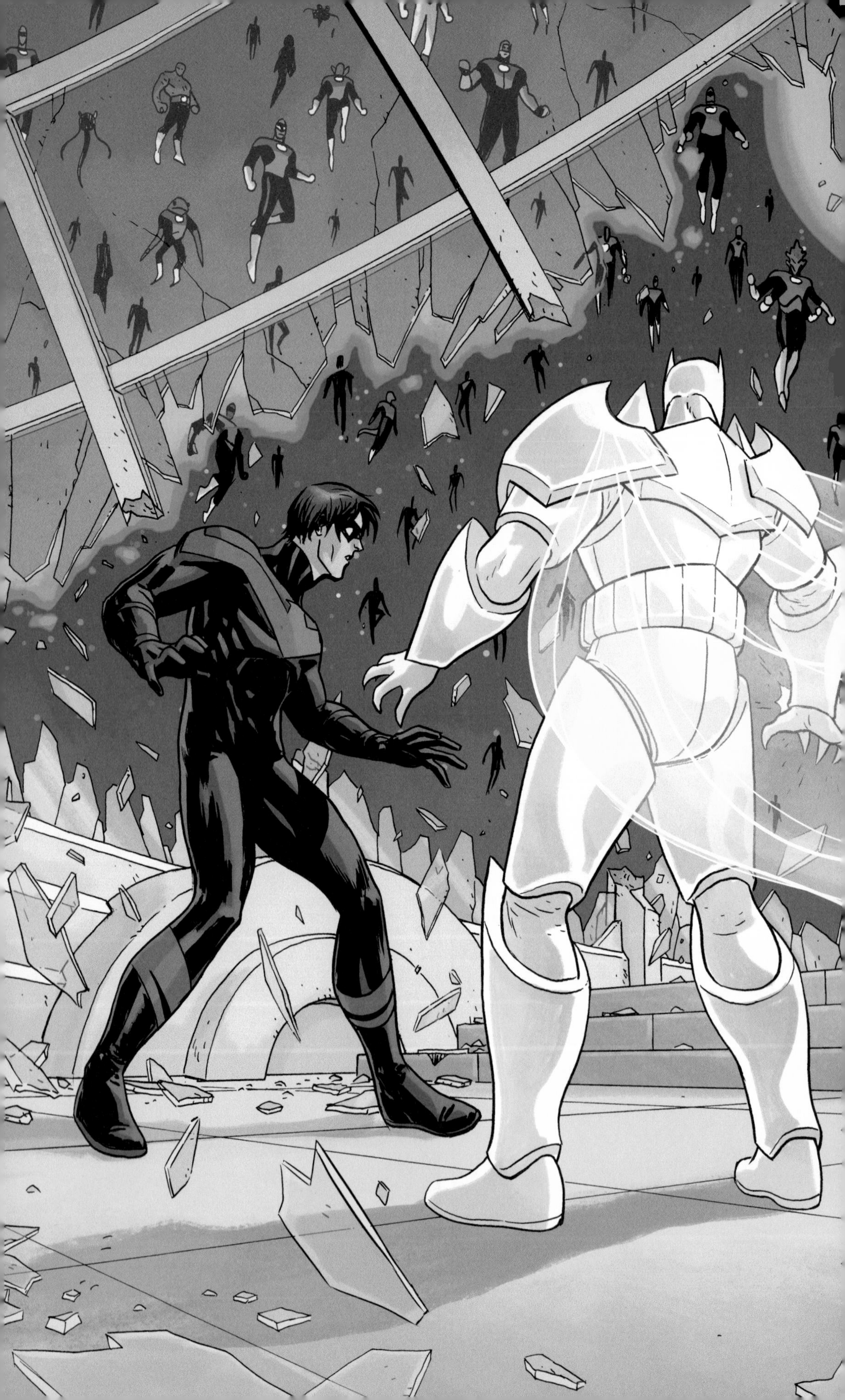

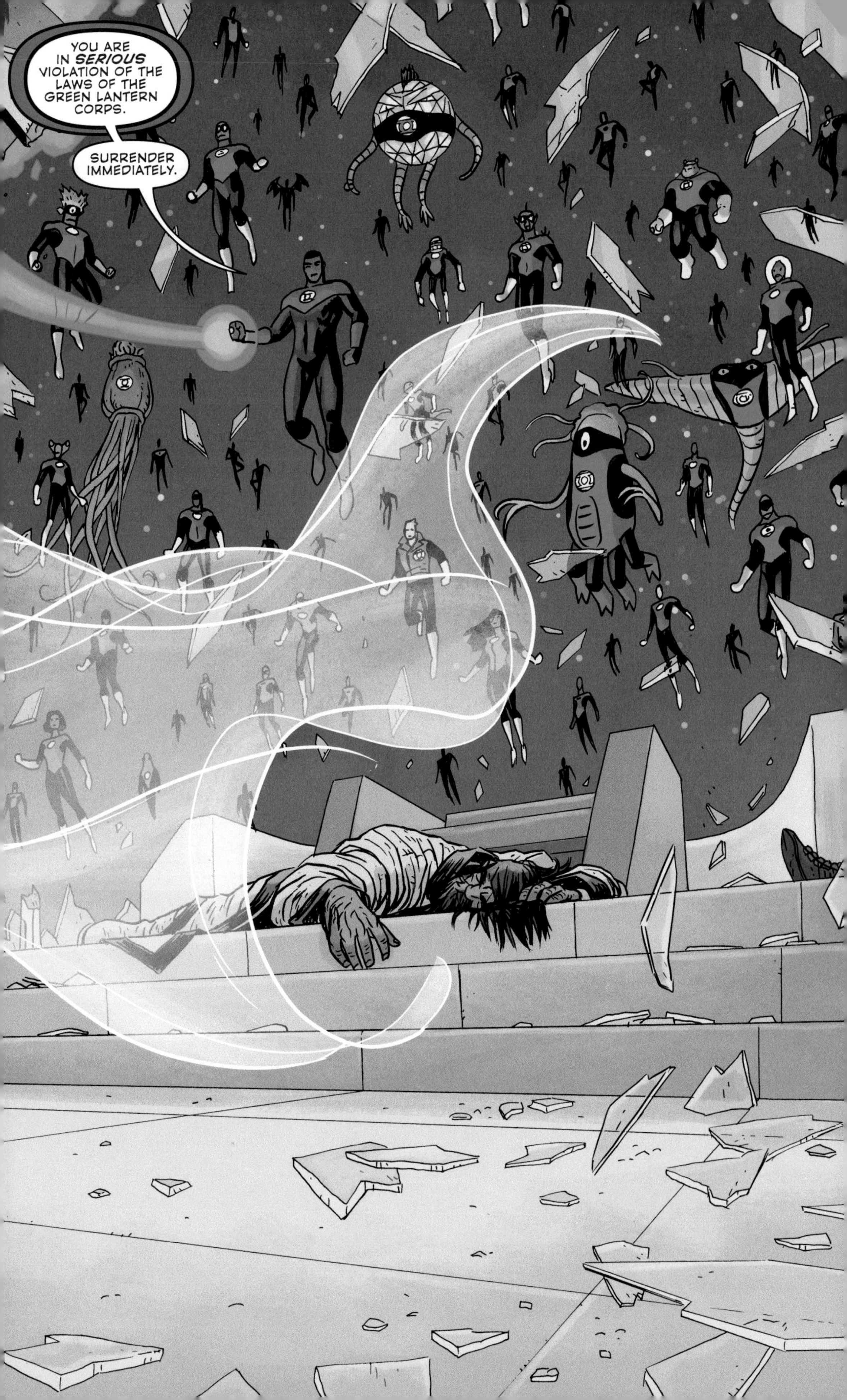
YOU ARE IN SERIOUS VIOLATION OF THE LAWS OF THE GREEN LANTERN CORPS.
SURRENDER IMMEDIATELY.

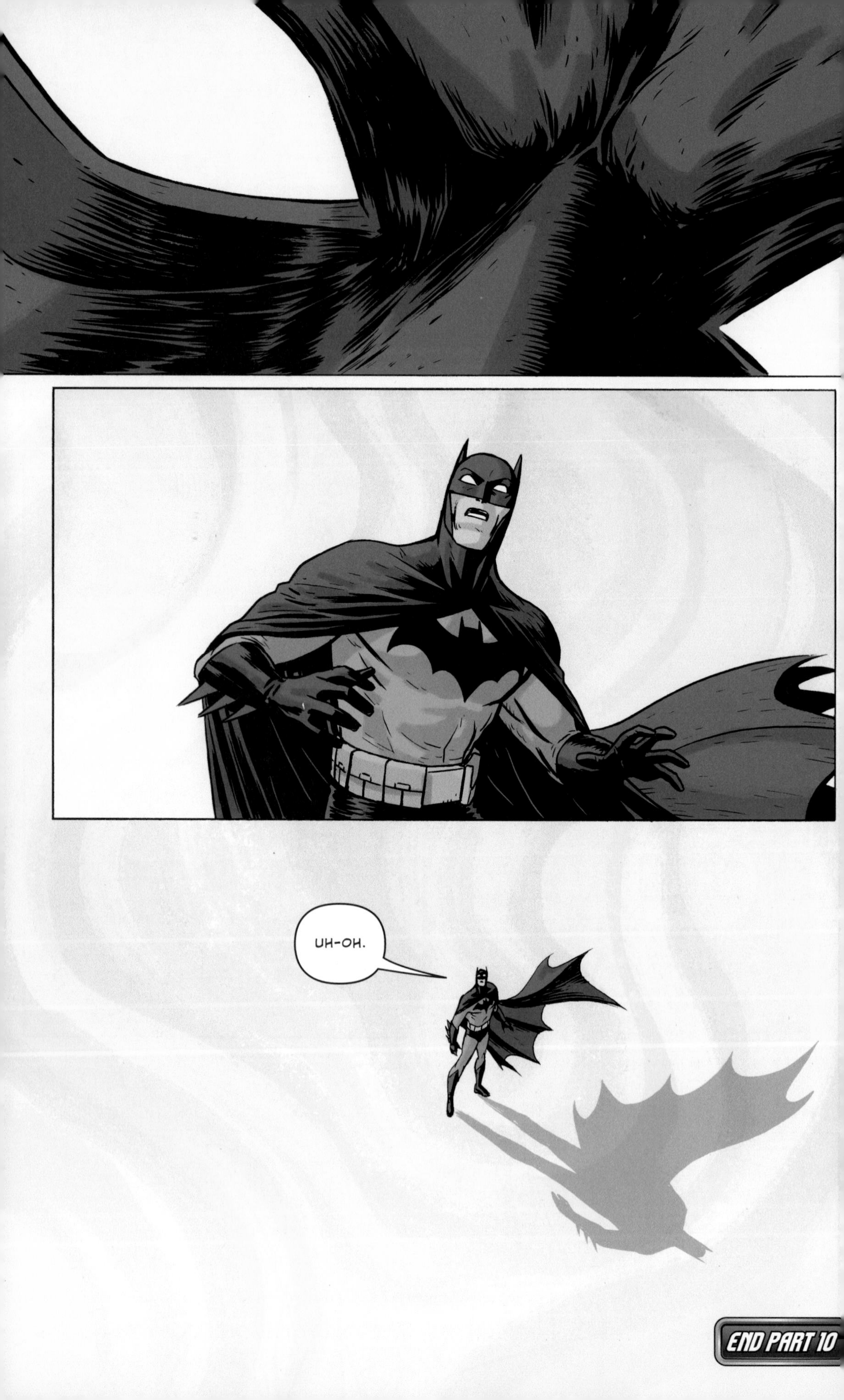
UH-OH.
END PART 10

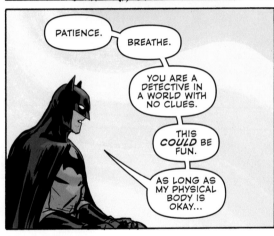

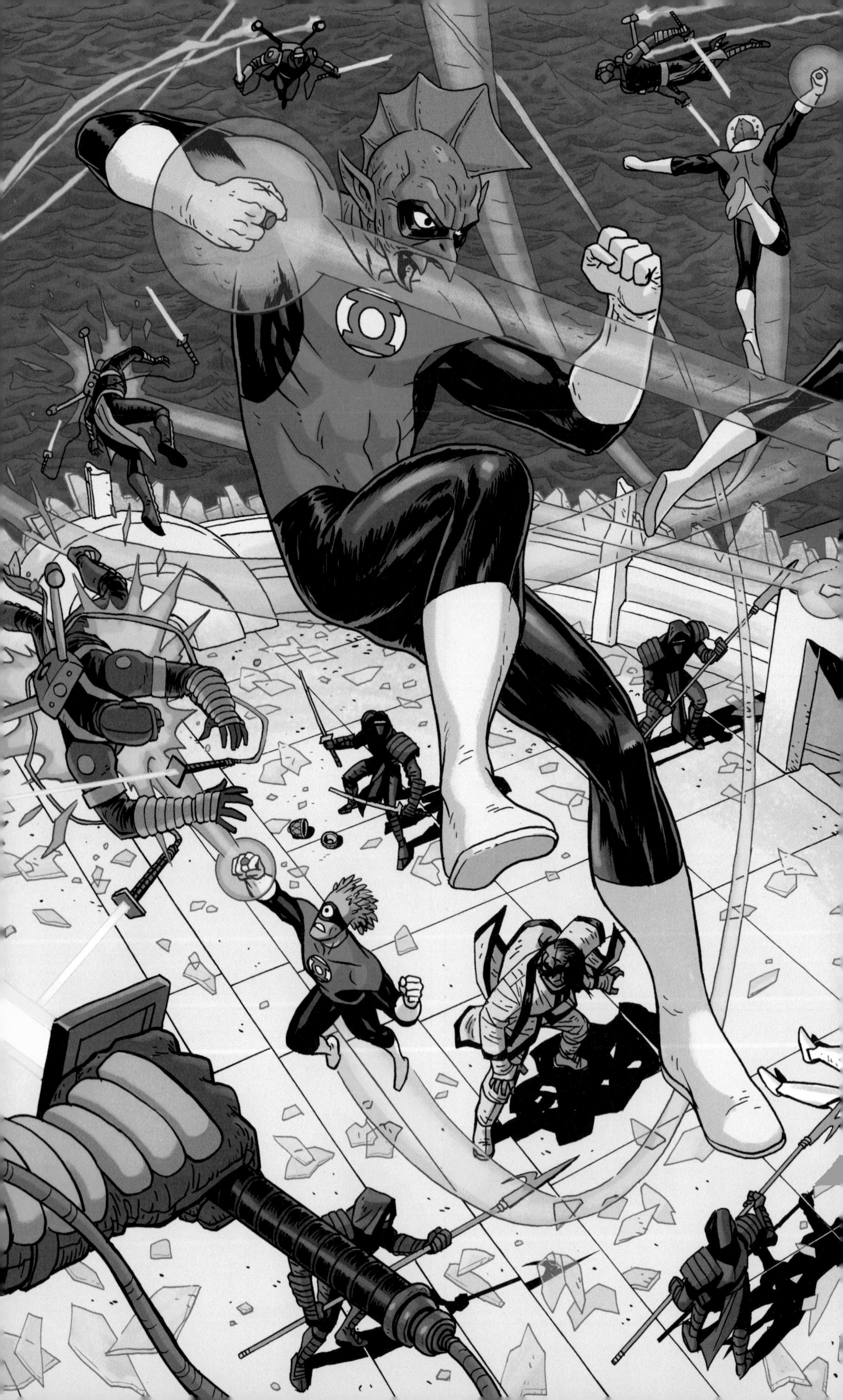

IN BRIGHTEST DAY, IN BLACKEST NIGHT.

NO EVIL SHALL ESCAPE MY—

GUARDIAN OF *OA*, I AM BATMAN.

OF THE PLANET EARTH.

WHAT DO I CALL YOU?

GREETING, BATMAN OF EARTH.

CONGRATULA*TIONS* ON BEING SELECTED AS THE PROTE*CTOR* OF *THE* GALAXY.

THANK YOU.

HOW WAS I SELECTED?

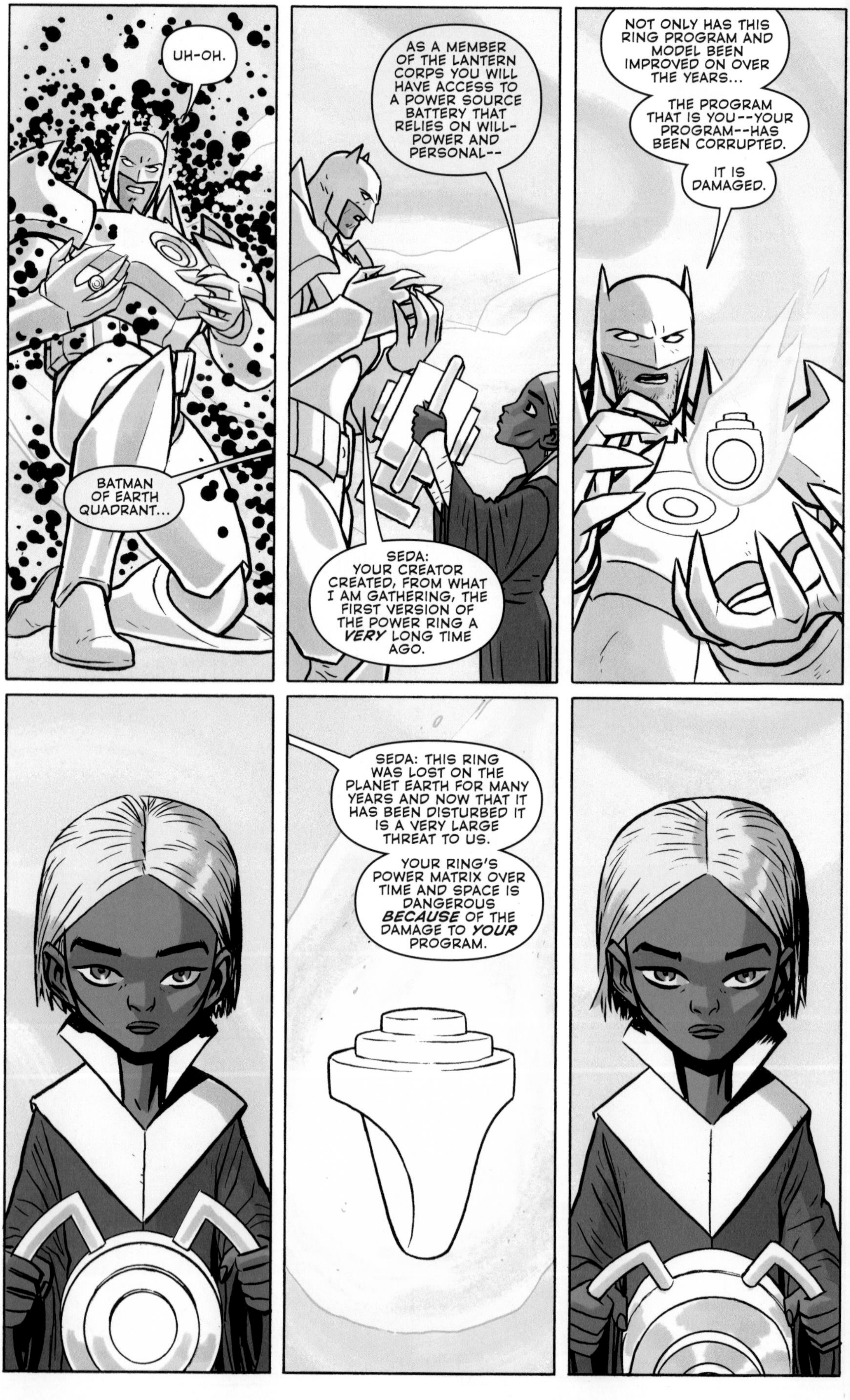
UH-OH.
BATMAN OF EARTH QUADRANT...
AS A MEMBER OF THE LANTERN CORPS YOU WILL HAVE ACCESS TO A POWER SOURCE BATTERY THAT RELIES ON WILL-POWER AND PERSONAL--
SEDA: YOUR CREATOR CREATED, FROM WHAT I AM GATHERING, THE FIRST VERSION OF THE POWER RING A VERY LONG TIME AGO.
NOT ONLY HAS THIS RING PROGRAM AND MODEL BEEN IMPROVED ON OVER THE YEARS...
THE PROGRAM THAT IS YOU--YOUR PROGRAM--HAS BEEN CORRUPTED.
IT IS DAMAGED.
SEDA: THIS RING WAS LOST ON THE PLANET EARTH FOR MANY YEARS AND NOW THAT IT HAS BEEN DISTURBED IT IS A VERY LARGE THREAT TO US.
YOUR RING'S POWER MATRIX OVER TIME AND SPACE IS DANGEROUS BECAUSE OF THE DAMAGE TO YOUR PROGRAM.

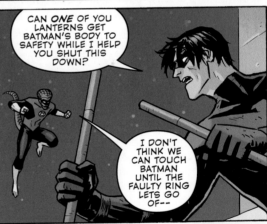

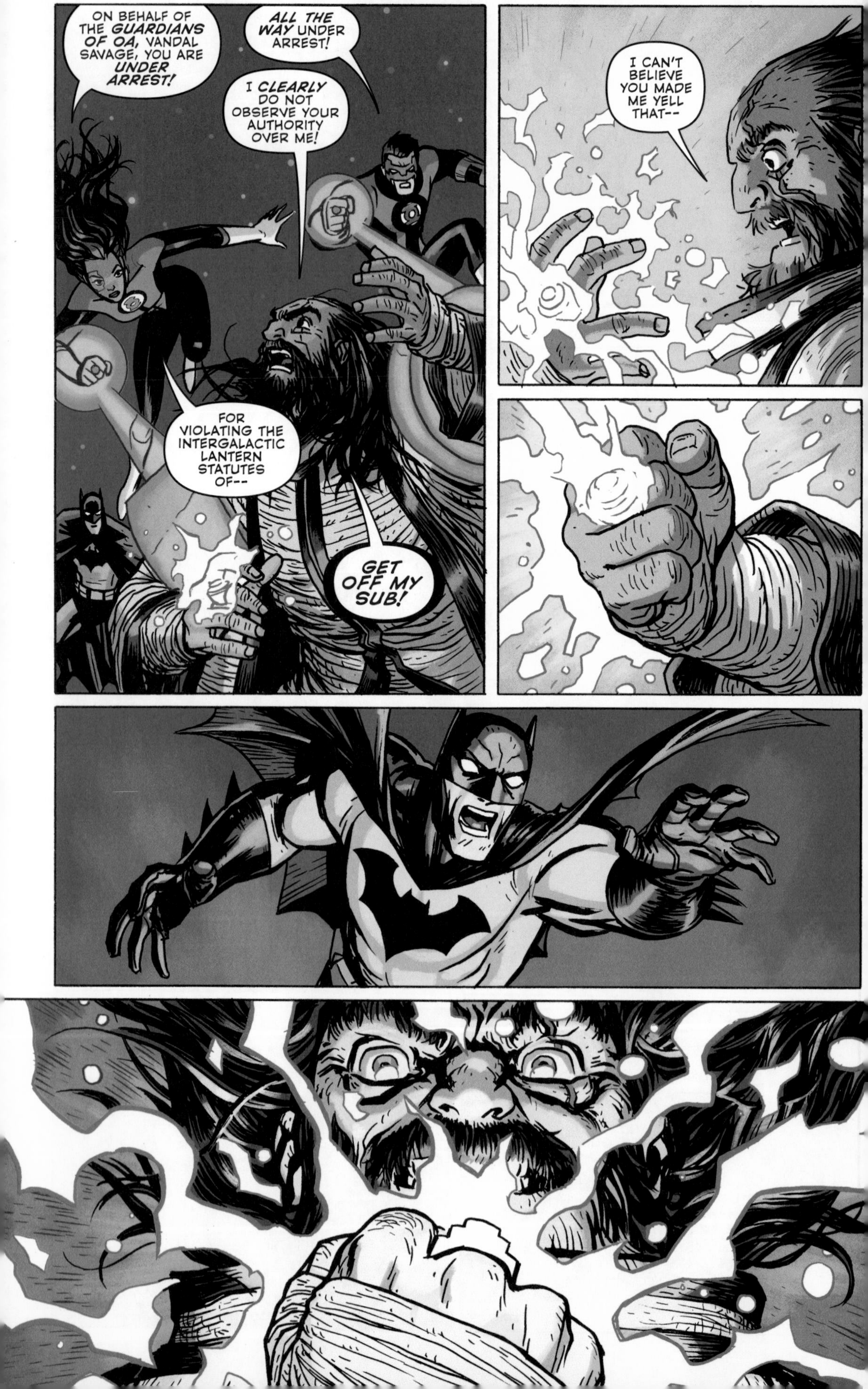
ON BEHALF OF THE GUARDIANS OF OA, VANDAL SAVAGE, YOU ARE UNDER ARREST!
ALL THE WAY UNDER ARREST!
I CLEARLY DO NOT OBSERVE YOUR AUTHORITY OVER ME!
FOR VIOLATING THE INTERGALACTIC LANTERN STATUTES OF--
GET OFF MY SUB!
I CAN'T BELIEVE YOU MADE ME YELL THAT--

THAT'S HIM?

WAKE HIM.

HE *IS* AWAKE.

POFFT!

AND RATHER ANGRY.

AGH! AGH!

DEAR LORD!

SO HAVE YOU NEVER HEARD OF PROFESSIONAL COURTESY?

THAT'S *NOT* ONE OF MY TRADEMARK RIDDLES, DEATHSTROKE...

I REEEEEALLY WANT TO KNOW.

I'M NOT A THIEF LIKE YOU, RIDDLER.

I'M FOR HIRE.

AND I WAS PAID *A LOT* OF MONEY TO HUNT *YOU* DOWN AND BRING YOU HERE TO GOTHAM.

GOTHAM? SLADE!

IF--IF THE ROLES WERE REVERSED, *I WOULD HAVE GIVEN YOU A* HEADS-UP AND A--

TSSS

WHERE IS *VANDAL SAVAGE?*

YOU RECENTLY STOLE AN ANTIQUE EGG OUT OF THE GOTHAM MUSEUM.

WE KNOW YOU SOLD IT TO AN IMMORTAL MANIAC NAMED VANDAL SAVAGE IN AMSTERDAM.

WHERE IS VANDAL SAVAGE NOW?

WHAT THE HELL?

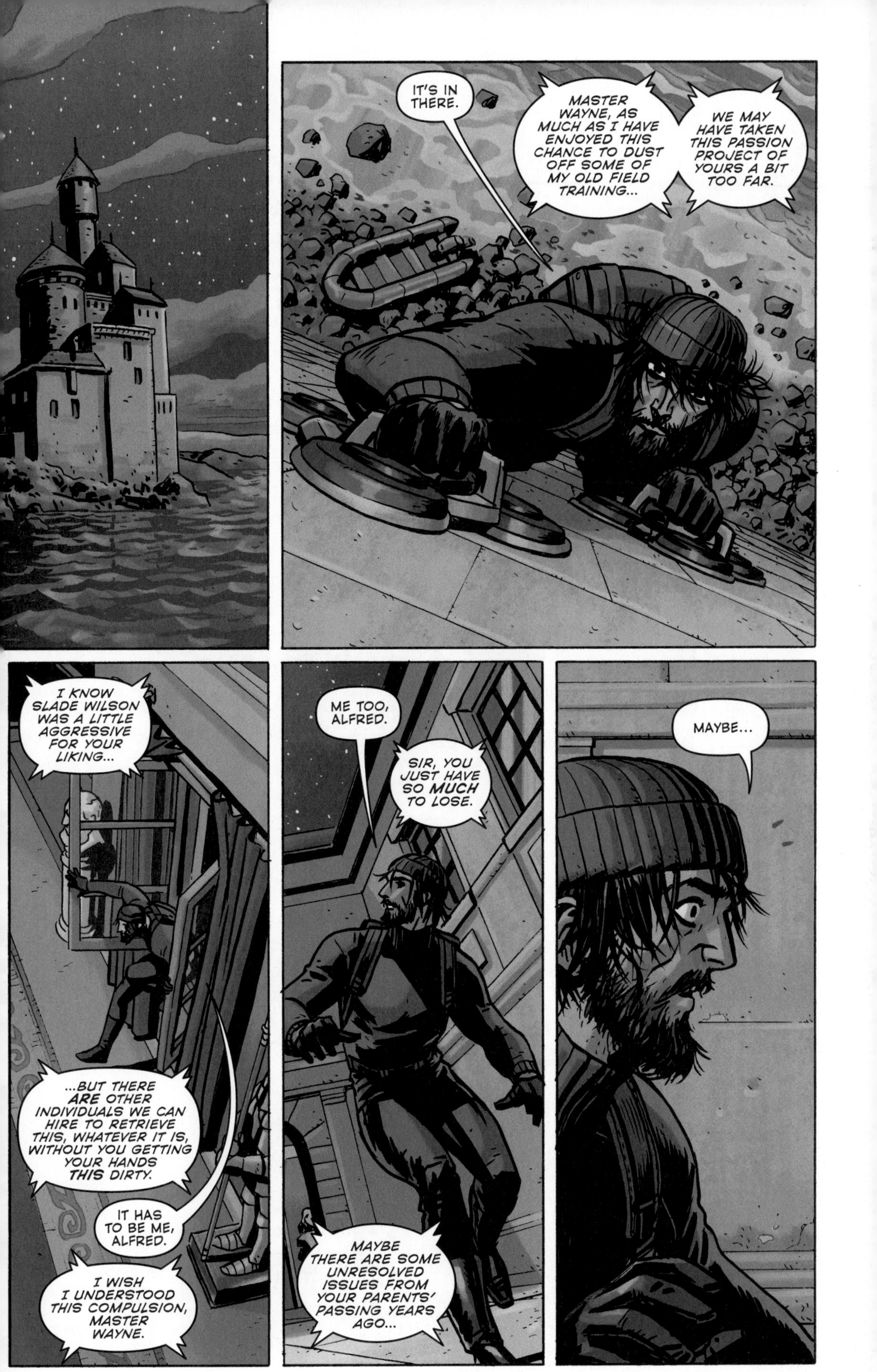
IT'S IN THERE.
MASTER WAYNE, AS MUCH AS I HAVE ENJOYED THIS CHANCE TO DUST OFF SOME OF MY OLD FIELD TRAINING...
WE MAY HAVE TAKEN THIS PASSION PROJECT OF YOURS A BIT TOO FAR.
I KNOW SLADE WILSON WAS A LITTLE AGGRESSIVE FOR YOUR LIKING...
...BUT THERE ARE OTHER INDIVIDUALS WE CAN HIRE TO RETRIEVE THIS, WHATEVER IT IS, WITHOUT YOU GETTING YOUR HANDS THIS DIRTY.
IT HAS TO BE ME, ALFRED.
I WISH I UNDERSTOOD THIS COMPULSION, MASTER WAYNE.
ME TOO, ALFRED.
SIR, YOU JUST HAVE SO MUCH TO LOSE.
MAYBE THERE ARE SOME UNRESOLVED ISSUES FROM YOUR PARENTS' PASSING YEARS AGO...
MAYBE...

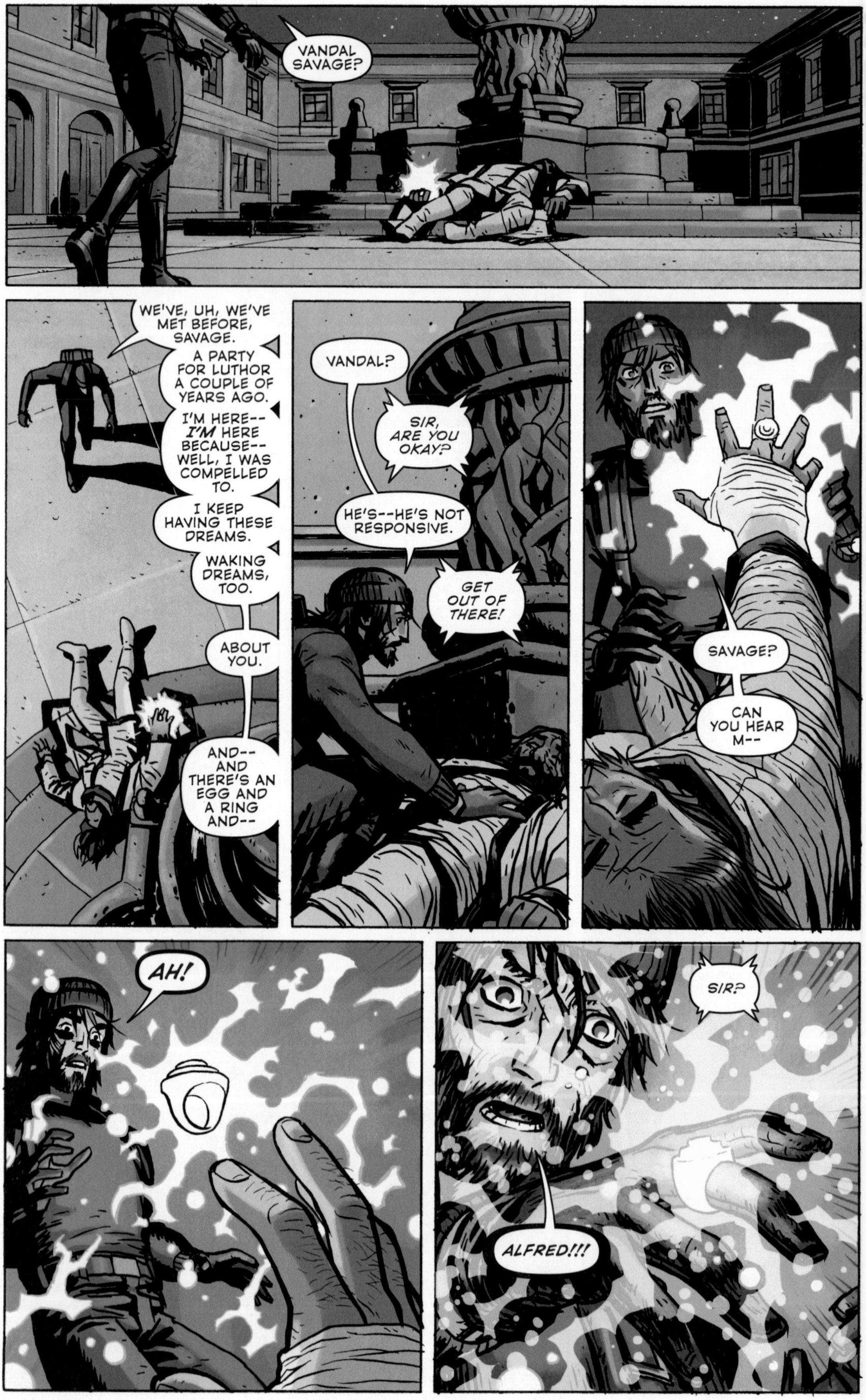
VANDAL SAVAGE?
WE'VE, UH, WE'VE MET BEFORE, SAVAGE.
A PARTY FOR LUTHOR A COUPLE OF YEARS AGO.
I'M HERE-- I'M HERE BECAUSE-- WELL, I WAS COMPELLED TO.
I KEEP HAVING THESE DREAMS.
WAKING DREAMS, TOO.
ABOUT YOU.
AND-- AND THERE'S AN EGG AND A RING AND--
VANDAL?
SIR, ARE YOU OKAY?
HE'S--HE'S NOT RESPONSIVE.
GET OUT OF THERE!
SAVAGE?
CAN YOU HEAR M--
AH!
SIR?
ALFRED!!!

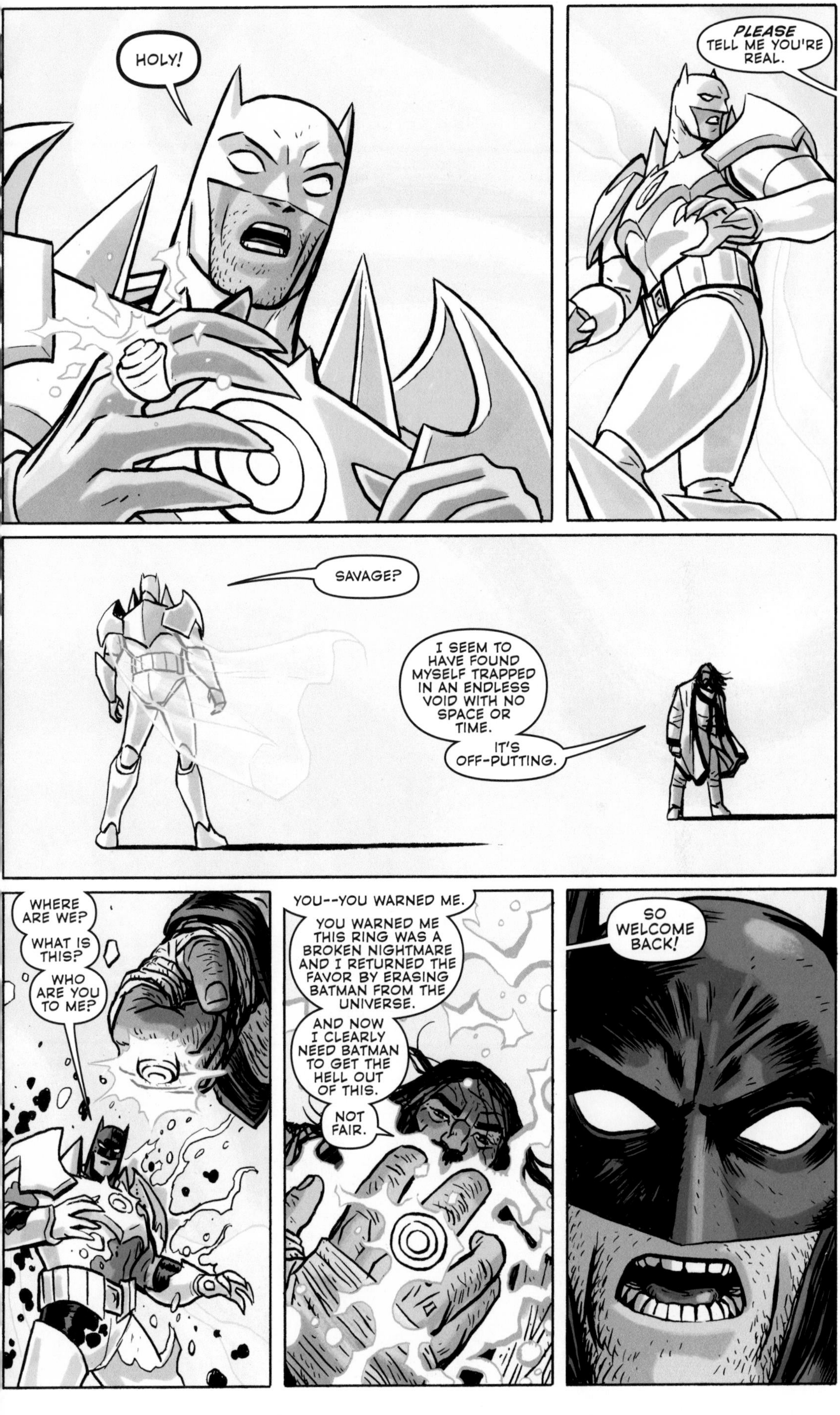
HOLY!
PLEASE TELL ME YOU'RE REAL.
SAVAGE?
I SEEM TO HAVE FOUND MYSELF TRAPPED IN AN ENDLESS VOID WITH NO SPACE OR TIME.
IT'S OFF-PUTTING.
WHERE ARE WE?
WHAT IS THIS?
WHO ARE YOU TO ME?
YOU--YOU WARNED ME.
YOU WARNED ME THIS RING WAS A BROKEN NIGHTMARE AND I RETURNED THE FAVOR BY ERASING BATMAN FROM THE UNIVERSE.
AND NOW I CLEARLY NEED BATMAN TO GET THE HELL OUT OF THIS.
NOT FAIR.
SO WELCOME BACK!

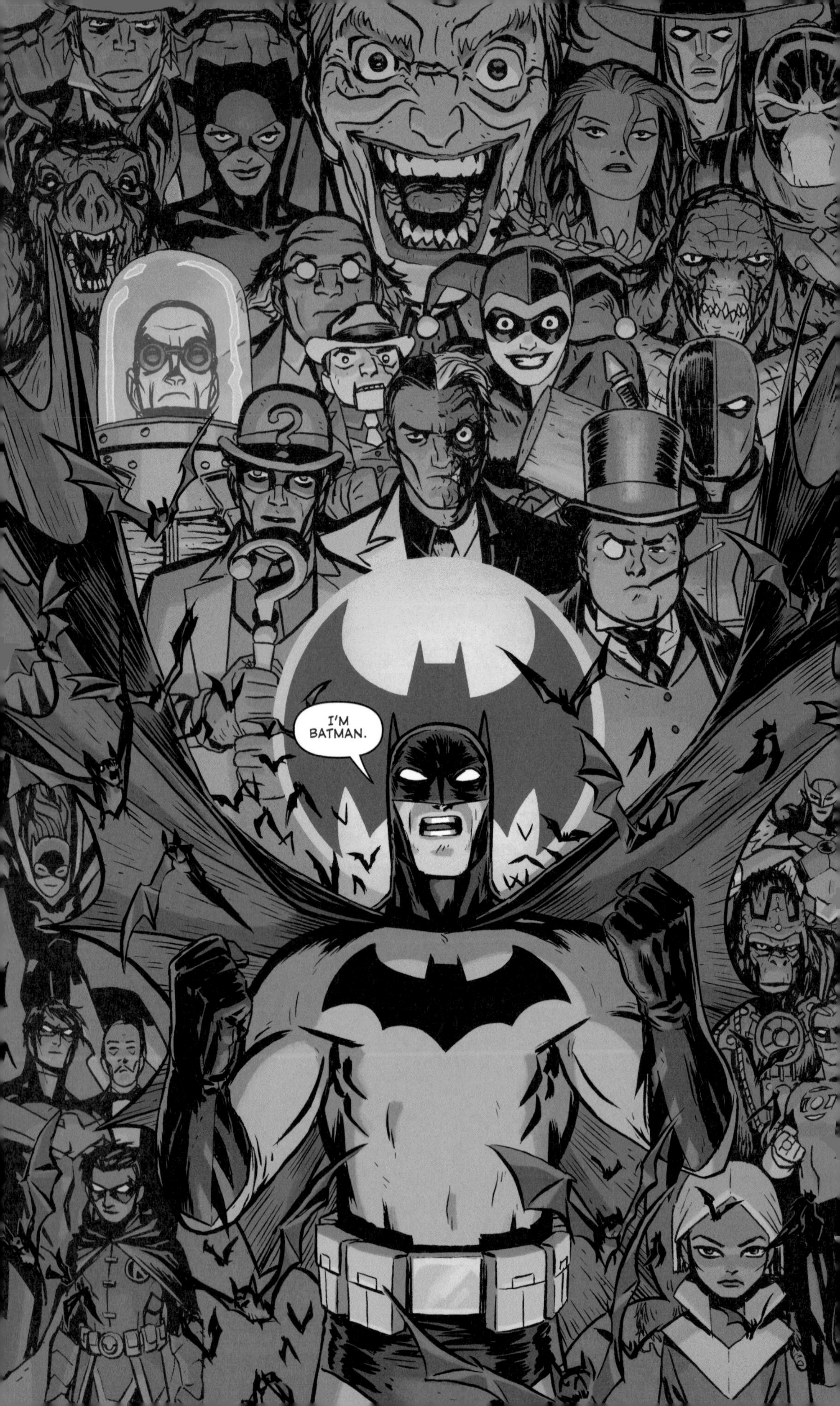
I'M BATMAN.

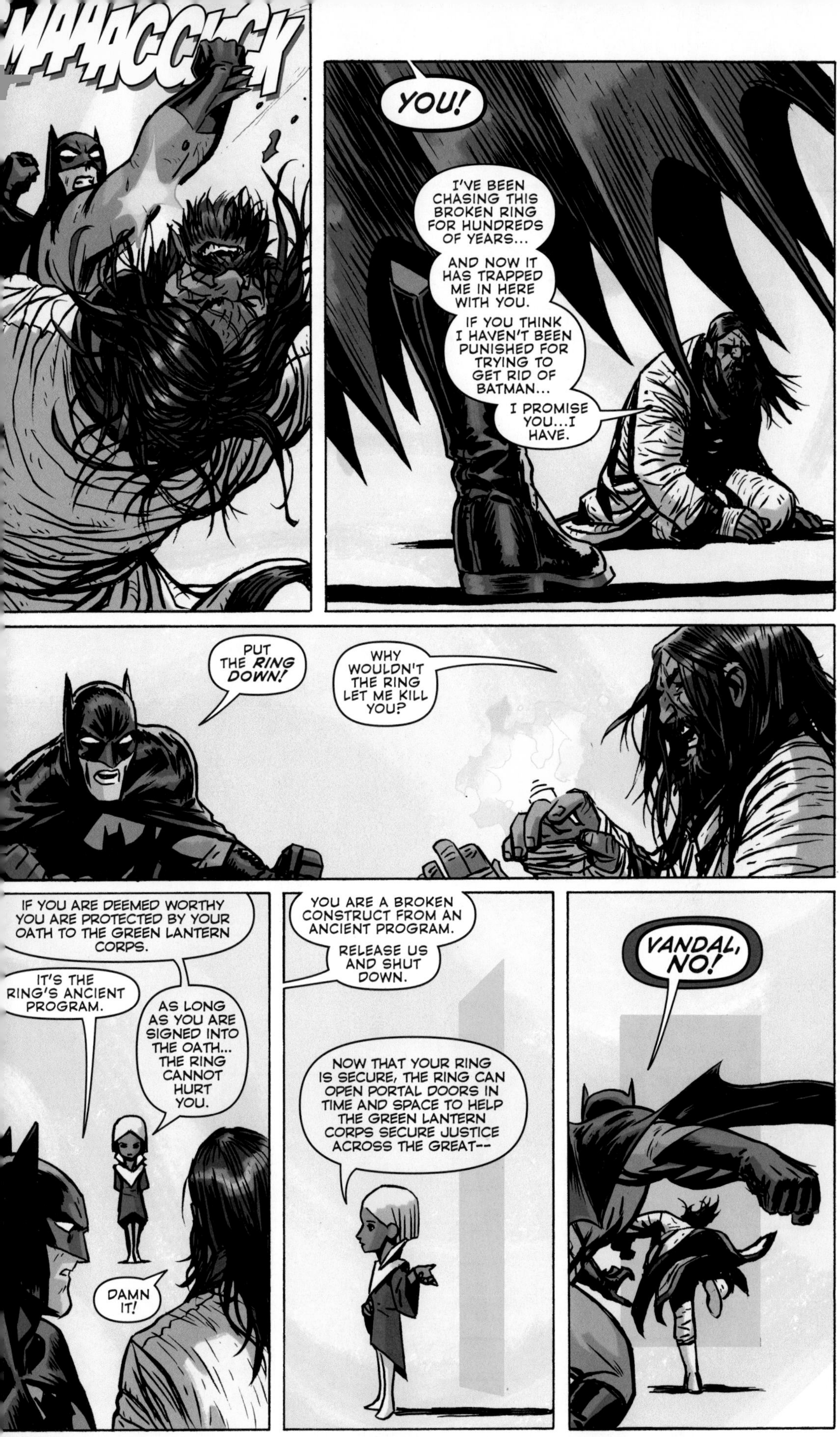
SHMAAACCKCK
YOU!
I'VE BEEN CHASING THIS BROKEN RING FOR HUNDREDS OF YEARS...
AND NOW IT HAS TRAPPED ME IN HERE WITH YOU.
IF YOU THINK I HAVEN'T BEEN PUNISHED FOR TRYING TO GET RID OF BATMAN...
I PROMISE YOU...I HAVE.
PUT THE RING DOWN!
WHY WOULDN'T THE RING LET ME KILL YOU?
IF YOU ARE DEEMED WORTHY YOU ARE PROTECTED BY YOUR OATH TO THE GREEN LANTERN CORPS.
IT'S THE RING'S ANCIENT PROGRAM.
AS LONG AS YOU ARE SIGNED INTO THE OATH... THE RING CANNOT HURT YOU.
DAMN IT!
YOU ARE A BROKEN CONSTRUCT FROM AN ANCIENT PROGRAM.
RELEASE US AND SHUT DOWN.
NOW THAT YOUR RING IS SECURE, THE RING CAN OPEN PORTAL DOORS IN TIME AND SPACE TO HELP THE GREEN LANTERN CORPS SECURE JUSTICE ACROSS THE GREAT--
VANDAL, NO!

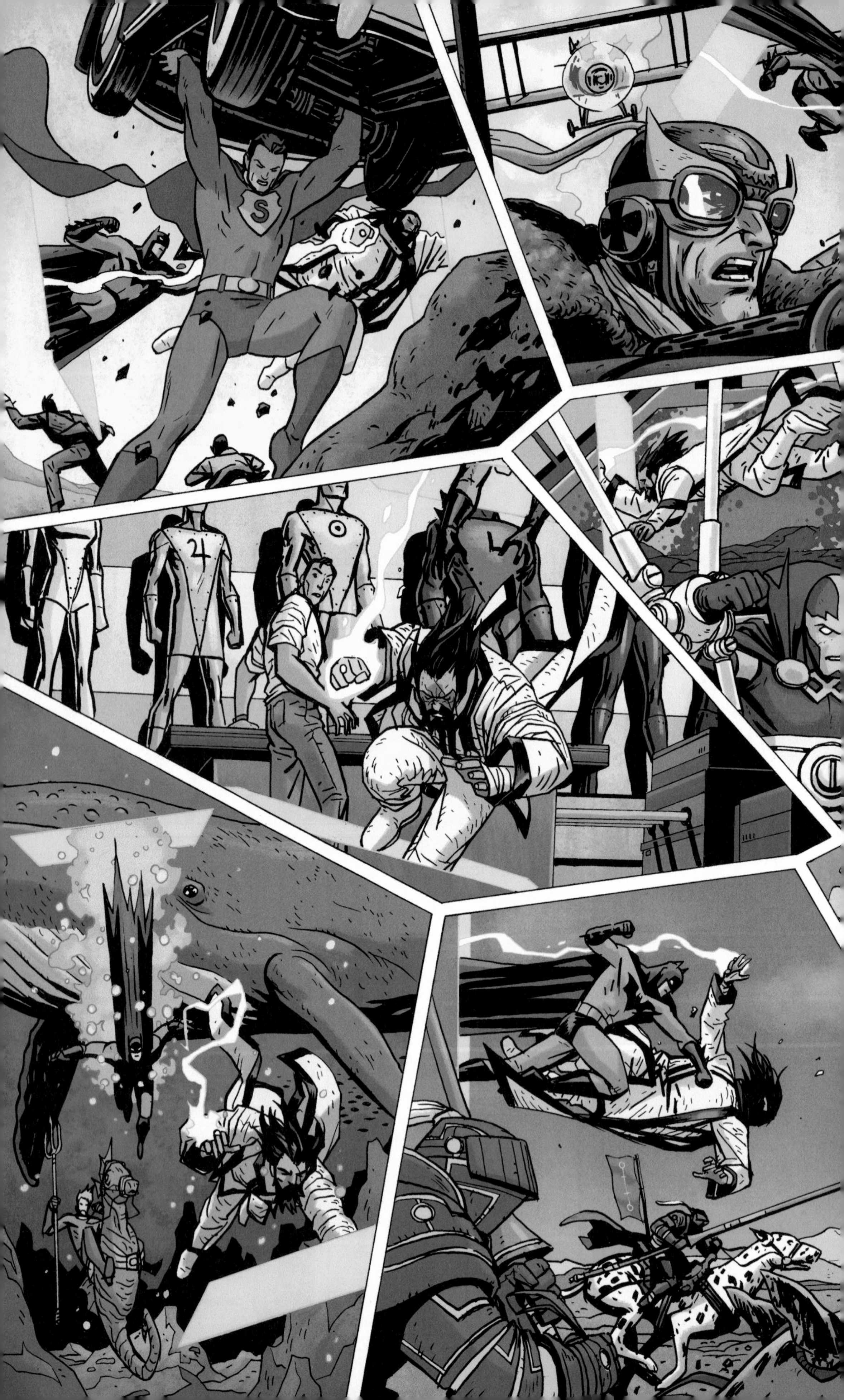

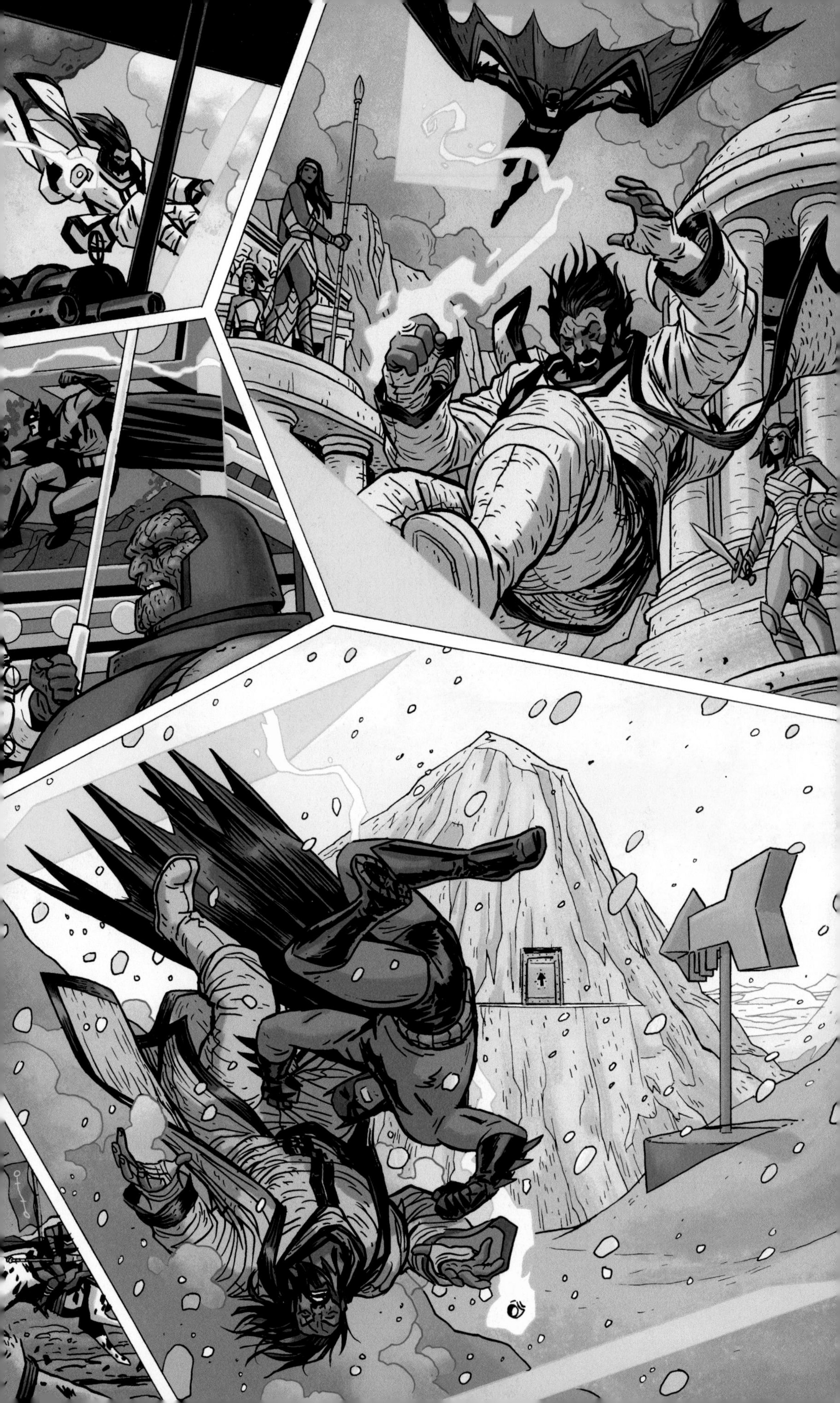

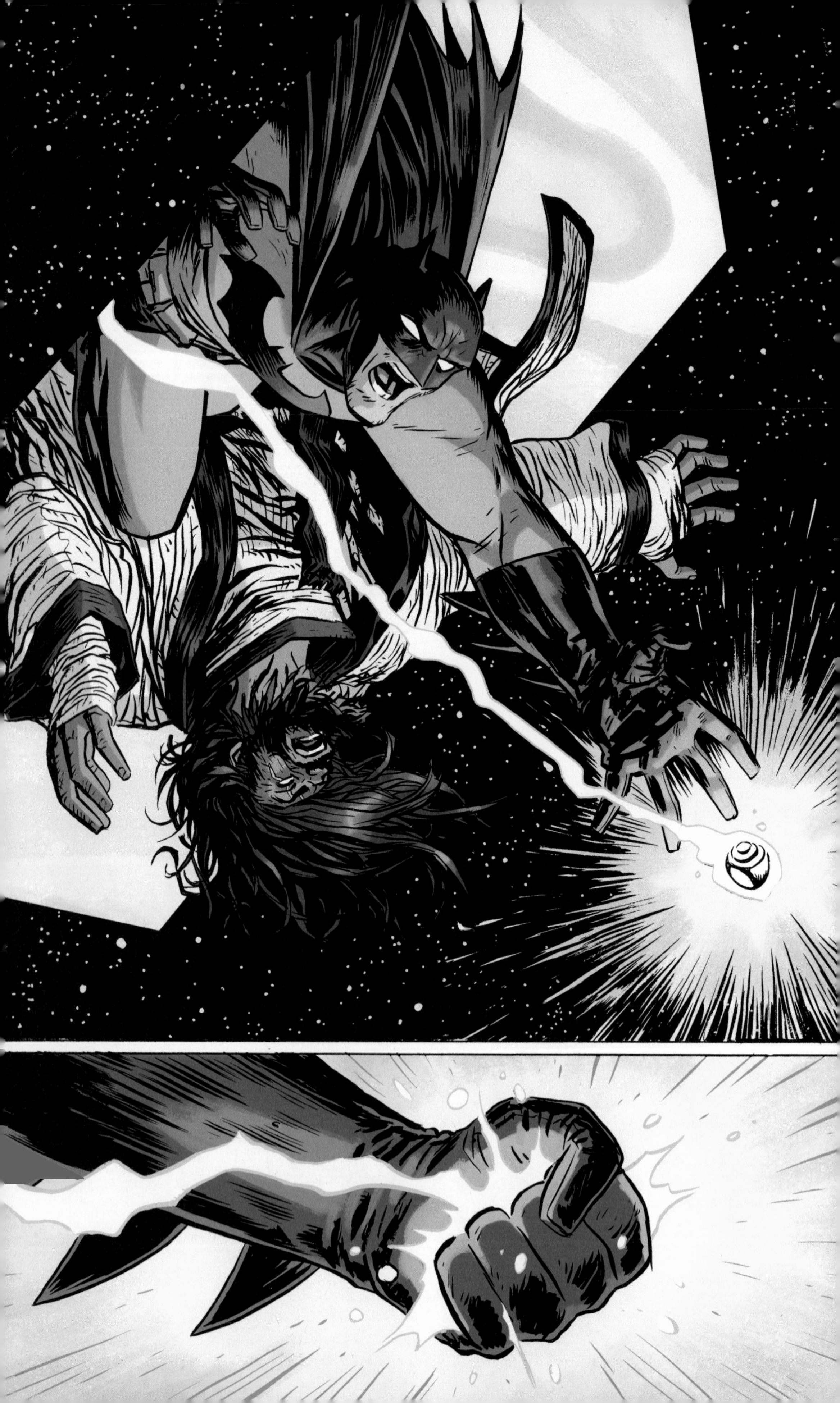

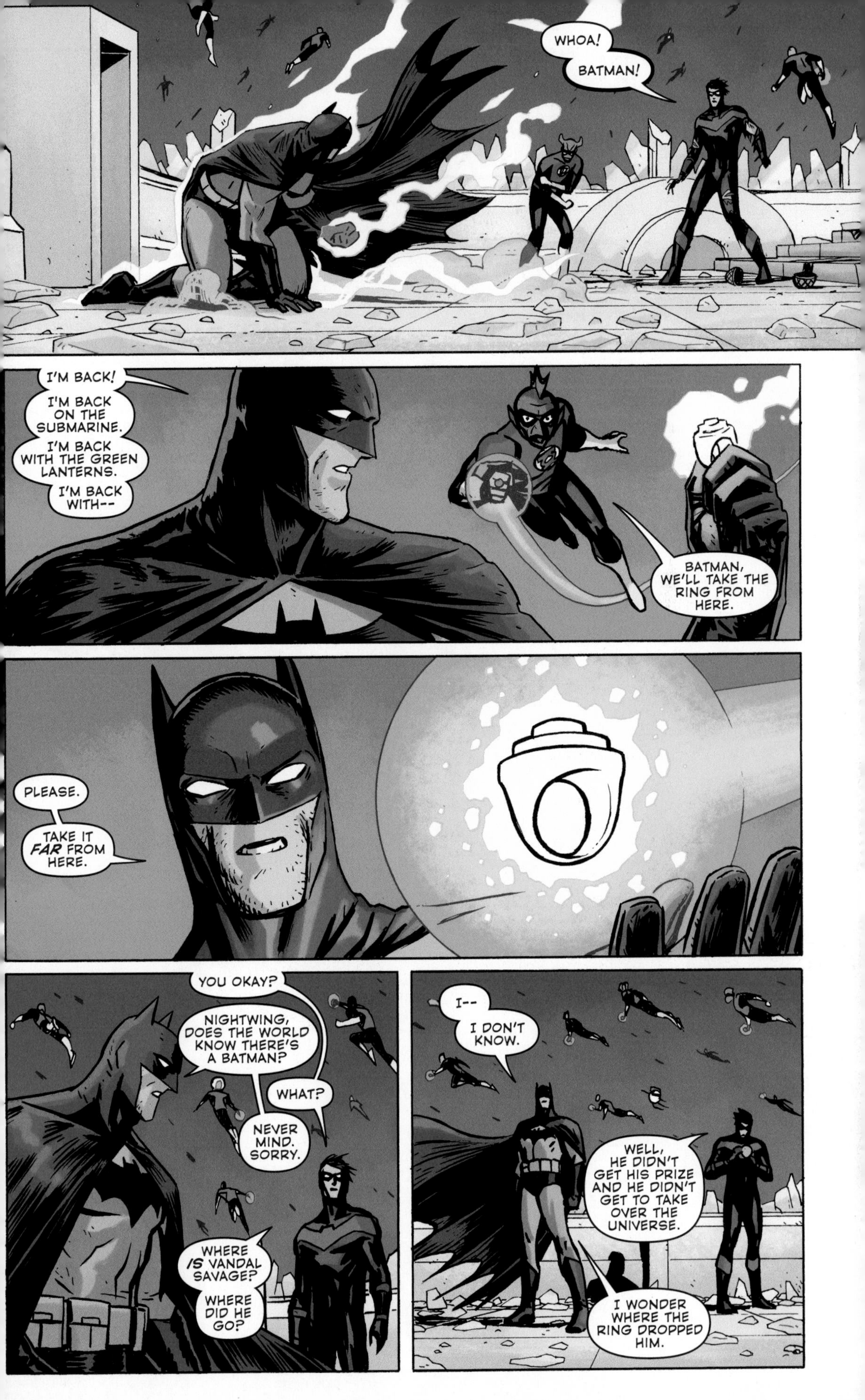
WHOA!
BATMAN!
I'M BACK!
I'M BACK ON THE SUBMARINE.
I'M BACK WITH THE GREEN LANTERNS.
I'M BACK WITH--
BATMAN, WE'LL TAKE THE RING FROM HERE.
PLEASE.
TAKE IT FAR FROM HERE.
YOU OKAY?
NIGHTWING, DOES THE WORLD KNOW THERE'S A BATMAN?
WHAT?
NEVER MIND. SORRY.
WHERE IS VANDAL SAVAGE?
WHERE DID HE GO?
I--
I DON'T KNOW.
WELL, HE DIDN'T GET HIS PRIZE AND HE DIDN'T GET TO TAKE OVER THE UNIVERSE.
I WONDER WHERE THE RING DROPPED HIM.

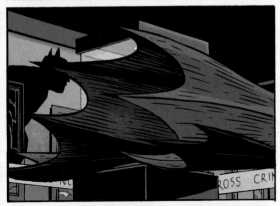

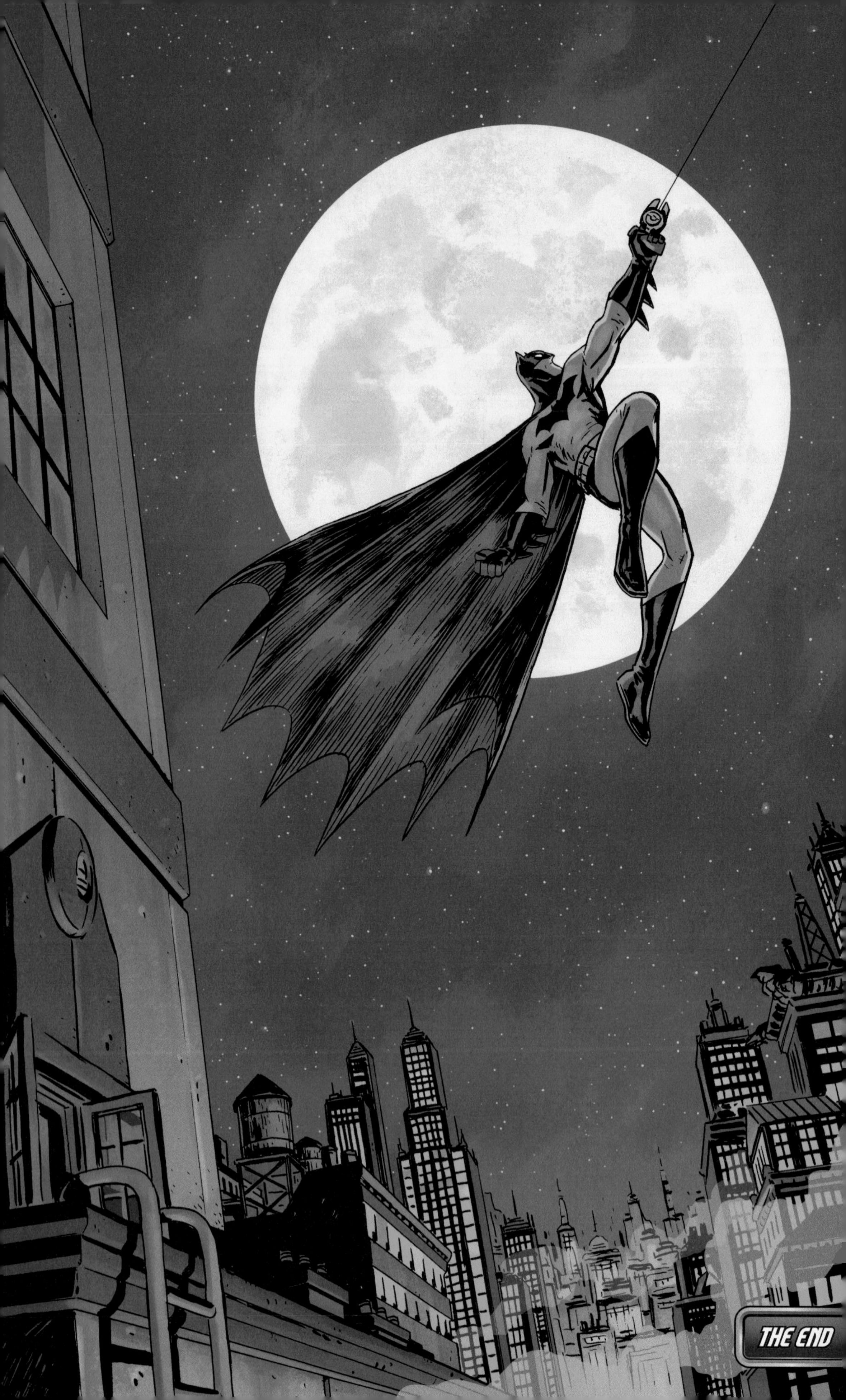
THE END

BATMAN: UNIVERSE COVER GALLERY BY
NICK DERINGTON

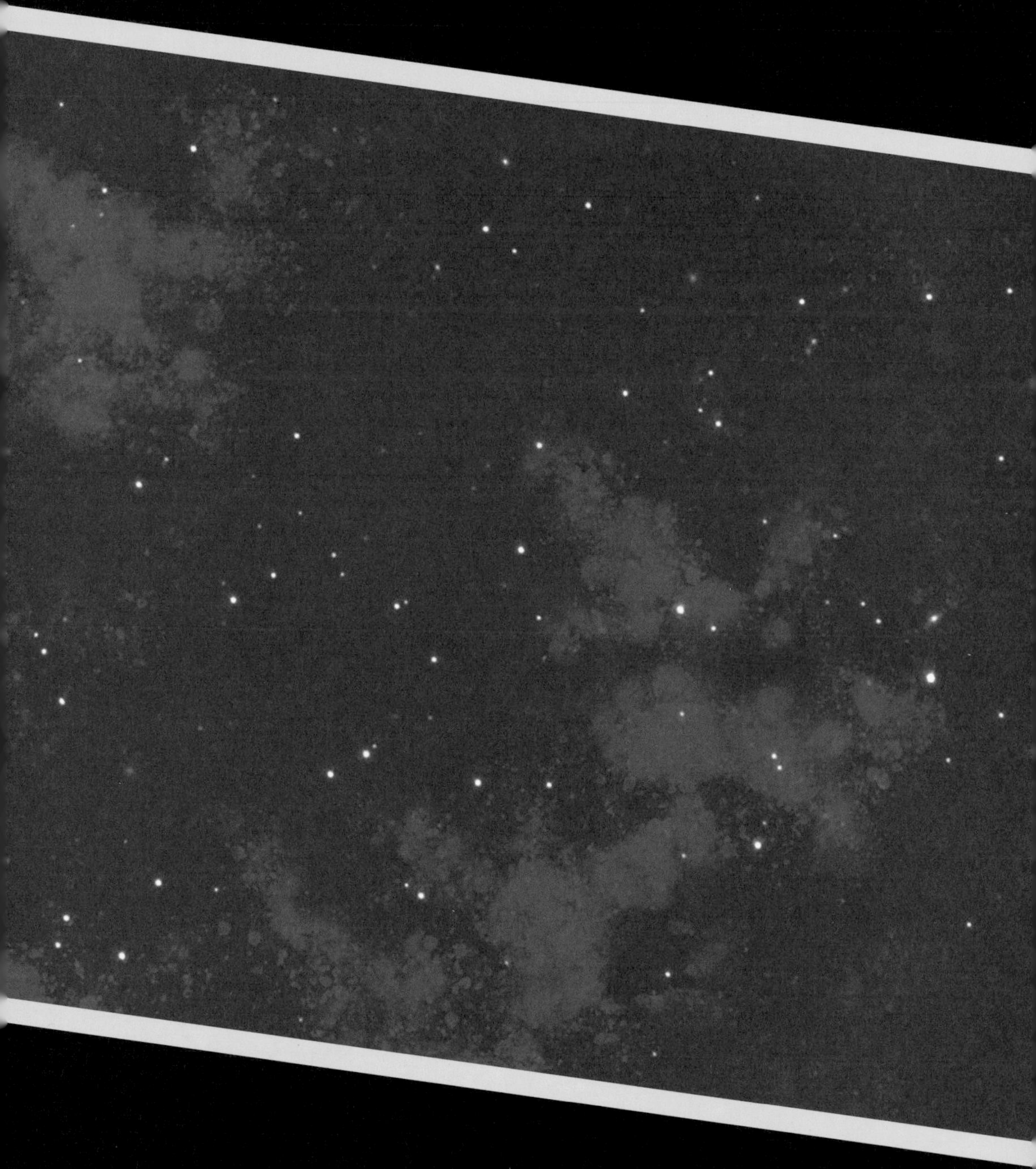

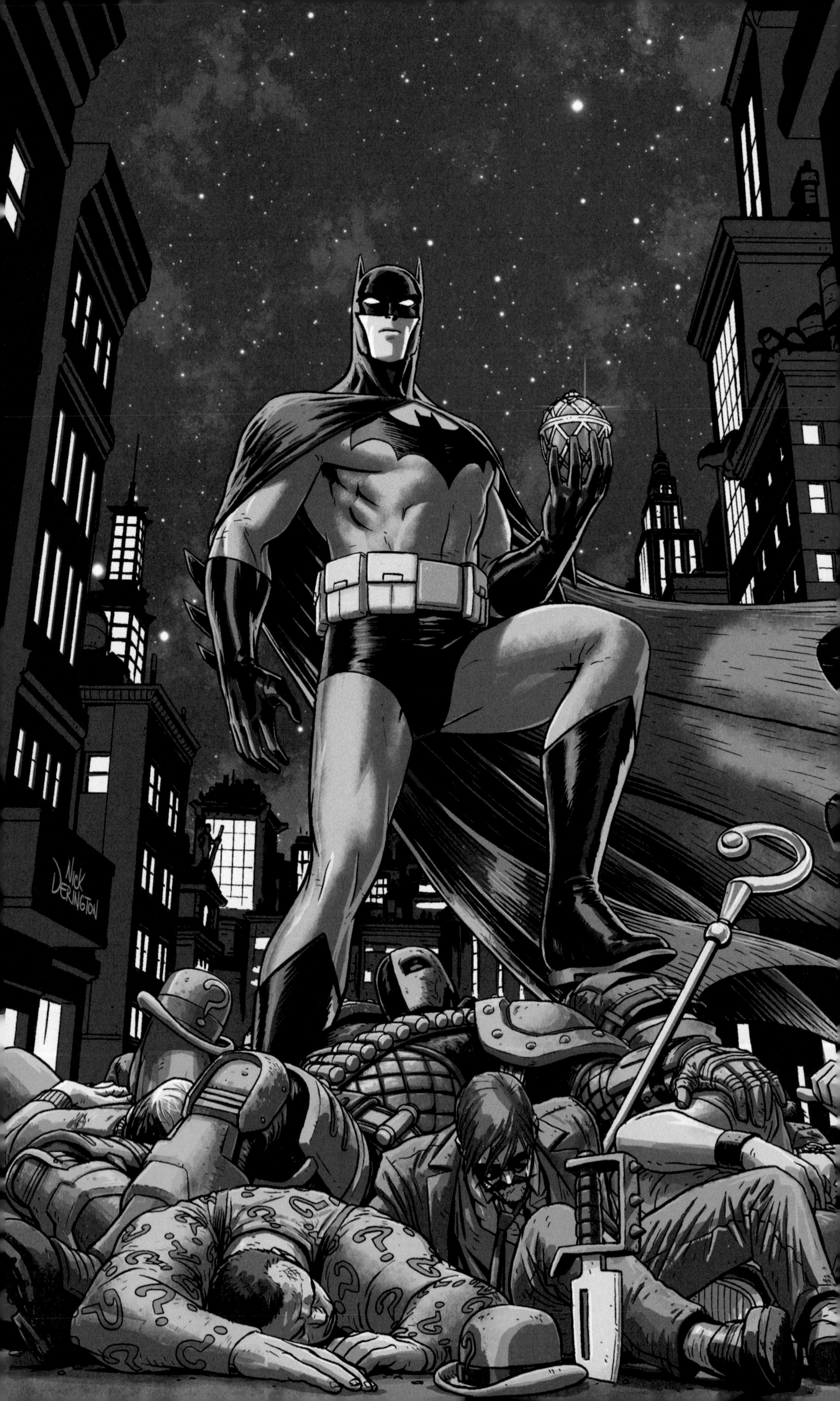
NICK DERINGTON

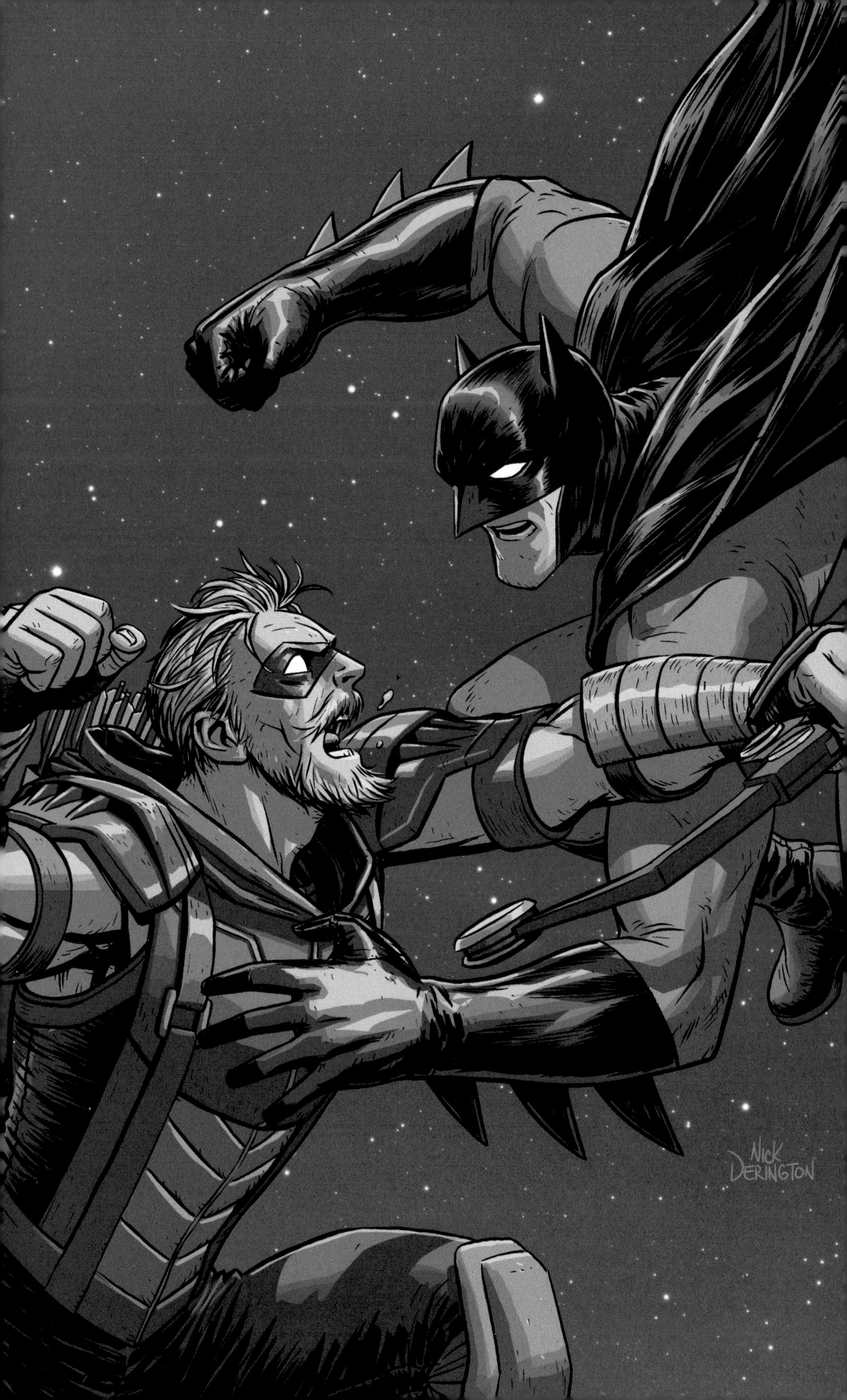
NICK DERINGTON

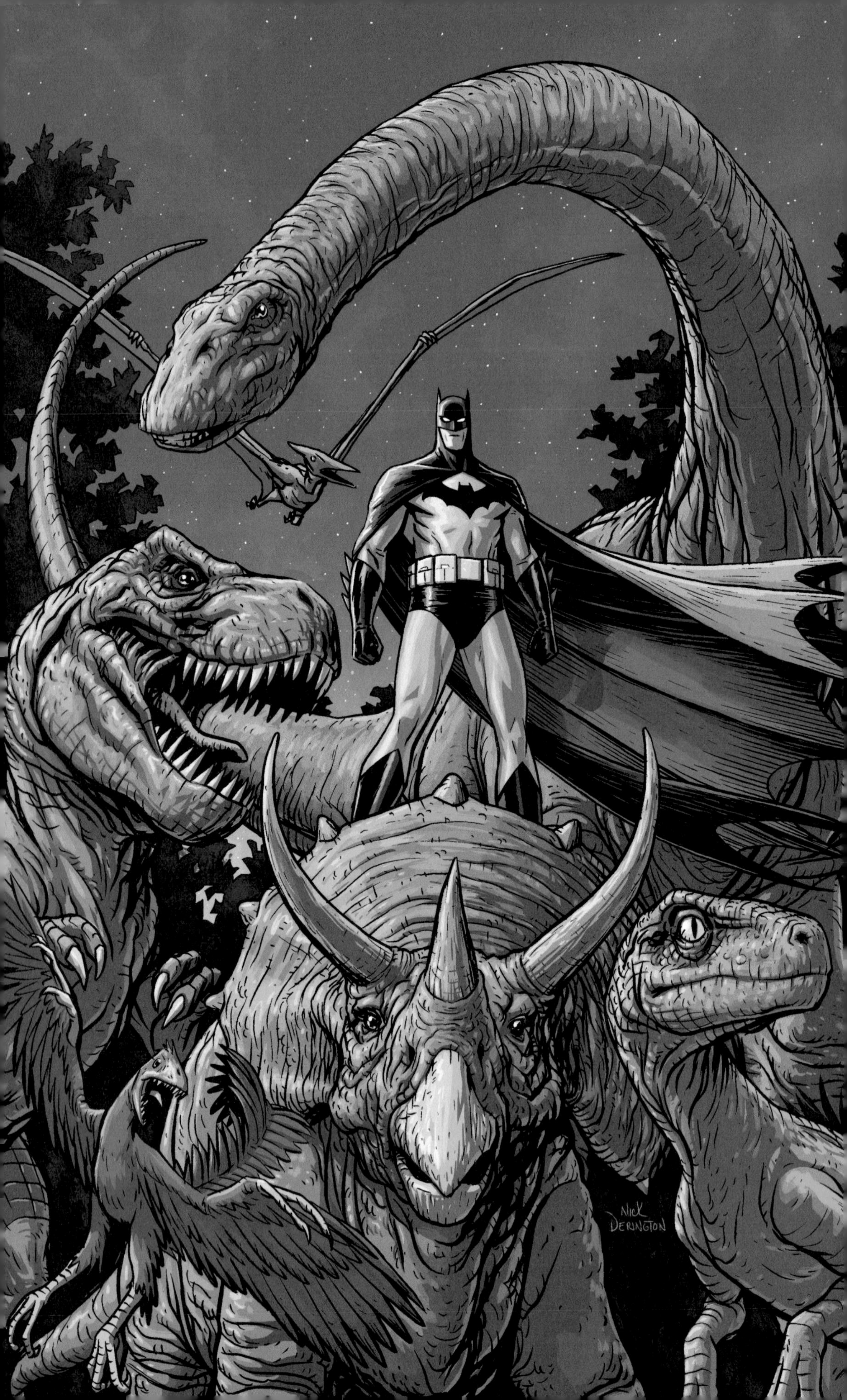
NICK DERINGTON

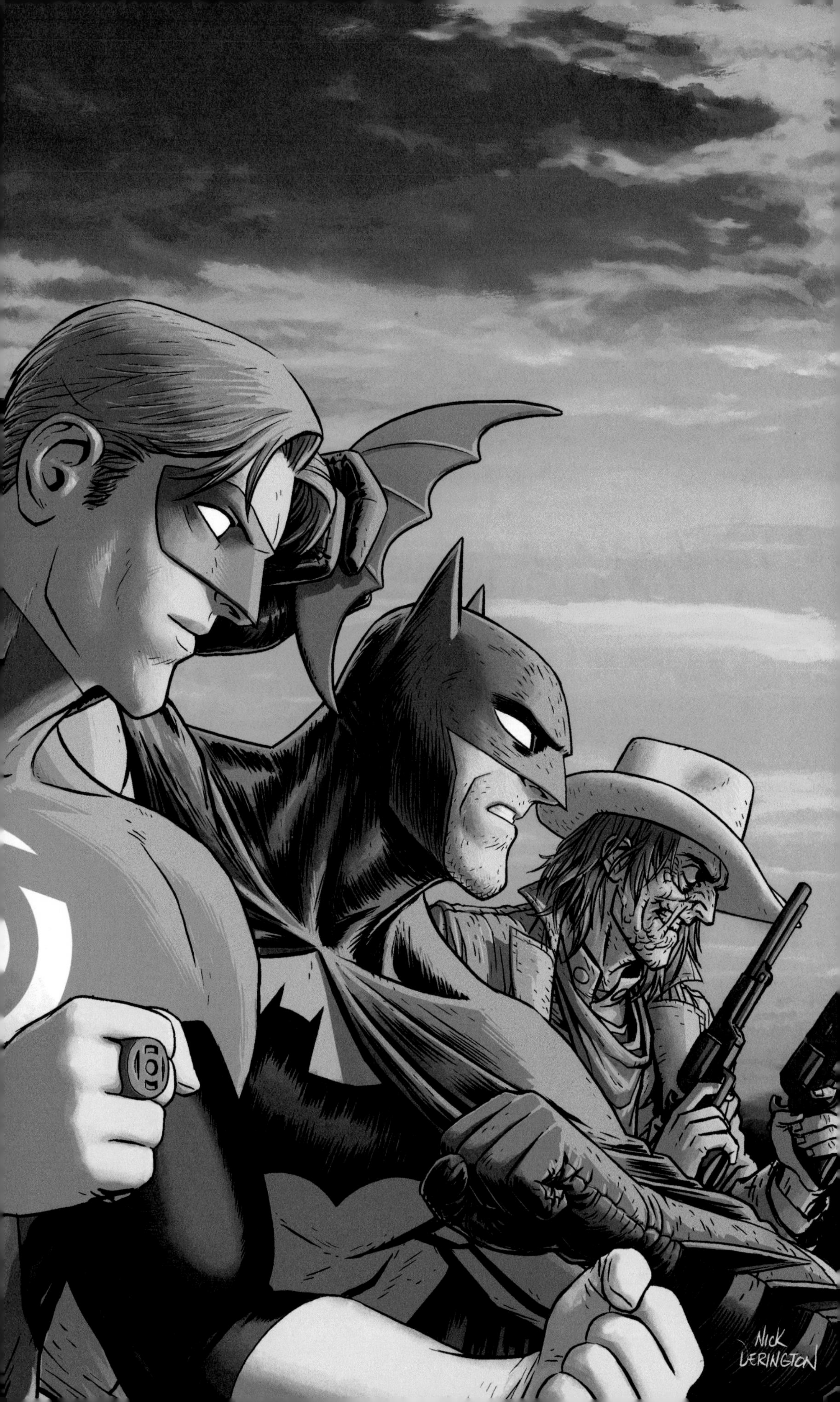
NICK
DERINGTON

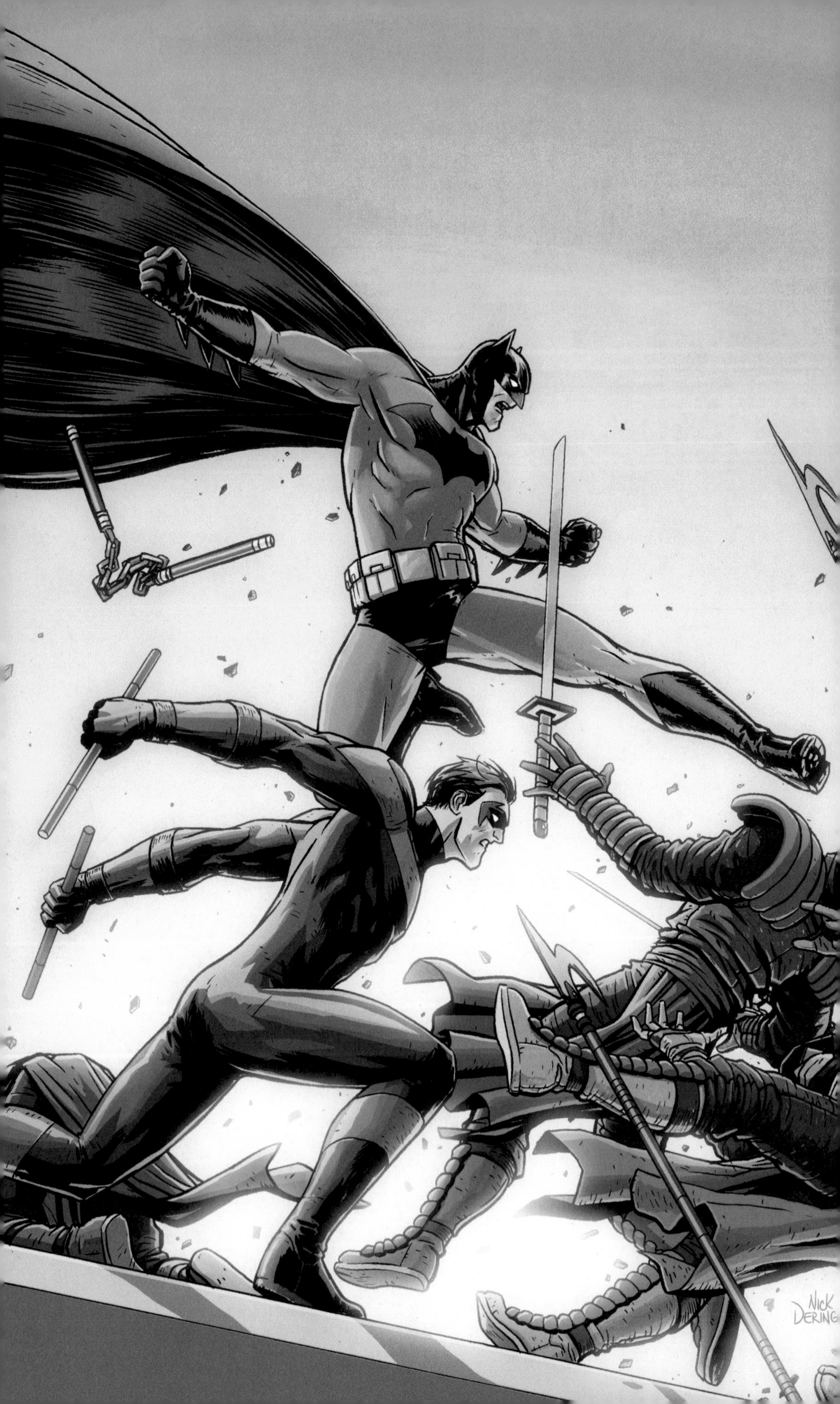
NICK DERING

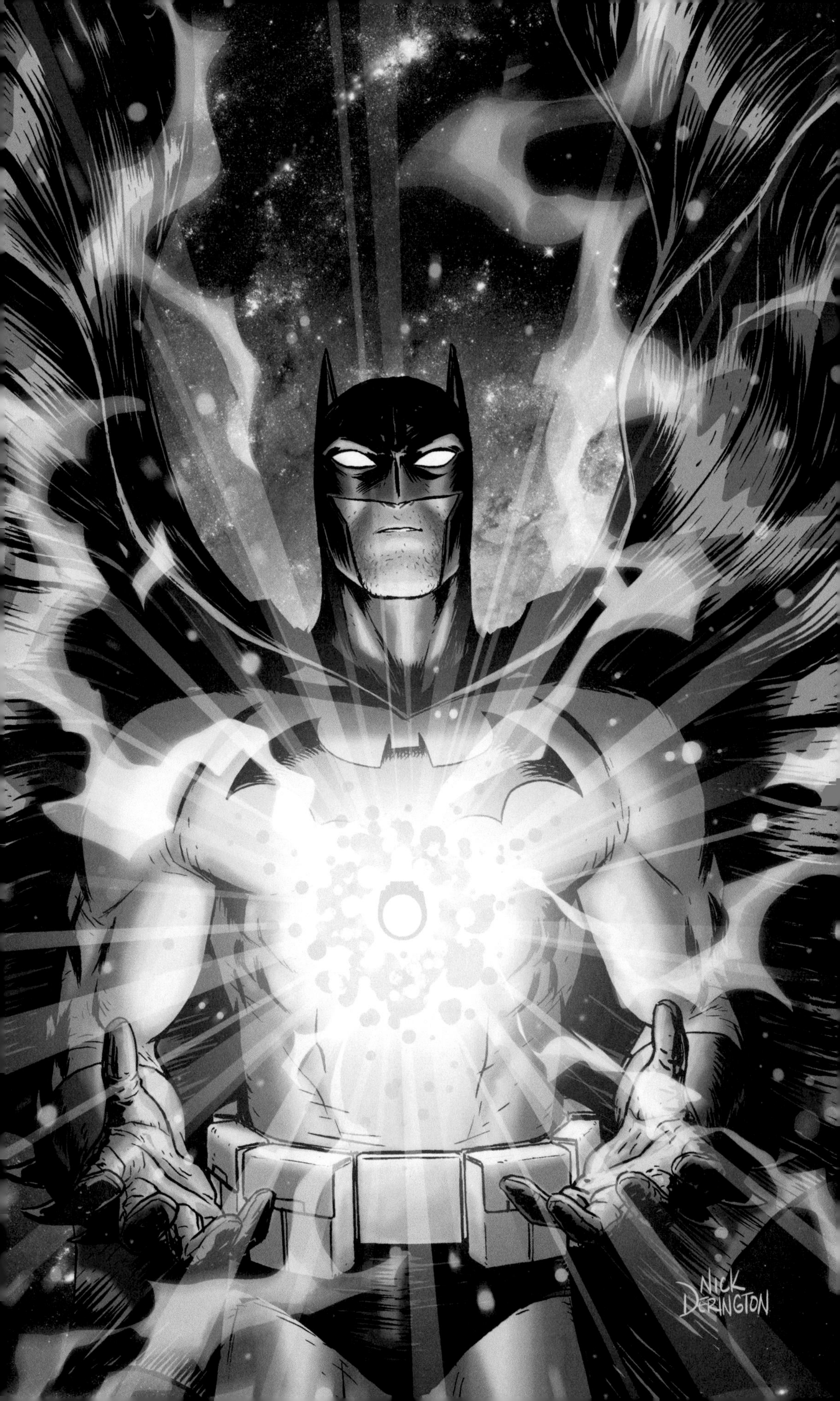
NICK
DERINGTON

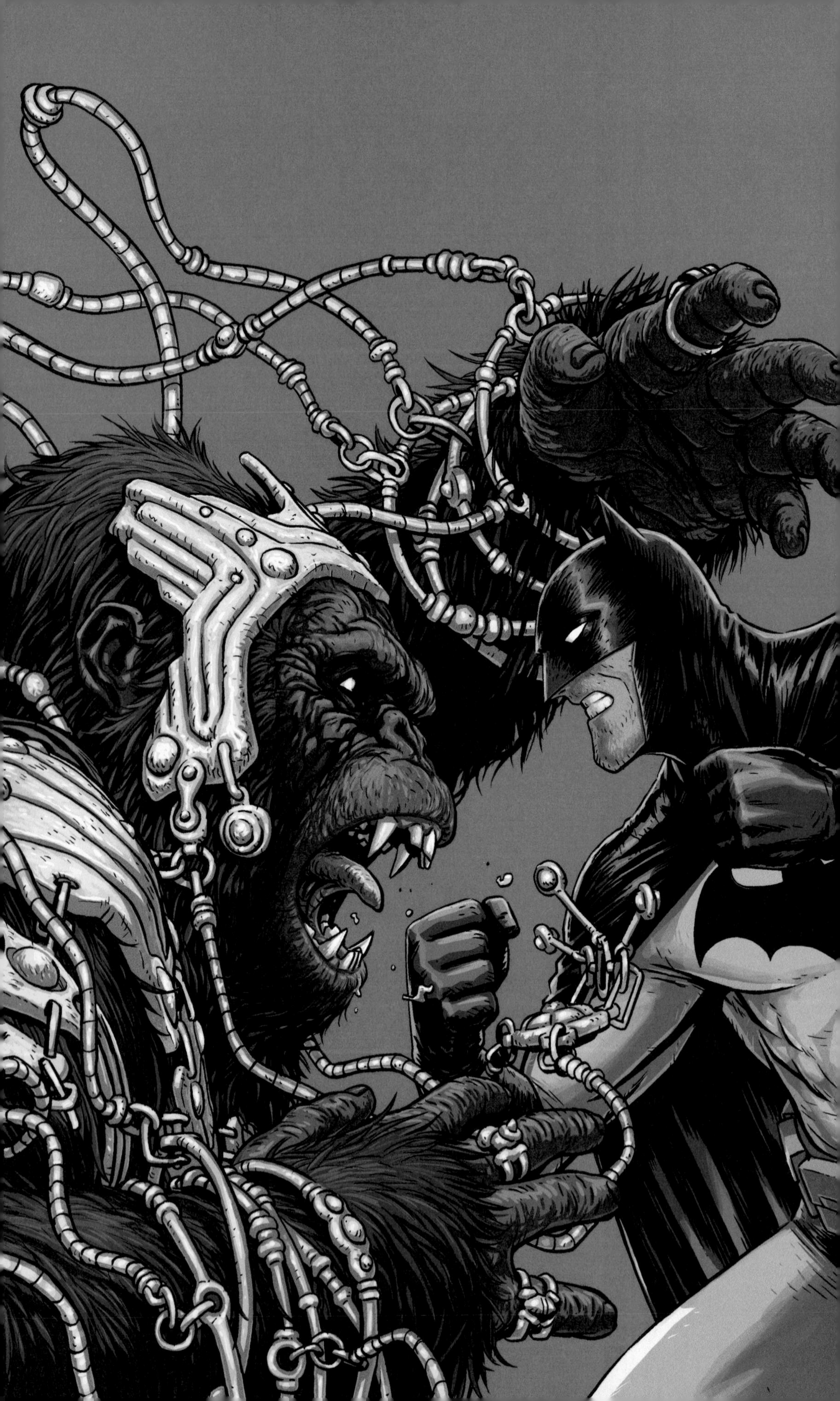

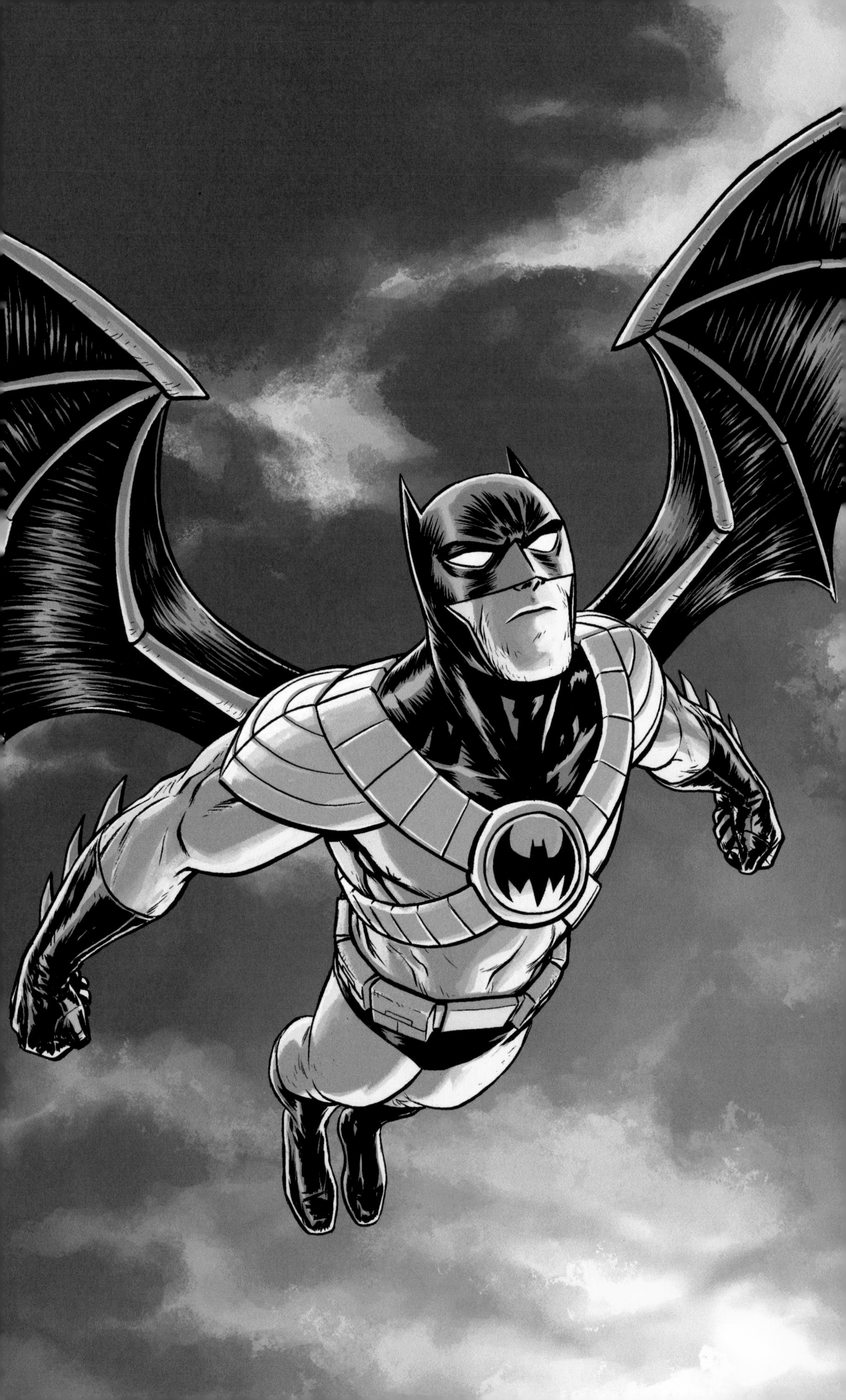

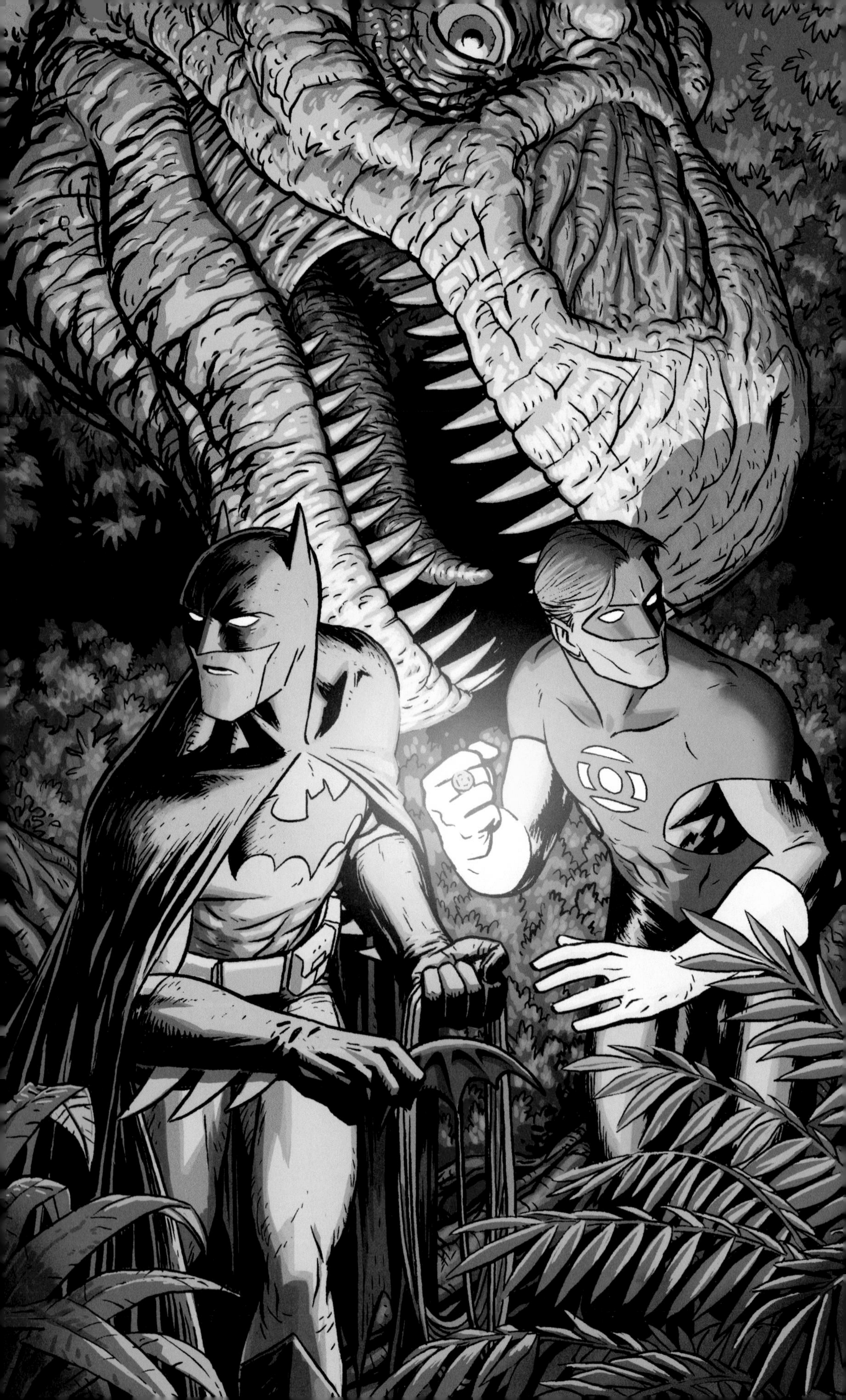

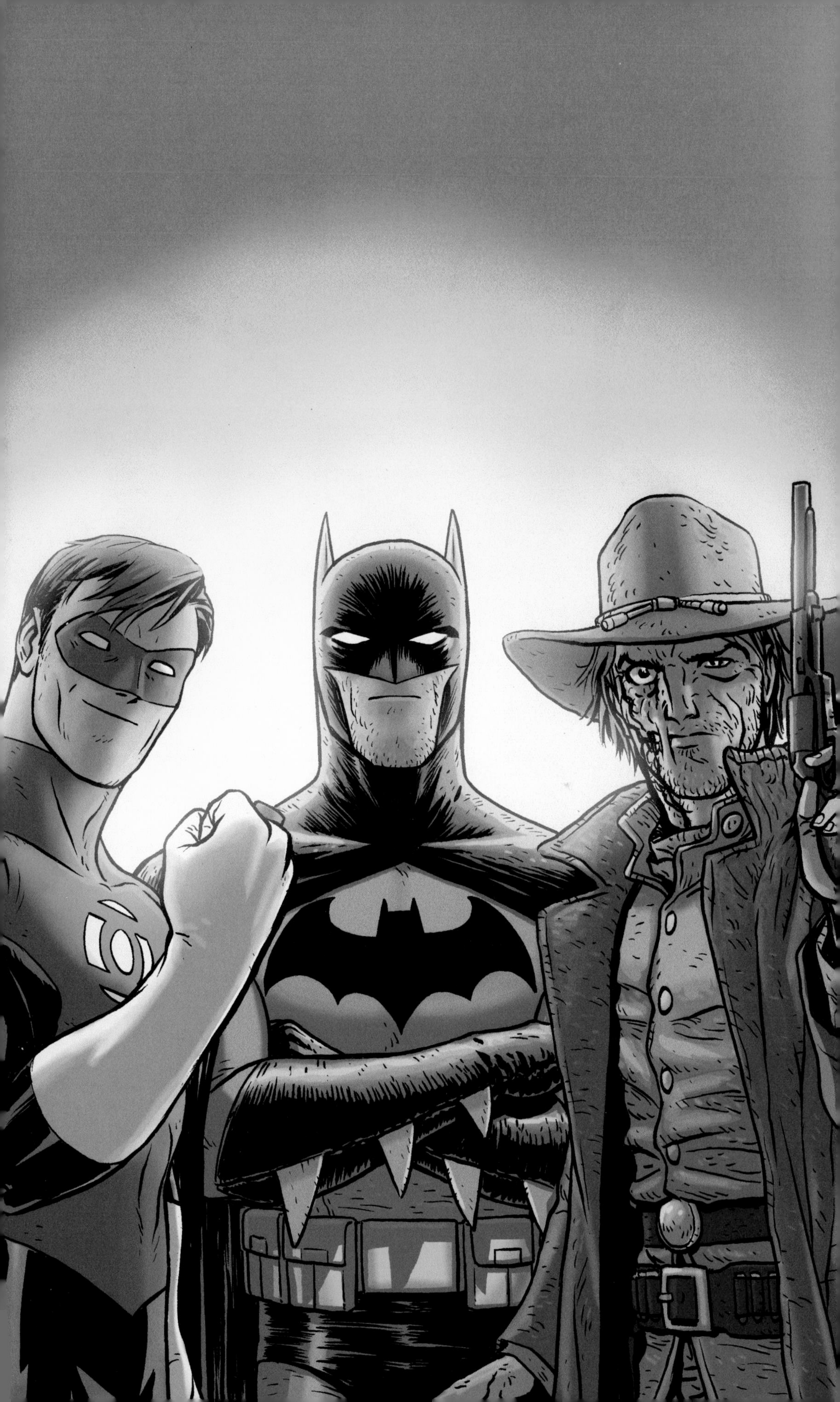

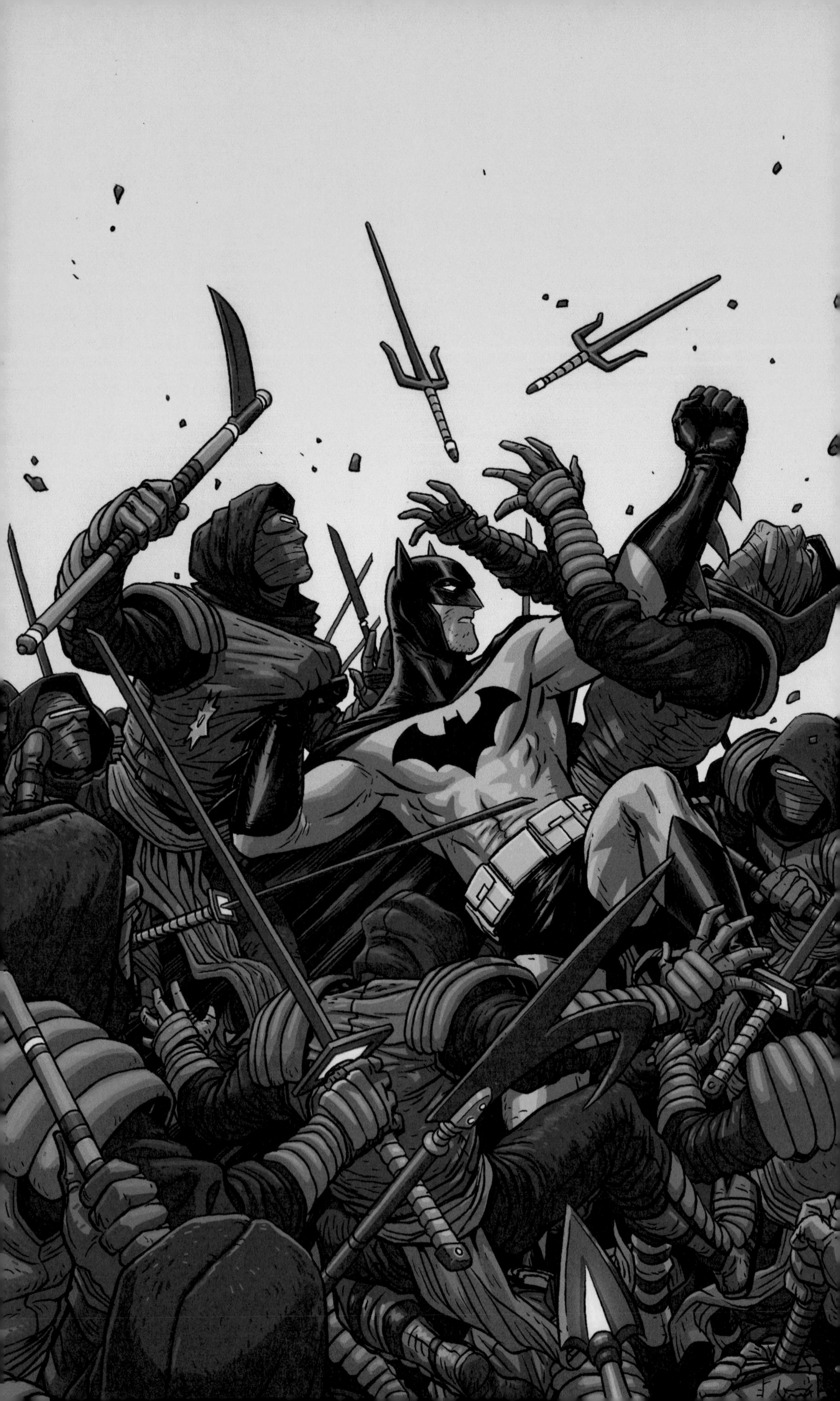

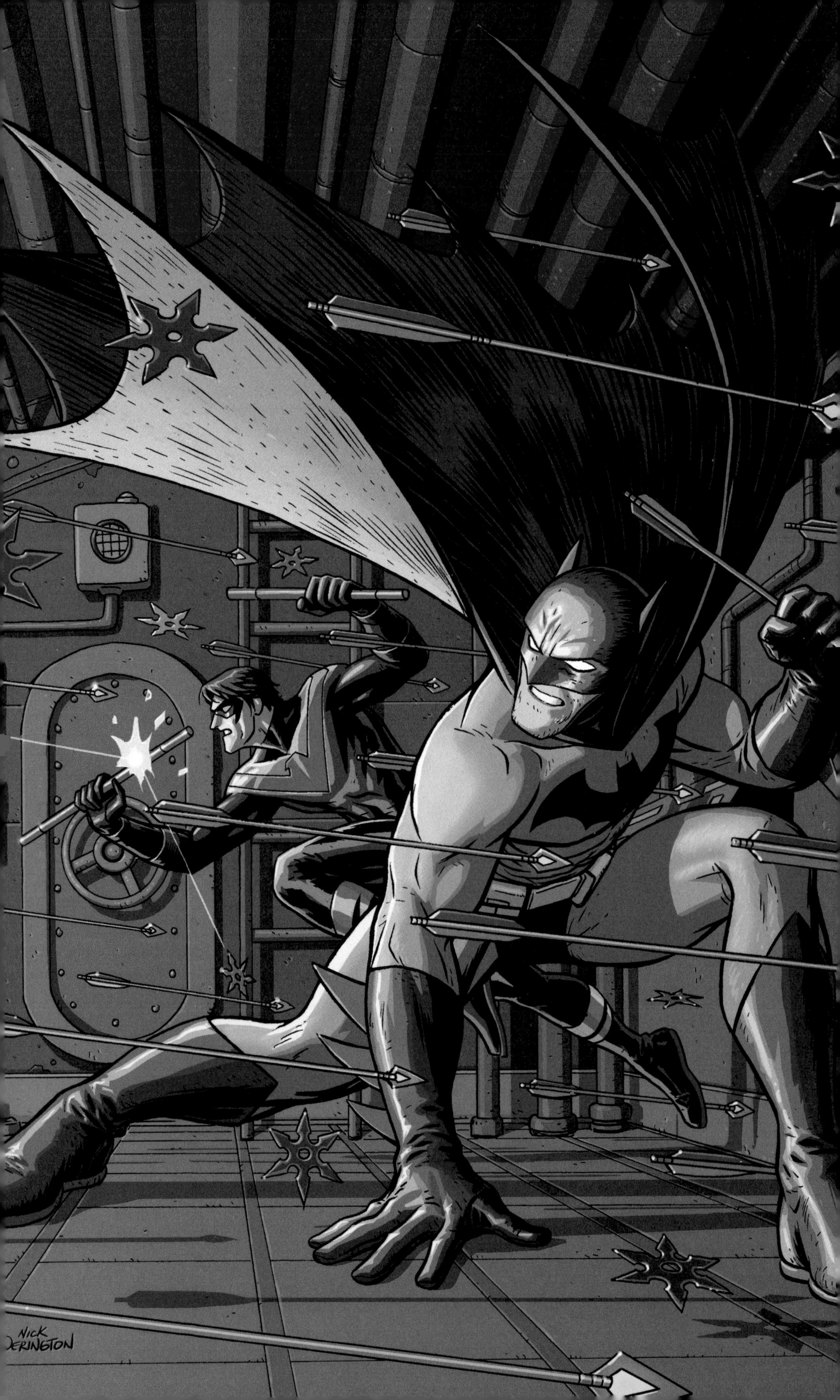
NICK DERINGTON

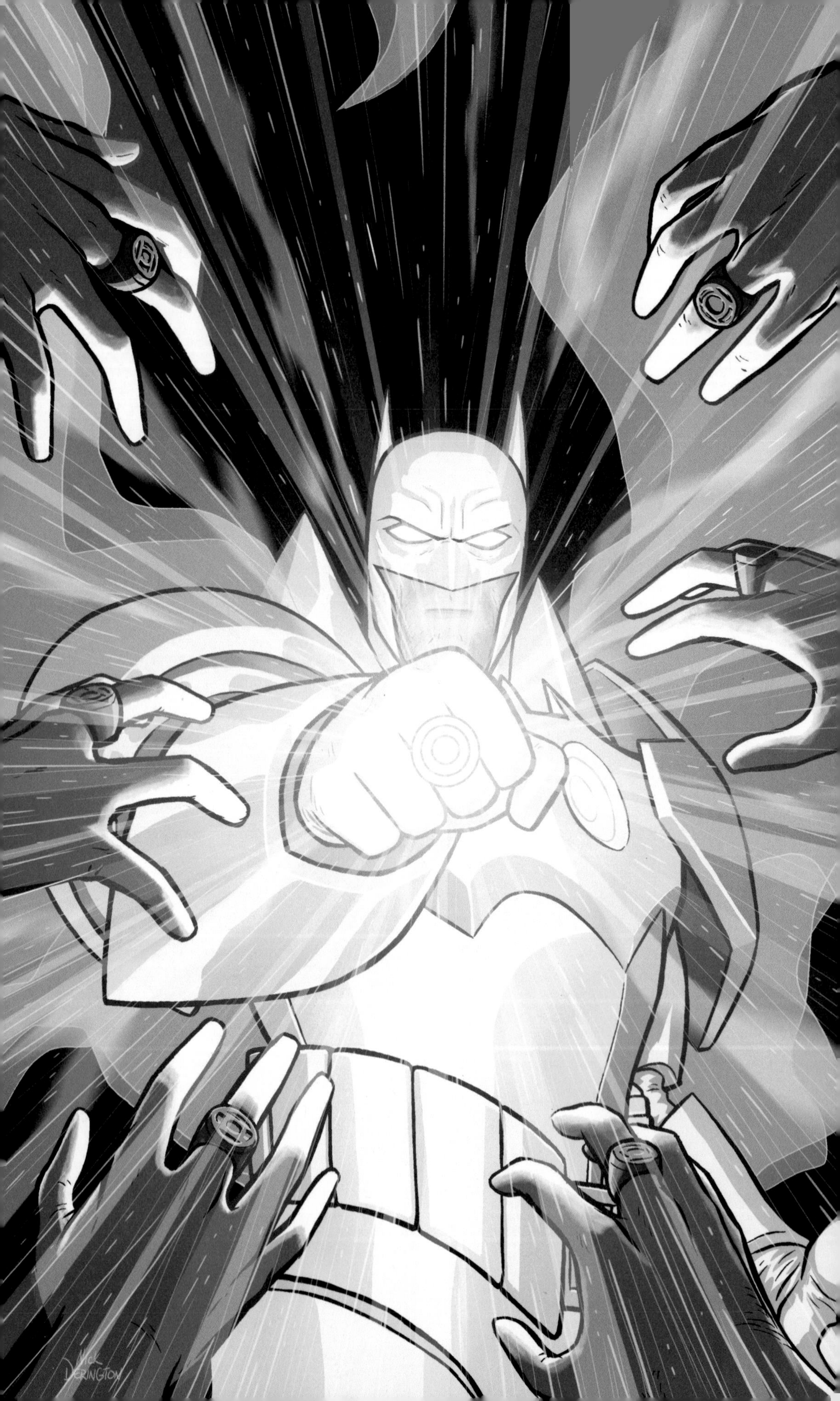

NICK DERINGTON

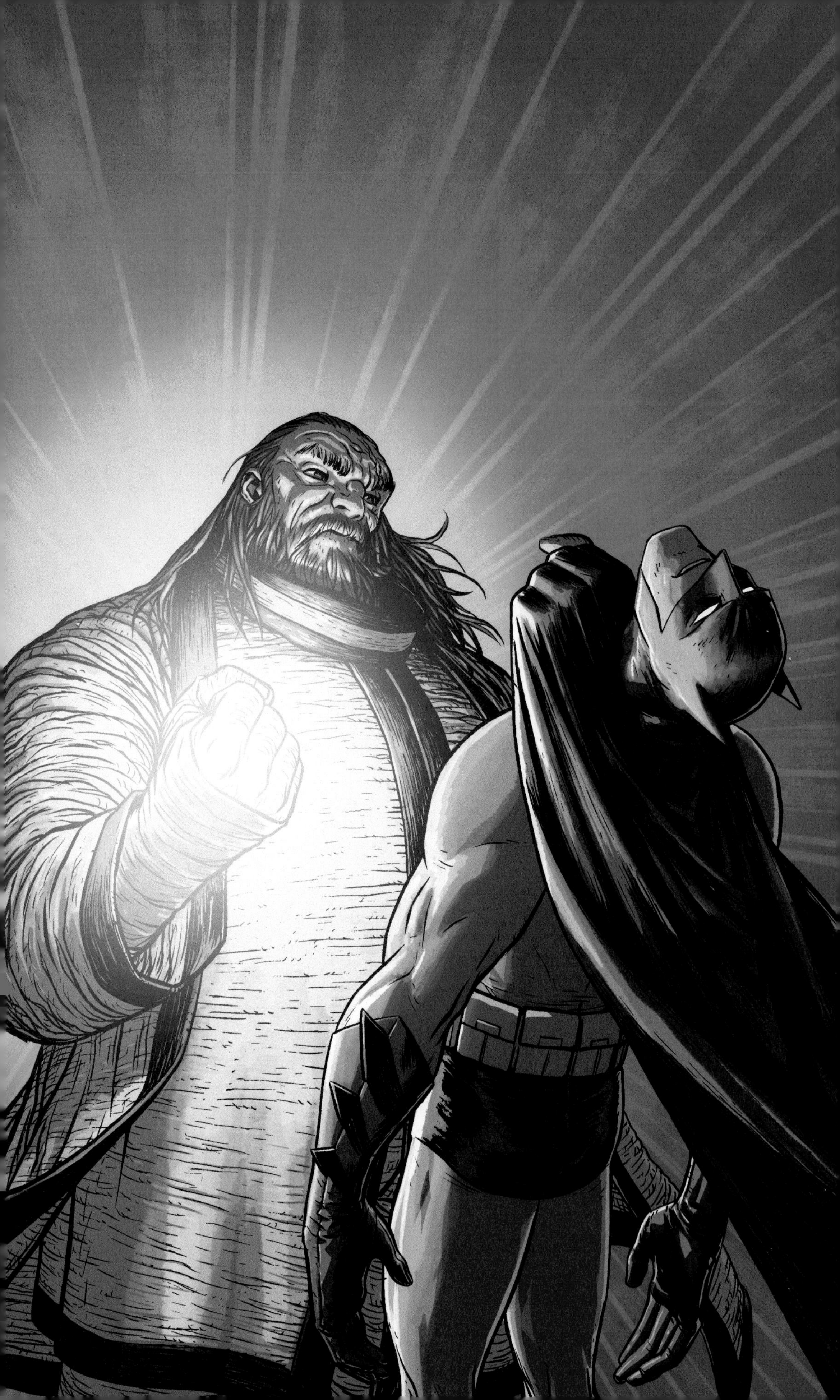

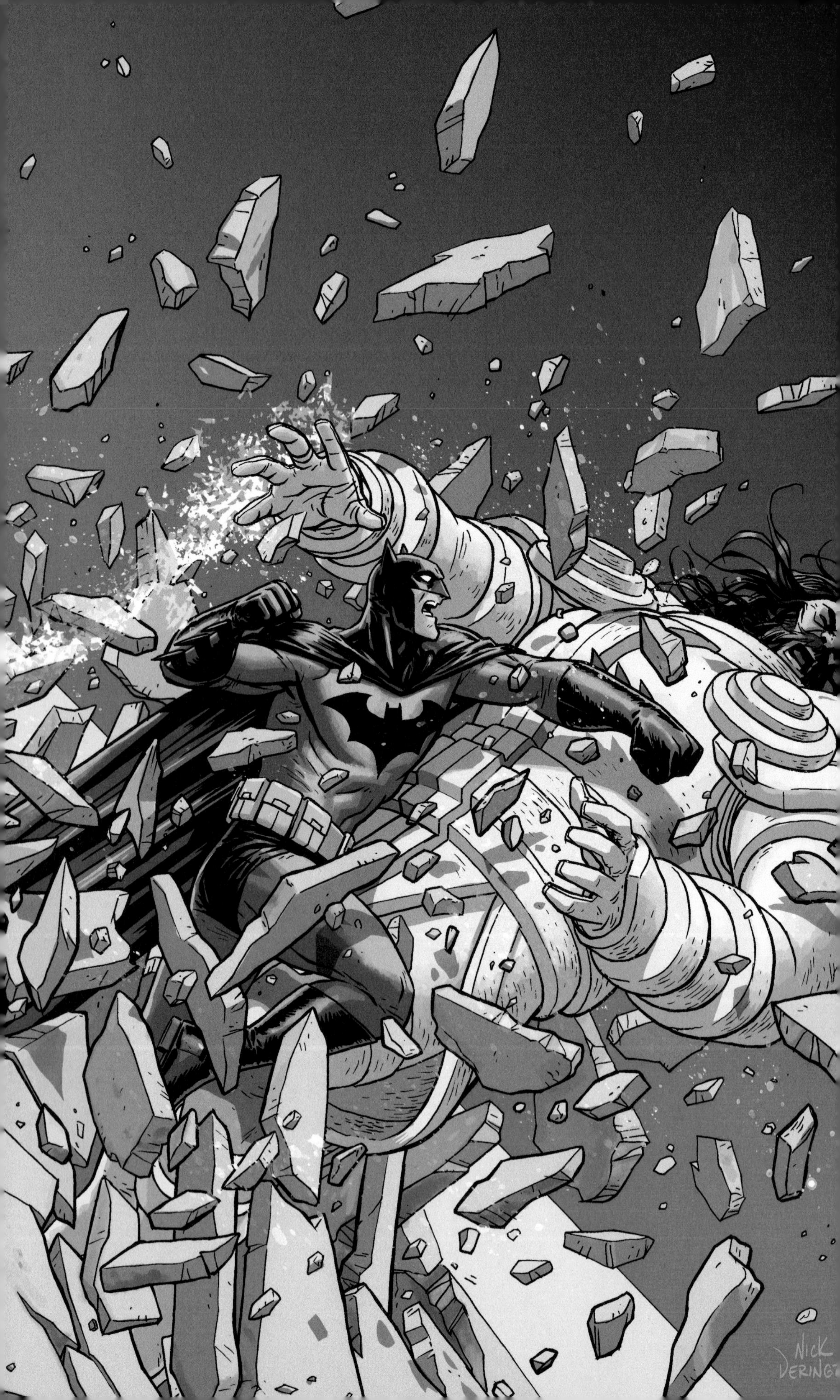
NICK
DERING

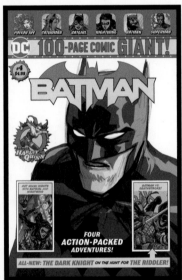

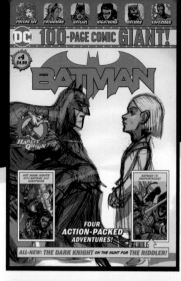

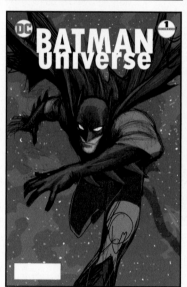

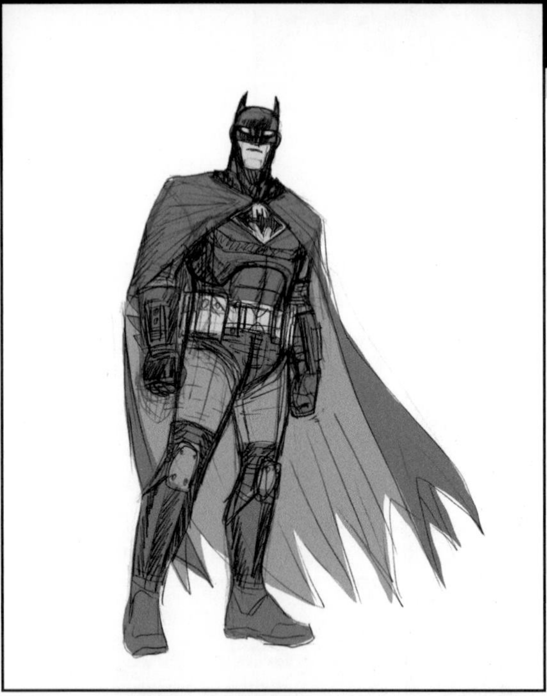

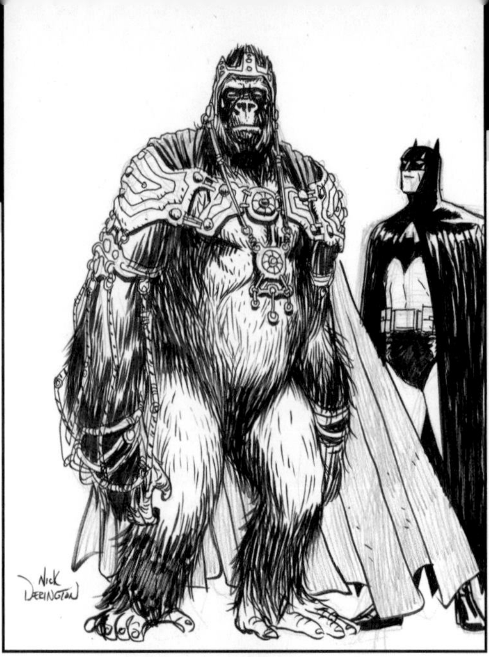
NICK
DERINGTON

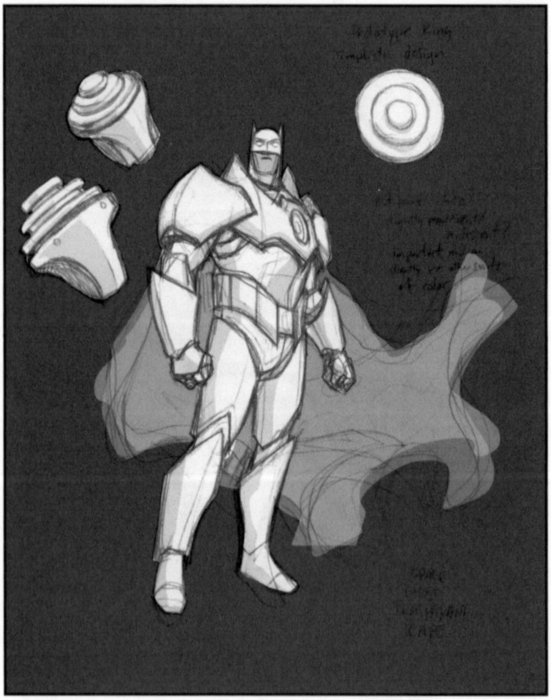

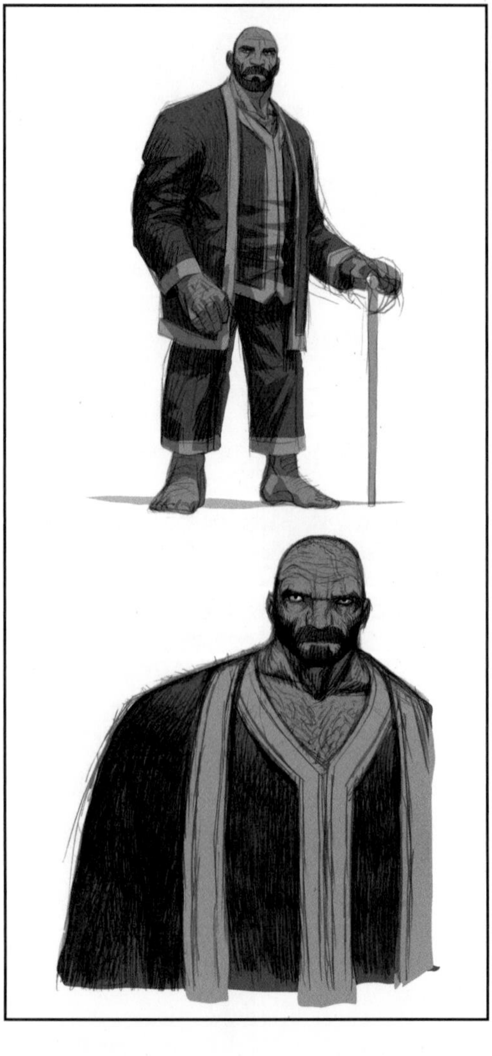

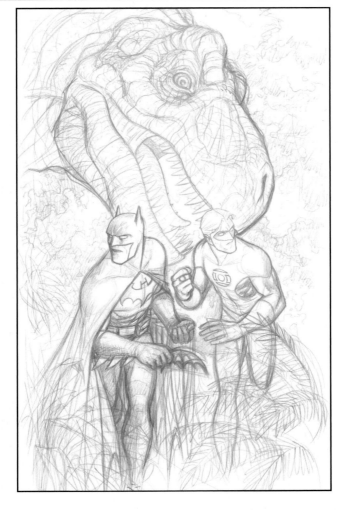

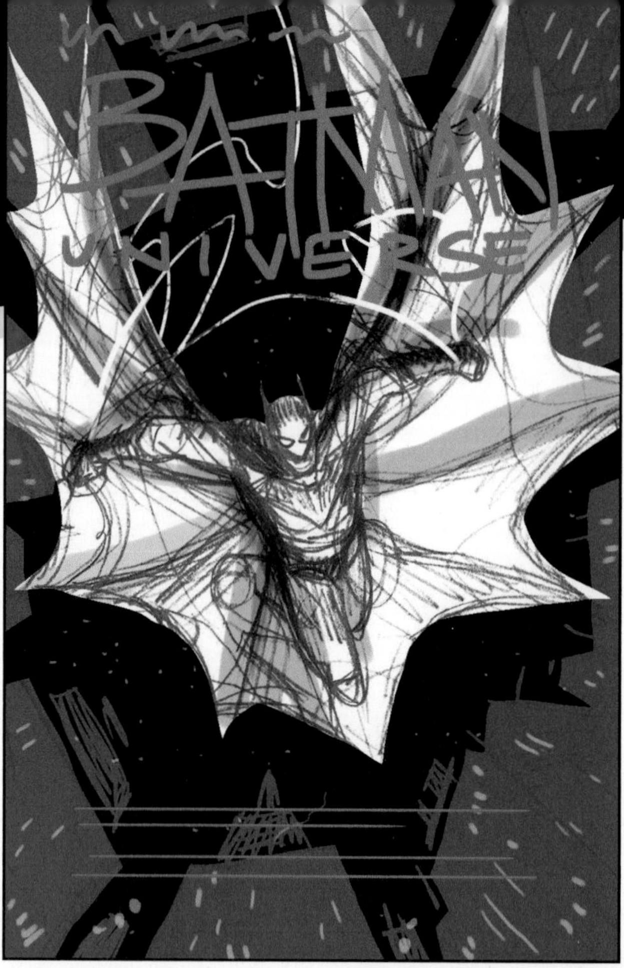
BATMAN
UNIVERSE

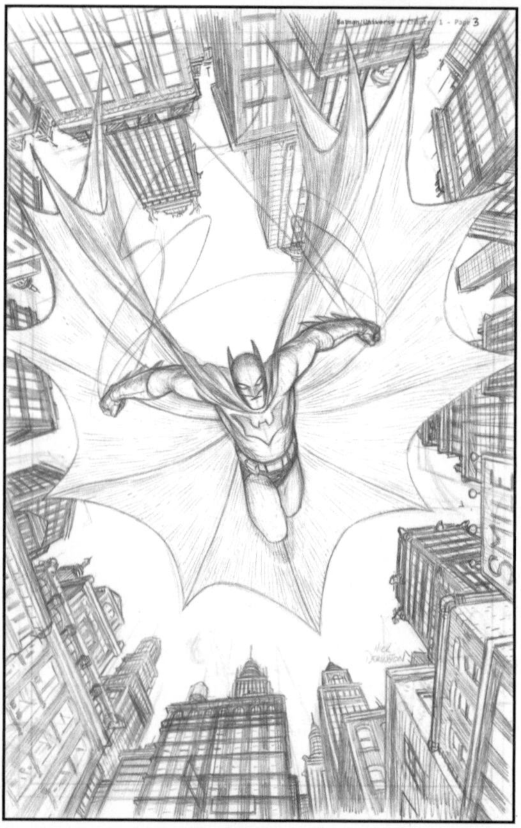

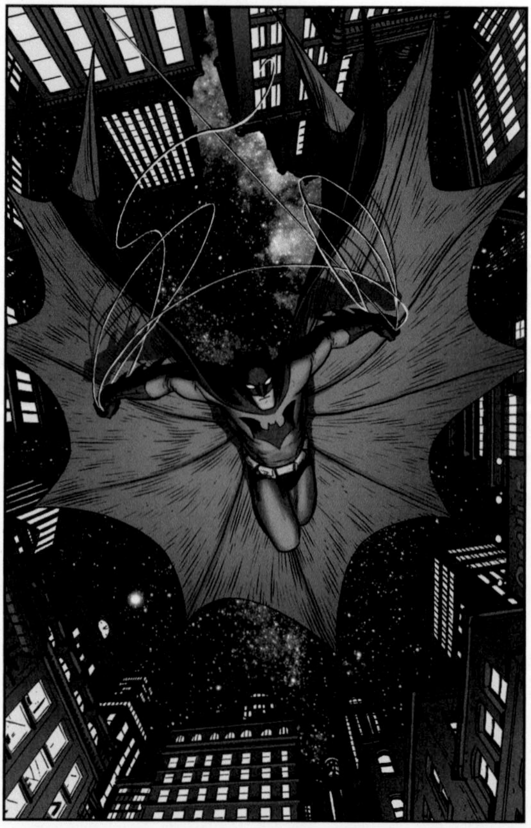

SUPERMAN
VOL. 1: THE UNITY SAGA: PHANTOM EARTH
BRIAN MICHAEL BENDIS AND IVAN REIS

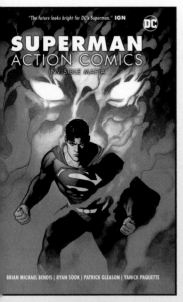

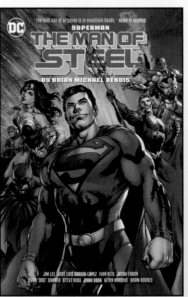

SUPERMAN:
ACTION COMICS: INVISIBLE MAFIA

SUPERMAN:
THE MAN OF STEEL

ACTION COMICS #1000:
DELUXE EDITION

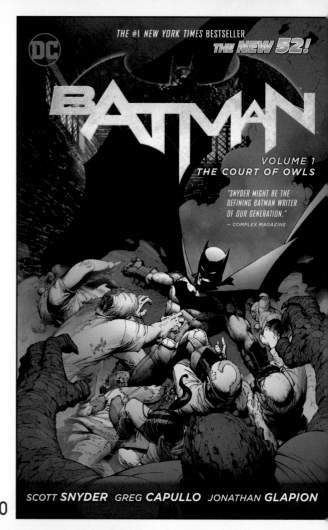
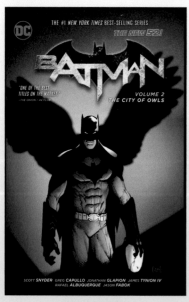

"...rilliantly executed."
...GN

"...orrison and Quitely have the magic
...uch that makes any book they col-
...borate on stand out from the rest."
...TV's Splash Page

...RANT
...ORRISON
with FRANK QUITELY
+ PHILIP TAN

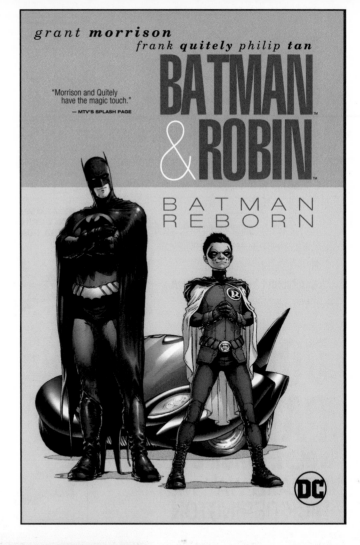

grant **morrison**
frank **quitely** philip **tan**

"Morrison and Quitely
have the magic touch."
— MTV'S SPLASH PAGE

BATMAN
& ROBIN

BATMAN
REBORN

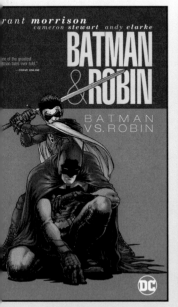

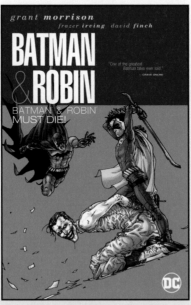

"Thrilling and
invigorating...
Gotham City that
has never looked
this good, felt this
strange, or been this
deadly."
**–Comic Book
Resources**

**VOL. 2:
BATMAN VS. ROBIN**

**VOL. 3:
BATMAN & ROBIN MUST DIE!**

DC's YOUNG ANIMAL

"For those who want to explore the weirder side of the DCU." **–IGN**

"A story of self-actualization, goodness, and coping that just happens to have biological Teddy Ruxpin like creatures and sassy robots in it." **–NEWSARAMA**

DOOM PATROL
VOL. 1: BRICK BY BRICK
GERARD WAY with NICK DERINGTON

DC's YOUNG ANIMAL — FOREWORD BY GERARD WAY

DOOM PATROL

VOL. 1:
BRICK BY BRICK
GERARD WAY
NICK DERINGTON
TAMRA BONVILLAIN

DOOM PATROL

CAVE CARSON HAS A CYBERNETIC EYE
VOL. 1: GOING UNDERGROUND

SHADE, THE CHANGING GIRL
VOL. 1: EARTH GIRL MADE EASY

MOTHER PANIC
VOL. 1: A WORK IN PROGRESS